THE
GUARANTEE

THE
GUARANTEE

A TRIAL LAWYER
EXAMINES SALVATION

LEWIS F COLLINS JR

XULON PRESS

Xulon Press
2301 Lucien Way #415
Maitland, FL 32751
407.339.4217
www.xulonpress.com

Paperback ISBN-13: 978-1-66284-309-9
Ebook ISBN-13: 978-1-66284-310-5

TABLE OF CONTENTS

FOREWORD

My journey in writing this book began as a parallel trek I'd made during my life as a Christian. I grew up in an Italian-Irish Catholic home and attended Catholic schools as a young boy. I deepened my faith by becoming an altar boy and was involved in my church's youth group, eventually becoming its president. I considered myself, throughout high school, a strong Catholic and Christian.

After completing college and law school I began to hunger for a deeper understanding of God's Word. My marriage and the birth of our first child created the need for a deepening of my faith. I needed it to grow even stronger. I thus began a faith journey that brought me to the Presbyterian PCA church, where I eventually served as an elder.

This spiritual journey continued when I moved my family from Sarasota to Tampa. The first church we joined there was a Southern Baptist church. Ultimately, the trail ended at a United Methodist church. These moves – to Tampa from Sarasota and from my Catholic upbringing to the Protestant church – were rather traumatic for my whole family, especially my wife and children.

As I mentioned, I was raised in the Catholic Church, as many Irish and Italian children were. My mother and grandmother were generational Catholics and both had grown up in church-going households. There was never a question as to which church we would attend; it would be the nearest Catholic church in our neighborhood.

As for my faith journey, I experienced stress for weeks. It was over having to tell my mother and grandma that I was *leaving* the Catholic church. As a third-generation Italian-American, like my grandmother and mother, I was born into the church. We were *very* Catholic. My grandmother, who still spoke quite a bit of Italian in our house, was my spiritual role model. When we made the family decision to change churches it was up to me to break the news to the matriarchs of my family.

I kept going over my announcement in my head, as I mulled over every word in an effort to avoid upsetting my cherished elders. I did not want them to think that I was abandoning my religion, just that I wanted something more so that I could gain a fuller understanding of my faith. After rehearsing the words dozens of times and finally screwing up my courage, I went home and broke the news. Like most things in life, my fears were overblown.

They both listened intently and, as the kind and understanding women they were, accepted the news with open minds. They essentially told me that if my change in churches gave me a better understanding of what it meant to be a Christian, they were fully supportive of my faith journey.

My wife and two girls were also affected by my sojourn. My wife, Mary Alice, had grown up in the Protestant church and converted to Catholicism shortly after we were married. I have always shared my innermost thoughts with my wife and best friend. She is thoughtful and kind as well as an exceptional sounding board. She has always shared my burdens and seemed to always know my mind. Even though she had just become a Catholic seven years earlier, she reinforced and agreed to the decision to chart our family's faith journey at a different church.

My two girls received their early religious teaching in the Catholic Church where my eldest, Courtney, made her First Holy Communion. Then, just two years later, we announced to the girls that we were switching churches. Courtney had little reaction but Sara was crestfallen. "You mean I don't get to wear the baby bride dress?[1]" she cried.

Later, when our son, Luke, came into this world, he was baptized in the Presbyterian PCA church we attended. Shortly after Luke's birth, we made a second momentous decision: to move from Sarasota to Tampa. When we took this fork in the road, however, it had an even greater impact.

While the two cities are a mere sixty-four miles apart, they are very different worlds. Mary Alice and the girls had put down deep roots in my hometown, so ripping them away from everyone and everything they knew was difficult. Courtney had just completed her sophomore year of high school, Sara would be entering her last year of middle school, and our baby, Luke, had just celebrated his first birthday.

I spent many hours on my knees asking for guidance for this consequential decision. I had practiced law for twenty years with the firm that had given me my start in the legal profession. This firm hired me as an errand boy in the summer before my senior year in college. They nurtured me throughout law school and gave me a job clerking in the two summers before I graduated. The partners in the

---

[1] At that time girls were asked to wear a white or ivory dress with white patent-leather shoes and white or ivory colored ankle socks for their First Holy Communion. The girls also wore a lace head covering. In Sara's beautiful eyes, this was a mini-bride's dress and she often talked about getting to wear the bride's dress on her First Holy Communion

firm taught me how to be a lawyer as I honed my skills in the profession. Twenty years later, the firm was undergoing a radical shift in the way its partners practiced law. Their new direction wasn't the path I wanted to travel, and after much debate and heartache, I knew I must leave the firm where I'd started my career and continue my profession elsewhere.

My prayers were answered when one of my role models in the legal profession answered a call I made to a Tampa firm that handled the same type of cases I did. When I asked Paul about whether he had a partnership opening with the law firm he founded, he was receptive. I had met Paul at a legal seminar where we were both speaking. I greatly admired his intellect and the warm and imaginative way he taught a very difficult legal concept to those in attendance. As I got to know him I began to understand the depth of this man. He had been educated as a Methodist minister prior to attending law school. His first plan was to use his legal education to further his work for Christ. In the process, he founded a law firm in Tampa that began as a sole proprietorship and was now a three-office, Florida-wide leader in its field.

He immediately invited me in for an interview and I met with him and Scott, the firm's managing partner. I quickly learned how God was guiding my way. I found out that Paul had just announced to his firm that he was retiring from the active practice of law to pastor a local Methodist church in hopes of reviving its sagging attendance. Paul's firm had never brought in a partner-level lawyer, but Scott, the managing partner, was willing to take a chance that this would work.

We had a very productive first meeting, followed by a succession of meetings with each of the partners. They made the decision to bring me into their firm and I was welcomed into my new legal home.

Make no mistake, these two parallel decisions were very heart-rending and traumatic, for both me and my family. I could not have started either journey without prayer and partnership. God and my wife affirmed my decisions and lightened the load that burdened these two journeys.

The decision that overturned my professional life also changed my trajectory as a lawyer. Leaving a law firm in my hometown, where I knew all of the trial lawyers by their first names, all of the judges, and most of the business leaders, was painful. The angst was authentic, yet leaving the firm that gave me my start in the legal field turned out to be the best professional decision in my forty-plus years of practice.

With the strong support of the managing partner, the blessings of the long-admired retiring founding partner, and the warm embrace of the rest of the partnership, I spent the second half of my legal career at the place I was meant to be. For twenty-one years, my firm in Tampa supported me in a way that I believe benefited the firm and me in equal measure. I was able to greatly expand the list of clients I represented and widen the depth of knowledge I needed to handle more complex and specialized cases. I was able to try high-profile cases in nearly every judicial venue in Florida.

God's hand was guiding me all along! However, leaving the church which I was born into, grown up in, and led my young family to belong was difficult. Telling my mother and grandmother, my two guiding lights, of my decision was hard. The choices were difficult and the process was gut-wrenching.

Trusting in God to guide my decisions concerning the best path to take brought the answers into clear focus. These significant changes, guided by God, turned out to be two of the best choices I have ever made (after asking Mary Alice to be my wife). My journey from my Catholic roots to the sanctification process that led to this book changed me in ways that I believe God intended – from the inside out. My understanding of what God wants of me has been sharpened. My comprehension of God's plan for me, His creation, has been more fully understood.

Along the way, I joined Bible studies and began my daily reading of God's Word. I eventually joined Hyde Park United Methodist Church in Tampa and founded a men's Bible study, which I co-lead. This study, *Raising a Modern-Day Knight*, was borne out of my participation in a knighthood ceremony for one of my friend's sons. The boy was coming of age and needed to understand that a *man* was not someone who was defined by the world, but by God.

This part of my faith journey, commenced when Jay invited me to be one of his son's mentors and a resource that his son, John, could lean on when navigating the journey from boy to man. I so enjoyed the teachings that this study provided that when my own son was nearing his thirteenth birthday, I went to my pastor and convinced him to begin a similar study.

This study, based on the book of the same name, was designed for men. It gave them the tools needed to raise a godly man. It emphasized the father's central role in the lives of their sons. This study was warmly welcomed by the fathers of Luke's closest friends. It was so embraced by the dads that, eleven years later, we are still together studying the Bible and supporting each other.

There will be many references in this book to these steps in my spiritual journey and the pastors, lay leaders, and Bible study members who influenced me in life. These Bible studies also opened my eyes to many biblical teachers and scholars[2].

---

[2] I would be remiss if I failed to mention the influence of my son's godfather, Jim, who first introduced me to C.S. Lewis (Mere Christianity) and Philip Yancey (The Jesus I Never Knew)

One thing that I began to realize in my trek – from having many unanswered questions to being a somewhat mature Christian – is that God desperately wants me back in fellowship with Him. He created each of us to live a life of joy and peace and to return to Him after our time on earth is through. I also learned, much to my surprise, that because God loves us so much, He has given us the freedom to reject Him. This seemingly strange dichotomy led me to question many things about my understanding of God's plan.

If God loves us:

Why does He allow us to experience heartache and pain?

Why does He allow us to reject Him?

How do I know I can find my way back to Him?

The answer to these conundrums is what led me to the title of this book.

In the almost fifteen years I've spent researching the material for the book, I have read, studied, and asked questions of my fellow Christians and my pastors. I also sought advice from the authors of the books I read. They provided answers to my questions within the pages of their works. That process led to the creation of the chapters that follow.

As you will discover, the format of this book is different from most published works. This is because it is written from the perspective of a trial lawyer. I have tried to convey the material in the form of a legal brief. When presenting a legal argument in a written brief, lawyers are required to lay out issues with heavy use of citations. Judges require that all positions taken by the advocate and the legal reasonings presented are based on prior published court decisions, statutes, or peer-reviewed legal treatises.

When making points in a brief the lawyer must provide these sources in the form of footnotes – so that the judges can easily confirm that the basis for arguments have sound foundations that can be readily checked and verified. I have therefore formatted the pages that follow so that you (as the judges of the facts cited herein) can easily verify the source material that forms the foundation of my *case*.

It is my fervent hope that I can provide you with a solid case for choosing a path that will lead you to the joy and peace of mind that I have experienced in my life's journey. I hope that this layman's perspective may provide a path for you to take on your trek through life. Perhaps I should sum it up this way:

> I hope no reader will suppose that *mere* Christianity is here put forward as an alternative to the creeds of the existing communions. It is more like a hall out of which doors open into several rooms. If I can bring anyone into that hall I shall have done what I attempted.
>
> But it is in the rooms, not in the hall, that there are fires and chairs and meals. The hall is a place to wait in, a place from which to try the various doors, not a place to live in. For that purpose the worst of the rooms (whichever that may be) is, I think, preferable[3].

So, welcome to the hall! I hope that I can provide some insight – and along the way some comfort – when divergent paths intrude into the road you are on in your journey through life. I sincerely desire that you may realize that God has guaranteed your salvation which, in turn, will lead to the reunification with your Creator.

---

[3] C. S. Lewis. "A Year with C. S. Lewis." P. 274. HarperCollins. iBooks.

CHAPTER ONE:

INTRODUCTION

Nothing is guaranteed...except death and taxes. We all know this truism. But this type of *guarantee* is hardly something we long for – in fact, it's something most people dread. These *dreaded* guarantees are the closest things we have to unqualified, ironclad, airtight promises.

One of the most famous guarantees in my generation was issued from a most unlikely source. It came from a brash young football player in an upstart football league – a league that had never won "the ultimate prize." This guarantee was made in the days leading up to Super Bowl III in 1969 which featured the New York Jets of the upstart American Football League vs the Baltimore Colts, the National Football League's best team. The first two Super Bowl matchups were won by the National League's Green Bay Packers, under legendary coach Vince Lombardi.

The American League teams in those first two contests were pummeled. In the week leading up to Super Bowl III, players on the Jets team were constantly taunted with the notion that they were not good enough to even be on the same field with the vaunted Colts. I remember sitting with my grandfather on his lanai in front of a small black and white TV watching Broadway Joe Namath, the impetuous, inexperienced quarterback of the American Football League champs – as he relaxed by the pool at a hotel on Miami's South Beach.

Namath, reclining on his chaise lounge, politely and patiently answered question after question about playing the highly favored Colts. The Colts, after all, were led by Johnny Unitas, a future Hall of Fame quarterback. Finally, Joe Willy had heard enough. In response to a final deriding question concerning the chances that the Jets could even stay on the field with Baltimore, he answered simply. *He guaranteed a win.* Namath's direct and powerful declaration was immediately seized upon by the throng of sports reporters. His "Guarantee" made headlines in every major newspaper. It led the NBC nightly news leading up to the big game. His teammates were as shocked as the media, yet, in a way, it gave them a peaceful sense of confidence as they made their final preparations for the Super Bowl. Although the game was close, the *guarantor* willed his team to an upset of the Colts, the first in the Super Bowl for an American League team. The guarantee also gave the other teams of this upstart league some measure of respectability and confidence. In fact, that *guaranteed win* was credited with eventually forcing the hand of the National League into agreeing to merge the two leagues into what is now the National Football League with its National and American conferences.

Before Joe Willy's bold guarantee, his teammates suffered from an inner feeling of not being good enough. Namath's fellow Jets later admitted that the national press corps had fanned their flames of doubt. But the guarantee, given by their leader, changed their hearts. It gave them a spirit of confidence that lead them to victory.

We often feel as if we are not good enough for God because we are habitual sinners. We know we all fall short of the expectations He has for us. We don't feel as if we are worthy to be on the same field as the *righteous* people we see every day. We are constantly hounded by questions of our status. Are we pure enough? Are we capable of winning God's approval? Are we acceptable to God? The doubts multiply to a point where we are tempted to give up.

Want the bad news?

The truth is, we are simply not good enough and we will never measure up to God's standards. We can never *will* ourselves to stay free of temptation. We can never live a sinless life. We can never play the perfect game. We all fall short of God's standard of a sin-free existence. Each day we confess our sins to God and ask for forgiveness, yet we commit those very same sins the next day. We have doubts about our ability to even *compete* for the eternal prize. We ask ourselves if we have done enough to be able to claim fellowship with God in perpetuity. How can we be certain that the *good side* of our ledger adds up to enough points to gain us the victory?

Are you asking yourself the same questions that Broadway Joe was hammered with in the days leading up to the Super Bowl? Perhaps, if *we* had a guarantee, we would feel the same sense of peaceful confidence that enabled the Jets to win the Super Bowl. But we are cynical and skeptical – just like the media before Super Bowl III. And our own experience with guarantees reminds us that they all come with exceptions and conditions. Beyond that, guarantees are only as good as the guarantor. What if Namath had gotten injured in practice before the big game? How good would the guarantee be then?

A word of caution – I am not a theologian. I did not get a degree in divinity, nor was my dad or grandad a preacher. I didn't even stay at a Holiday Inn Express last night! In fact, I spent my entire career as a trial lawyer. I was not an advocate representing Christians in constitutional challenges before the highest tribunals – but as a civil trial lawyer representing defendants in civil litigation. My clients were manufacturers, corporations, and insurance companies who were sued for alleged civil wrongs: such as breach of contract, personal injury, product liability, commercial litigation, or other assorted civil cases that brought parties into court to resolve their conflicts.

What does any of this have to do with the salvation that God offers? How does the practice of civil litigation qualify me to write this book? Perhaps it doesn't, but it may provide me with the tools needed to investigate and examine God's great grant of guaranteed salvation. It may allow me to put those claims on trial and call into question the foundational aspects of this promise.

I have tried to embed in this book a great many quotes and the work of scholars who understand this subject much better than I. As a lawyer, this is the way I was taught to make a legal argument – by citing case law, legal journals, and statutes to underpin and bolster the arguments I made for or against a proposition.

The philosopher William James advised that "[i]n the metaphysical and religious sphere, articulate reasons are cogent for us only when our inarticulate feelings of reality have already been impressed in favor of the same conclusion."

This, in fact, is something trial lawyers always fight against – a juror making up his or her mind before hearing all the evidence. The civil justice system is aware of preconceived notions and inherent biases that every human brings into a courtroom when called for jury duty. This is why, during the selection process for jurors (known as voir dire[4]) the lawyers and the judge try to unearth and deal with such notions and preconceptions when selecting a fair juror. In fact, when the jurors are elected to sit in judgment of a case they must

---

[4] Voir Dire is a latin phrase meaning "speak the truth." Jurors are required to be candid about their jobs, their experiences and background so that any preconceived notions or biases can be rooted out before they are selected for the jury

all take an oath, under penalty of perjury, to treat each party the same and wait until they hear all the evidence before making up their minds.

I hope you will do as jurors have to do when taking their oath by listening to all the evidence before making a decision. I hope you wait until all the evidence is presented in the succeeding pages and the closing argument is made in the last chapter.

The presiding judge would tell the jurors selected to sit in judgment on a case that this was their solemn duty. While I cannot make you take the same oath (nor would I ever ask you to do so) I do hope that you will listen to all the evidence presented in the pages of this book before coming to your own conclusions.

The Catholic writer Walter Percy put it this way. "Fiction doesn't tell you what you don't know. It tells you what you know but don't know that you know[5]."

Spiritual writing, according to Philip Zaleski and Philip Yancey, is supposed to accomplish something just as subtle. It should make a point inside the reader before the reader consciously acknowledges it.[6] That is just the goal I hope to achieve with this book.

The following pages are my attempt to make sense of all of the doubt I felt about whether I would be acceptable to God. The questions I asked were fundamental. How could I be sure? In essence, I wanted a guarantee that would erase the doubt I felt about my salvation. So, I started at the source. I believed the answers were right in front of me in God's Word - the Bible. I embarked on my fifteen-year quest to find the answers. I used my training as a trial

---

[5] www.quotes.thefamouspeople.com
[6] The Best of Spiritual Writing 2012. iBooks.

lawyer to conduct discovery[7]. Through the process of discovery, I was able to understand the facts of the case I was tasked to handle.

Through my investigation of the case for salvation, I examined God's word in light of historical facts. I wanted to see if there was a logical consistency in the Bible. I tested this through the use of techniques I learned in law school and honed in the forty-plus years I practiced law. I also conducted research by examining the pronouncements of gifted Christian writers to see if their understanding of Christian doctrine on salvation was logically consistent with my understanding of biblical principles. In short, I attempted to determine if the proof that exists could form the basis for a winning argument to a tribunal that there is a guarantee of salvation, given by God.

I believe that trial lawyers are good at investigating the truth of positions and, as such, are perhaps in a unique position to determine the veracity of claims. In fact, a trial lawyer figured prominently in the trial of Jesus.

Joseph of Arimathea was a Scribe, a Pharisee, and a member of the powerful governing body of the clergy – the Great Sanhedrin. When Jesus was betrayed by Judas and brought before this august body, they were determined to convict Him swiftly, and without an adequate examination of the evidence that formed the basis of the charge leveled against Him. After the pronouncement of the claim of blasphemy made by his accusers and the opening statement by the prosecutor, all but two of the sixty-member Sanhedrin collectively

---

[7] Discovery is the phase in a case where both sides seek documents and take depositions to find all the facts surrounding the issues in the case. It is an arduous and painstaking process that allows both parties to probe the positions of their opponent in an attempt to bolster their own position. This process allows each lawyer to decide which are the best facts supporting their side and simultaneously determining what facts best undermine their opponents position so as to be able to present their client's case in an eventual trial.

rose and said they needed to hear no evidence. They wanted to convict Jesus on the spot, without any further examination.

It was this trial lawyer, Joseph, who tried to stop the proceedings and insisted on compliance with the rules of the tribunal. He wanted to give Jesus the right to plead His case and warned against rushing to judgment without adequate facts. Unfortunately, Joseph's lone voice could not stop what the leaders wanted – and got. But this solitary voice of a trial lawyer was important nonetheless.

In my career, I handled hundreds of cases that dealt with various forms of guarantees, each involving different types of assurances. Lawsuits are, by their very nature, disputes over something: someone's version of the facts of an accident, the wording of a document, or the ability of a product to live up to the promises made about its expected or intended ability to perform a specific function. Underlying most of these disputes was the intention or purpose of a guarantee given by a manufacturer, service provider, or insurance company.

In my job as a trial lawyer, words mattered so very much. They could make the difference between winning and losing a case. It was my job as my client's legal representative to advocate to the Judge or the jury presiding over my case to present proof that formed the basis of my client's position. I was responsible for making legal arguments based on my client's view of how their actions matched their promises. Whether their product, service or actions were true to the guarantee they made. I spent my whole professional life trying to convince the ultimate authority (the judge or trier of fact, the jury) of the justness of my client's position. Sometimes my entire case would hinge on the interpretation of a single word or discrete action.

The words God uses are like that – but even more so. When God says *will*, it doesn't mean *perhaps*! This book will examine that ultimate question – how can we be guaranteed that we will receive salvation? How can we be assured of our admittance into heaven and into eternal fellowship with our Creator?

The great theologian, Eugene Peterson said that "[t]he reason many of us do not ardently believe in the gospel is that we have never given it a rigorous testing, thrown our hard questions at it, faced it with our most prickly doubts."[8] I have attempted to use my experience as a trial lawyer to do just that. This book is my attempt to examine – and cross-examine – what I thought was the most difficult question I faced as a person who grew up in the faith – how do I *know* I am going to heaven? How can I pass my own judgment on the "blessed assurance" that the hymn claims one has in Jesus? How can I be guaranteed that, at the end of my life, I will go to heaven, given that I have never had a dramatic conversion experience? How can I be assured of my salvation even though I never had the flash of revelation that was experienced on the road to Emmaus?

Now that I am retired from the active practice of law, I have the time to put my doubts to this rigorous microscopic examination suggested by Peterson. I investigated the question that was always whispered in my ear when my faith was tested: *How do you KNOW that you are saved?* Tapping my experience as a trial lawyer I embarked on this journey to bring this question to a jury of my peers – fellow sinners who have fallen short of the standards laid out by God. Over the past fifteen years, I have studied the Bible and, as set forth above, read the views of many noted Christian authors from diverse religious backgrounds.

As a litigator would do, I tried to put the concept of salvation to the test, to conduct discovery into all of the facts that I could find that are relevant to this issue. I endeavored to probe the question

---

[8] "A Long Obedience in the Same Direction." InterVarsity Press, 2012-04-25. iBooks. P. 108

at hand so that I could make a closing argument in support of or against the proposition of a guarantee of redemption.

While I was educated as a lawyer and spent my entire career in the courts contesting highly charged civil litigation, I came to this very serious question of faith as one without theological training. I'd been trained as an attorney. However, I will try my best not to use legal jargon nor engage in questions of doctrinal analysis of religious beliefs. I come to this question as a sinner looking desperately for grace.

A. Assurance = Guaranteed

Guarantees come in many forms. And despite numerous iterations, a key aspect of all types of guarantees is that they are designed to give the recipient an assurance of something. A guarantee is given to provide a consumer with the peace of mind needed to make a leap of faith – to purchase a product or enter into a transaction. The legal definition of guarantee is a "formal pledge to pay another person's debt or to perform another person's obligation in the case of default." The Cambridge Dictionary[9] phrases it as "a promise that something *will* be done or *will* happen." Guarantees were designed to convince someone to behave in a specific way. Based on my understanding, a warranty is a promise by a manufacturer that a certain product is free from defects and that it will perform optimally as promised. A guarantee, though similar to a warranty, is an *assurance* by the manufacturer that a certain product is of high quality and will withstand the test of time. Both warranties and guarantees are used to give customers confidence that they are purchasing quality products that are free from defects. This marketing concept is simple: a manufacturer

---

[9] www.dictionary.cambridge.org

uses a guarantee as a *tool* to give the assurance to consumers that what they are buying is worth their hard-earned dollars.

For instance, when you are considering whether to spend thousands of dollars to buy a new car, you want the promise that it will operate as the ad proclaims – and perform thusly for a long time. This type of guarantee is called a warranty. To entice you to purchase that shiny new model, the manufacturer agrees to guarantee their workmanship and the mechanical condition of that vehicle for a specified period of time. Based on this promise we plunk down our money knowing that if something goes wrong with the car, its manufacturer will *make it right*. We have a written promise from the maker that it will fix what goes wrong – assurance that the manufacturer will make it right.

With this written promise in hand, we believe that we can make the purchase with confidence that the car will perform as the ad has pledged. The warrantee, however, has conditions, exceptions and exclusions. You know, the fine print that many people complain will water down most of the promises made by the manufacturer. You, the purchaser, must also do something more than just buy the car and fill it with fuel if you are seeking to claim the assurance made when you bought this beautiful piece of machinery. You have to properly maintain the car for the warranty to be valid.

What if we could get a guarantee from our Maker? How confident would you be that the Maker will honor the warranty if you fail to follow the law set forth in the Old Testament? What if you violate those commandments? What if there are conditions, exceptions and exclusions that would allow the Giver of the guarantee to void the warranty? What if you do wrong? Will God still make it right?

B. Insurance Contracts

During my career, I also had to deal with policies of insurance. These documents were involved in many of the cases I handled. To successfully represent my clients, I needed an intimate knowledge of what form these documents took, the intent of the parties entering into these agreements, and how the insurance policy interfaced with consumer and commercial occurrences and transactions. Luckily, I majored in risk management/insurance in college and used much of that education to assist in the cases I handled. I bring this up because insurance policies are another form of guarantee.

Insurance policies were first created in England in 1686 to protect vessel owners and shippers from the loss of their ships and cargo from causes as diverse as storms or pirate raids. Owners of ships and the producers of the cargo they carried sought an agreement that contained a guarantee against financial loss of the ship and its cargo. The first insurance carrier, Lloyds of London, was formed by a group of vessel owners and shipping companies in an effort to make owners "whole" if the ship and its cargo were lost at sea. The Lloyds syndicate of policyholders tried to spread the risk of loss among themselves to lessen the economic burden when a ship of one of its policyholders was lost. In this way, the company that suffered the loss of cargo or ship was *guaranteed* that they would be *saved from economic peril* if the loss occurred to an ocean-going vessel. These policies, however, contained limitations, exceptions, and exclusions. Clauses in the policy limited the amount of recovery that could be obtained and, in some cases, prevented any recovery at all. The guarantee, therefore, was not ironclad or airtight.

Insurance policies have also been referred to as policies of "assurance." They provide *assurance* that a person or business would not lose everything due to an unforeseen event. The vessel coverage was contingent on the timely payment of premiums by the insured. The guarantee will only hold true, of course, if this precondition of premium payment was met.

There are now many types of insurance policies. These insurance products cover a range of risks, from life, health, and disability to homeowners, auto, and boat insurance. The basic premise is, however, the same: protection from financial harm if a certain risk occurred.

If you purchase automobile liability insurance, the insurance company promises to protect you from loss if you incur an accidental rear-end collision with the motorist in front of you. This form of protection is a guarantee against financial loss as a result of damage or injuries caused to others by your careless act. If you are negligent and injure another person, the insurance company will shoulder the blame for your carelessness and *save you* from the damages you caused. In order for this assurance policy to be effective, however, you are required to pay your premiums and cooperate with your insurance company in handling the claim made against you.

Most people are aware, however, that auto insurance policies come with exceptions, conditions, and limitations. For instance, if you intentionally injure someone, your policy does not provide coverage. There is no coverage afforded for damages you intentionally cause. The policy also has a limit on the number of damages that it will pay for in a loss. This guarantee is limited to the amount of coverage you select and the types of wrongful events it covers.

Another example of an assurance policy is life insurance. In this contract an insured person secures an agreement from the insurance company that, in the event of their demise, the company will pay their heirs a sum of money. This policy is a form of guarantee that protects your loved ones from the financial loss they will experience when you die. Like all other insurance contracts, it contains contractual exceptions and limitations.

For example, if a person does not truthfully fill out the insurance application and represents that he or she is a non-smoker – when in fact they have smoked most all of their adult life – this misrepresentation can void coverage. In such a situation, the insurance company simply returns the premiums paid and the policy is canceled. The guarantee of paying the policy limits to your kin thus ceases to exist.

Governments have also gotten into the *business* of issuing guarantees. The Federal Deposit Insurance Corporation (FDIC) is a United States government corporation providing assurance to depositors of funds in US commercial banks and savings institutions backed by the "full faith and credit" of the US Treasury. The federal flood insurance program is also one of these government-backed programs that protect homeowners and businesses from the destructive force of flooding. While the issuer of the guarantee is different (a private insurance company vs. a governmental entity), the concept is the same. In the instance of the government providing the assurance, the governmental entity will "save you harmless" from loss due to the bank or savings institution going bankrupt, or a flood destroying your property. In each instance, the guarantor (the entity guaranteeing something) agrees to protect you from the consequences of an unexpected occurrence or act.

While there are differences (in a legal sense) between guarantees, warranties, and indemnity agreements, the concept of protection and assurance from financial harm or loss runs as a common thread through these instruments. All these forms of guarantees are methods designed to protect people from ruin and to offer *peace of mind* by knowing that if a sudden, accidental, and unforeseen event causes significant financial loss, there will be something in place to protect them and "make them whole." While the insured property is vastly different in each form of assurance agreement, the concept remains the same.

The person giving the guarantee makes a promise in writing that specifies if something untoward happens, they will make it right. The guarantor will save you (or your heirs) harmless from the consequences of an act or occurrence. The type of policy or agreement identifies the type of "act" that protects the insured. The rear-ending motorist is protected from having to pay damages to the person hurt by their careless act, the ship owner is protected from the consequences from a hurricane, the depositor is protected from losing his or her savings if the bank is dissolved and the heirs are protected from the insured's loss of income in the event of death.

These promises are made to encourage us to act in a certain way: to buy a car, deposit our money in the bank, or purchase our house on the banks of a beautiful river. These "man-made" assurances drive commerce by allowing companies to ship goods across the sea, to produce that new model of car, to build a home – thus allowing businesses to provide a wide array of products to an international market. A life insurance policy provides peace of mind, knowing that when we make our premium payment, we have the assurance that if we die, the people who depend on us will not face financial hardship.

As I noted above, the idea behind insurance from loss was first developed in Great Britain. The English law definition of a contract of indemnity (i.e. an insurance contract) is "...a promise to *save a person harmless* from the consequences of an act."

As we will examine in this book, God gives each one of us a guarantee to "save us harmless from the consequences" of our sin. This promise from God is in writing and can be claimed by everyone.

C. Examination of God's Guarantee

This book is my attempt to investigate the facts behind the guarantee from the point of view of a lawyer investigating a new lawsuit. I have tried to evaluate the *case* for salvation. I have used my education, training, and experience to examine the issues underlying this claim, to put this claim of a *guarantee on trial* so to speak, through the techniques and logical methods of analysis that were my tools of the trade in the practice of law. I tested the truthfulness of testimony and documentary evidence in the cases I handled for my clients. I have used the same skills to subject the guarantee of salvation to the *rigorous testing* mentioned by Eugene Peterson.

In a trial, each lawyer is allowed the opportunity to cross-examine a witness. This process of examining a claim that the witness has made is used to ferret out the truth. In fact, cross-examination has been hailed as the greatest tool ever developed to determine the truth. I used the art of cross-examination to throw hard questions at this notion of salvation.

I have attempted to put God's offer of salvation through rigorous tests. I have examined the covenant made by God as if this contract between God and humankind were on trial. I have done this in the hope that will you find, as I have, that the guarantee of salvation is real and has been given by God as a *paid in full* promise to anyone who asks. It is the most ironclad claim that mankind could ever hope to receive. And it is given by an impeccable source. Once given, it will never be taken away by the Giver – it can only be rejected by the recipient. It is the most valuable guarantee ever imagined – eternal fellowship with God where every tear shall be wiped away and every sorrow will be turned into joy.

D. Are Death and Taxes the Only Unqualified Guarantees?

The Apostle Paul in the book of Romans said:

> While we were still weak, at the right moment, Christ died for ungodly people[10]. It isn't often that someone will die for a righteous person, though maybe someone might dare to die for a good person. But God shows his love for us, because while we were still sinners Christ died for us. So, now that we have been made righteous by his blood, we can be even **more _certain_ that we will be saved** from God's wrath through Him. If we were reconciled to God through the death of his Son while we were still enemies, now that we have been reconciled, how **much more _certain_ is it that we will be saved by his life?** And not only that: we even take pride in God through our Lord Jesus Christ, the one through whom we **now have** a *restored relationship* with God[11]. Romans 5: 6-11 (Common English Bible) emphasis added.

The legal dictionary I used throughout my career as a lawyer, Black's Law Dictionary, defines *certain* as: "*Ascertained; precise; identified; definitive; clearly known; unambiguous; or, in law, capable*

---

[10] Sinners like me

[11] No longer ungodly

of being identified or made known, without liability to mistake or ambiguity, from data already given[12]*."*

Therefore, the keyword used by the Apostle Paul in describing our salvation in chapter five of Romans is the word *certain*. Synonyms of this word include: free from doubt, inevitable, unquestionable, indisputable. These are very powerful words indeed.

Using certain in a sentence relative to the above bible verse can illustrate the point that Paul, I believe, seeks to make. As analogized from a *dictionary.com* definition, the certainty of salvation means that the recipients should be:

1. free from doubt or reservation; confident; sure: *I am certain that I am saved.*

2. destined; sure to happen (usually followed by an infinitive): *I am certain that I will be united with God in heaven.*

3. inevitable; bound to come: *Paul knew that Jesus provided the only path back to God.*

4. established as true or sure; unquestionable; indisputable: *It is certain that I have been saved from my sins.*

5. fixed; agreed upon; settled: *On a fixed day (my death) I will be in heaven with God; for an agreed-upon payment has already been made (by Christ's death). It is therefore settled: I am saved from God's wrath (His inability to have sin in His presence) because I have been absolved of my sins.*

6. definite or particular, but not named or specified: *A certain person (Christ) died for my sins. I am, therefore, certain (that Christ saved me).*

---

[12] Black's Law Dictionary, see also: Cooper v. Bigly, 13 Mich. 479; Losecco v. Gregory, 108 La. 648, 32 South. 9S6; Smith v. Fyler, 2 Hill (N. Y.) 049; Civ. Code La. 1900, art 3556.

7. that may be depended on; trustworthy; unfailing; reliable: ***This guarantee, given by God and confirmed through the resurrection of Christ, can absolutely be "taken to the bank!".***

Therefore, it is by faith that we believe and by that faith we have the guarantee - the assurance of salvation. Faith is the *assurance* of things hoped for, the *conviction* of things not seen. Hebrews 11:1. In their book, *The Wonder of Christmas*, authors Ed & Rob Renfro say this:

> Our God has scars – scars He received because He came to life in the same cruel world that we live in. Let life do you what it will. Let life take your dreams, your health, your loved ones, and your ability to figure things out and make sense of it all. But don't ever let it take from you the ***certainty*** that God is with you and will ***never*** forsake you. You are never alone. If you hold on to that promise, it will be enough to see you through[13].

It is my hope, by writing this book, that you will bask in the joy of the guarantee. That you will conclude, as I did, that God has established an unbreakable and guaranteed contract that assures salvation for all who accept this agreement. The law requires that a contract is not binding unless both parties understand the terms of the agreement and that a price (consideration) is paid for it to be consummated.

---

[13] Emphasis added, p. 104

God's contractual agreement with you is fully detailed in the most widely read book ever: the Bible. This book specifically spells out the terms of the agreement – God's covenant. The consideration for this agreement, or price to be paid, has been paid in full for you by His Son's death on a cross. I will also lay out an argument later in this book about the authenticity of the Bible and why this guarantee is set forth in a reliable document.

As you will no doubt surmise once you read this book, one of my favorite writers is Philip Yancey. He writes in a way that is, to me, *conversational*. It seems as if he is sitting in my living room and answering questions that, to my amazement, I have yet to ask. He explains the subject he is dealing with in a way that is easily understandable.

This way of communicating is very important when trying to convince someone of justness of your position. I tried to prepare the witnesses I put forth in trials this way. I would ask experts who were going to testify to explain his or her complicated engineering testimony in a fashion that a jury of everyday people can understand. Similarly, I have tried to emulate Yancey's writing style but with my own twist, from my own viewpoint. In his book, *Vanishing Grace*, Yancey so eloquently puts it this way:

> When I write, I want readers to consider a viewpoint I hold to be true, and I assume the same applies for those who write from the perspective of other religions or no religion at all. In doing so, I want to express my viewpoint in a way that communicates grace, which means compassion and

empathy for those I write about as well as respect for those who reject what I believe.[14]

This is my promise to you and I hope when you finish reading the following pages, that you conclude I met this laudatory goal.

---

[14] p. 145. iBooks

Chapter 2

Is a Trial Lawyer's Viewpoint important?

My primary focus, as you can tell, is an examination of the guarantee of eternal life. To prepare for this book I conducted an investigation of that offer of salvation. I wanted to determine if this offer was something that can be counted on – something that is certain. That issue is at the heart of this book.

A. How a Lawyer Examines Issues

As mentioned earlier, a trial lawyer undertakes the defense of a civil case by conducting an investigation called "discovery." This term is emblematic of the process. It involves discovering what the lawyer needs to evaluate his or her case and what is relevant in resolving the dispute at the center of a lawsuit. It consists of obtaining documents, asking witnesses questions under oath (depositions), and retaining experts to help in the analysis of the facts and data obtained during this phase of the case.

The purpose of this process is to determine what evidence is or is not relevant to the issues involved in the cause of action. It is an investigatory and winnowing process that will lead to a settlement of the case or a final determination by trial. I have attempted to use this same type of discovery system to examine the issue of God's promise of eternal life.

I started my discovery of the issue of *guaranteed salvation* at the end. I know that starting at the end is not something that comes naturally. The end, after all, is something that only happens in the future. When I was practicing law, I taught the associates who worked with me that when they received a new case assignment, the first thing they should do is to imagine their closing argument to the jury. A *closing argument* is the last thing that happens in a trial before the jury deliberates. For the lawyer, the closing argument is the *end* of the trial.

My advice was usually met with blank stares. "How can we start at the end?" Lawyers, they would say, "are supposed to be logical thinkers and logic dictates that we should start at the beginning." The associates had a hard time understanding that at the beginning of a case, a good trial lawyer always starts at the end. Starting at the end was a method I used to allow me to visualize what I wanted the closing argument to be.

Visualizing the end is not a tool that only trial lawyers use. In golf, a player is taught to visualize the way her next shot will travel so the ball ends up in the place the player wants. The greatest golfers play an entire round in their minds - visualizing each shot on every hole - before they hit their first drive.

> In order to get the most out of every performance learning how to visualize your golf shot will be crucial. When done correctly, it can put you in the right golf state of mind. Visualization doesn't require any type of physical skill to learn. However, it can be one of the most powerful tools to use on

the course. Many of the leading golf pros use visualization during practice or right before a competition. Visualizing a great performance on the course, right before you take [the first] shot is a tactic many pros swear by.[15]

In one of my favorite movies, The Greatest Game Ever Played, director Bill Paxton displays the ability of the two main characters to use visualization to successfully compete against each other in the 1913 US Open. The movie tells the true story of a blue-collar amateur golfer from Massachusetts, Francis Ouimet, who was pitted against the greatest golfer of his era, Harry Vardon, from Britain. Each golfer draws on his own method of visualizing how a round would be played by *seeing* how the ball will get in the hole before it is even struck. In this way, the golfer can plan his strokes to accomplish the ending he desires.

Fiction writers also use this tool. I learned from my wife, a writer, that the secret sauce used by mystery authors as they craft a *who-do-ne-it* plot twist is to write the ending first. Once the ending is established, a talented writer can write her book so that the story goes through many twists and bends but winds up "fitting the ending." In this way, the storyline and characters can be written in a fashion that they flow to a crescendo just as the story ends. The reader never sees the plot twist coming and can't, for the life of them, figure it out until the last chapter. Surprise endings are made possible by writing the ending first.

I wanted my associates to "write the ending," one that could convince a jury to do justice for the client who sent us their case. If they imagined the ending first, they could build their case so

---

[15] https://visionsgolf.com/how-to-visualize-your-golf-shots/

that the evidence they discover in a case fits the way they want the jury to decide the matter entrusted to them. By doing so, the associates could build their case by presenting the evidence in a way that would allow the evidence to withstand the "slings and arrows" of the contrary position being argued by their opponent. Such a method enables the lawyer to concentrate on the evidence that fits the desired ending. As Johnnie Cochran famously said in the OJ Simpson murder case "if it doesn't fit, you must acquit!"

B. The Opening Statement

I believe that God has already written the ending of your story. He knows how it will end. In fact, the ending of your story on earth is the beginning of the story of salvation that God has guaranteed. The end is where I believe we should begin our examination of the guarantee because salvation is finally delivered to you at the end of your life.

With this in mind, let me begin my opening statement to you, the jury.

> May it please the court. Ladies and gentlemen of the jury, my client has a guarantee, the strongest ever given. And I'm here to prove to you that this guarantee is backed by the most ironclad agreement ever conceived. The evidence will show that this guarantee is clearly set forth in a written document with clear and convincing language. And, if that is not enough, this contract is like no other. There are no exceptions, conditions, or limitations.

It is issued by a Grantor who has never withdrawn or changed the terms of the guarantee. Furthermore, despite proof that my client repeatedly breached his promise to fulfill his end of the bargain, the guarantee remains in full force and effect. This is so because the agreement allows for such breaches – even if they are committed 7 times...or 70 x 7!

Throughout this trial, I will present evidence to you that supports these rather bold and astonishing statements of the nature and scope of the guarantee. You will hear testimony from eyewitnesses who will attest to this covenant guarantee - people who actually witnessed the bedrock facts underpinning this agreement. I intend to prove that these statements are historically accurate and documented in such a way as to establish the credibility of the terms and provisions of this agreement.

Documentary proof will also be admitted into evidence that is factually relevant. These documents are reliable and their source, as I will show you, is both persuasive and believable. You will also hear from world-renowned experts who will testify about the validity of the guarantee and how it came to be. These experts have studied the issues involved in this case and will provide explanations of the theories advanced in support of the validity of the guarantee.

You will also be presented with evidence and theories by my able opponents. They will posit contrary positions to the validity of the guarantee and will question and attack the Giver of the guarantee. They will also seek to admit into evidence documents to dispute the positions that I will advance in this case. They too will seek to admit the testimony of expert witnesses that are expected to testify to positions that are contrary to the case I will present. Let me say that I welcome this evidence and I will meet the testimony with rigorous cross-examination and contrary conclusions. As an advocate, I will take on each piece of evidence brought forth by my opponents and provide you, the jury, with sufficient rebuttal evidence so that, at the end of this case, you will have enough proof to decide the issues in this case for yourself.

I trust that you will heed the judge's admonition given to you when you were selected for this jury: to listen to all the evidence presented by both sides before making up your minds. I believe that if you do this, you will see that the positions I have taken in this opening statement are not only true but that you will be moved to accept the guarantee of salvation offered by your Creator.

Thank you in advance for your time and attention to the evidence to be presented in this case.

This is the roadmap that I have laid out for you so that you can visualize the ending of this book. This book is designed to convince you that the guarantee of salvation given by God is real and unbreakable. My closing argument at the end of this book (please no peeking!) is made possible because I was able to start at the end - because the end has already been written.

The happy ending of this story has been put in writing and distributed in hundreds of different languages and versions. It is there in print for anyone to read. The ending of this story of salvation was the resurrection of Jesus from the dead. The resurrection was our assurance that the debt accrued by our sin has been paid in full. We know the ending, so we can now navigate the journey of our lives and write our own book of salvation.

C. **Logic and Virtue**

The primary method of analysis for lawyers is the deployment of the syllogism of logic. This logical analysis allows a lawyer to take established facts and arrive at a conclusion based on given or proven facts. This is also referred to as deductive reasoning. However, logic and virtue often conflict. I believe this conflict comes about when man tries to apply human standards to God. For instance, the law of man says that killing another human being is a much greater crime than stealing.

As a result, the punishment for these two crimes is vastly different. There is a logical relationship between the severity of the crime and the sentence that is meted out in response to a conviction for that crime. In God's view, any crime against God (any type of sin) is viewed as punishable by death[16]. God treats all sin the same. God,

---

[16] For the wages of sin is death ... Romans 6:23 NIV

being completely without sin, is completely righteous and therefore cannot tolerate any sin (or a sinful person) in His presence[17].
Murder is just as despised by God as someone being angry with their
neighbor[18]. Adultery is just as bad as lust[19] (ask Jimmy Carter[20]).
Jesus said that even if you kept every command of God, you will still
sin and be denied fellowship with God, i.e., no entry into heaven.
"For I tell you that unless your righteousness *surpasses* that of the
Pharisees and the teachers of the law, you will *certainly* not enter the
kingdom of heaven." Matthew 5:20, NIV, emphasis added.

So, let me get this straight, if I get angry at my neighbor and
you kill your friend, our punishment by God is the same? Yes, that
is God's standard. It hardly fits our notion of fair play, due process,
and logic. So how can we use a lawyer's tools of the trade to figure
this all out?

The story of Abraham, the father of the nation of Israel, is a
great example of the conflict between virtue and logic. The conflict
that comes about when we judge God's conduct by man's standards.
We all know how that story goes. God anointed Abraham as the
founder of the nation of Israel. In fact, God told Abraham that he
would be the father "of many nations" (Gen. 17:4, NIV). After his
son, Isaac was born, God decided to test Abraham's faith against
God's covenant promises. God told Abraham to take his son (or as
God put it the "son he loved") and journey far from home. Once
there Abraham was told by God to kill his beloved son as a sacrifice. Just a pleasant father/son outing! Read Genesis 22:1-10, NIV.
More detail on this later!

---

[17] More on this later (Chapter 4)

[18] Matthew 5:21-22 NIV

[19] Matthew 5:27-28 NIV

[20] Playboy Magazine, September 28, 1976

It doesn't take a lawyer to see the ethical quandary into which God has seemingly put the father of Israel – a crisis of virtue, so to speak. God has decreed that "Thou shalt not kill" and also that killing is a sin – which is an affront to God. Yet God is commanding Abraham to kill his own son – and then to dispose of the evidence as a burnt offering to God. As the famous philosopher Soren Kierkegaard noted:

> ... if it stands fast that Abraham is the representative of faith, and that faith is normally expressed in him whose life is not merely the most paradoxical that can be thought but so paradoxical that it cannot be thought at all. He acts by virtue of the absurd, for it is precisely absurd that he as the particular [that he intends to kill his son] is higher than the universal [that murder is unethical].

Abraham is therefore at one instant a tragic hero. He is either a murderer or a believer[21].

God, therefore, put Abraham in a logical no-win dilemma. This Kobayashi Maru[22] test by God positioned Abraham in a tough ethical quandary. Should he obey a direct command from God and kill his son or should he follow God's (and man's) law as set forth in the Ten Commandments? Well, we all know the rest of the story. As Abraham raised his knife to kill his only son, God intervened and provided a substitute - a ram - as the sacrificial offering to God. Abraham survived his test of faith – just as God knew he would.

---

[21] Fear and Trembling, Chapter 3. Soren Kierkegaard

[22] The test given to Star Fleet cadets to test their mettle. Put them in a no-win scenario and see how they perform under such conditions (see: Star Trek II: The Wrath of Kahn)

God's grace intervened and saved Isaac with a substitutional animal. That word – grace – will play a central role in this examination of the certainty of the guarantee.

In order for God's grace to flow down, Abraham had to put his faith in God and trust that God would redeem him and spare the life of his son. When Abraham put his trust in God, he was confidently moving forward with fulfilling God's command. Nothing that Abraham did or could do would bring him the salvation he desired. Placing his trust in God is what prevented his son's death. Grace, by definition, is the free and unmerited favor of God, as manifested in the salvation of sinners. Grace is the outpouring of forgiveness of sin, which assures us of salvation.

As John MacArthur explains, grace is unmerited and freely extended. As I discovered, this grace is also the logical extension of who God is, relative to His children. MacArthur said that the best example of this grace (that I believe is a logical syllogism) comes from the book of Romans, chapter four[23]. The reasoning goes as follows:

1. Grace saves us and is received by faith in God alone
2. Nothing we can do merits the grace of God
a. Doing good works is not enough – or else we will brag about all we have done to merit grace
3. Therefore, by definition, grace is from God and is not due to our own good works... or else grace would no longer be grace.

Sound legal reasoning thus establishes that grace is a gift from God and cannot be "won" or "bought" by anything we do. But, can we do something to "lose" or "sell" this grace? Is grace guaranteed?

---

[23] One Perfect Life, John F. MacArthur, p. 214

That question sits at the core of the issue that I grappled with my entire adult life. The issue that drove the research I conducted and resulted in the writing of this book. From my viewpoint as a trial lawyer, I will attempt to answer these questions using the tools of discovery and logical analysis.

I am heartened by this verse of Romans that comes smack-dab in the middle of chapter four: "Therefore, the promise comes by faith, so that it may be by grace and may be ***guaranteed***..." (Rom. 4:16, NIV). Paul, writing to the Jews and Gentiles, provided with certainty the assurance that faith in God brings a guarantee of forgiveness of sins and thus salvation.

Some people, however, are skeptical and will argue that there are no true *facts* in the legal sense because the statements of Saint Paul in Romans are not facts. I plan to address this skepticism in detail in later chapters but I want to comment on the notion that everything must be proven with total knowledge. The law does not demand perfect knowledge or depend any less on reasonable inferences and deductions that we rely on in everyday life. I understood this principle in my practice and it has been affirmed in a number of court decisions.

My favorite quote on the subject came from a dissenting opinion in 1919 written by the brilliant US Supreme Court jurist Oliver Wendell Holmes in the case of *Abrams v. United States*[24]. He said that "...all life is an experiment. Every year, if not every day we have to wager our salvation upon some prophecy based on imperfect knowledge." As a lawyer, I recognized the same. Each case had conflicting evidence, differences of opinion from experts, and *holes* in the testimony that warranted deductions or logical inferences.

---

[24] 250 U.S. 616, 630, 40 S. CT. 17,22

The great mathematician Pascal made a *wager* on salvation and the existence of God based on logic. This wager is grounded on the imperfect knowledge equation of salvation. It was described by him in the vacuum of an argument without any facts whatsoever. It involves a logical analysis of the issue of salvation as determinative of the outcome of different decisions or circumstances. It's called *a wager* because it contemplates someone wagering on whether God exists and, therefore, whether His guarantee of salvation is true. It relies on the mathematical principle of game theory which is defined as "the branch of mathematics concerned with the analysis of strategies for dealing with competitive situations where the outcome of a participant's choice of action depends critically on the actions of other participants"[25]. The wager uses the following logic (excerpts from *Pensées*, part III, §233):

1. God is, or God is not. Reason cannot decide between the two alternatives

2. A game is being played... where either heads or tails will turn up

3. You must wager. This is not optional.

4. Let us weigh the gain and the loss in wagering that God is. Let us estimate these two chances. If you gain, you gain all; if you lose, you lose nothing.

5. Wager, then, without hesitation that He is. (...) There is here an infinity of an infinitely happy life to gain, a chance of gain against a finite number of chances of loss, and what you stake is finite. And so our proposition is of infinite force when there is the finite to stake in a game where there are equal risks of gain and of loss, and the infinite to gain.

---

[25] Oxford International Dictionary

6. But some cannot believe. They should then at least *learn your inability to believe...* and *Endeavour then to convince* themselves.

Was that as difficult for you to understand as it was for me? Let me try to paraphrase this so it can be understood. It is as follows:

1. If you believe in God and God does exist, you will be rewarded with eternal life in <u>heaven</u>: thus, an *infinite gain*.
2. If you do not believe in God and God does exist, you will be <u>condemned</u> to remain in <u>hell</u> forever: thus an *infinite loss*.
3. If you believe in God and God does not exist, you will not be rewarded when you die: thus, you sustain a *finite loss* during your lifetime.
4. If you do not believe in God and God does not exist, you will not be rewarded, but you have lived your own life in your own way - not the life God wants us to lead: thus, you have received a *finite gain*.

Therefore, using logic and deductive reasoning, Pascal concluded that it was a much better choice to believe in God rather than not. Mind you, this is based on no facts, documents, testimony, or analysis of experts.

I will discuss Pascal's Wager in more depth in chapter eight when I examine the reasons why the Bible is a true and reliable source of information about God's guarantee of salvation.

D. The Most Valuable Truth-Seeking Method

Cross-examination is the greatest legal engine ever invented for the discovery of truth. You can do anything with a bayonet except sit on it. A lawyer can do anything with cross-examination if he is skillful enough not to impale his own cause upon it. — JOHN HENRY WIGMORE

Yes, cross-exam is a valuable tool used by lawyers to reveal the truth. And, I believe, the art form known as cross-examination explains the reality of God. Ravi Zacharias[26] explains it this way: "... Proverbs 18:17 (NLT): 'The first to speak in court sounds right—until the cross-examination begins.' In other words, often when we hear one side of a case presented, the evidence sounds persuasive. But then we hear the other side of the story, and suddenly we see the initial case crumble in the light of new facts and arguments."[27]

Throughout this book, I will attempt to use this essential legal method to extract the truth about salvation and the promised guarantee given by God and paid for with the death of His Son on the cross.

---

[26] This book was written before the allegations and revelations about Mr. Zacharias came to the fore, however, references to his book are included

[27] *The End of Reason.* Zondervan, 2008. iBooks.

Chapter 3

The Giver of the Guarantee

Any guarantee is as good as the person or entity that issues the promises made. As the old saying goes, a guarantee is as good as the paper it is written on. The legal term for the issuer of a guarantee is the "grantor." Even the most powerful nation on earth cannot issue an ironclad guarantee. US Treasury notes are backed by the United States government. A pretty good guarantor, one would think. However, how good was the guarantee during the stock market crash of 1929?

The US Constitution even contains a guarantee of sorts. Article IV, Section 1 of the United States Constitution, is called the Full Faith and Credit Clause. It is so named because it addresses the duties that states within the United States have to respect, specifically the "public acts, records, and judicial proceedings of every other state." It is supposed to guarantee that the laws or judicial proceedings of one state are to be enforced in another state. As an example, Florida is supposed to give full faith and credit to a divorce decree given by the state of Nevada.

Since this is in the constitution it is an iron-clad guarantee, right? By now you must surmise the answer is "it depends" because, after all, I am a lawyer.

As Lee Corso likes to say on College GameDay, "not so fast my friend." This supposed guarantee has been the subject of much litigation and, as a result of a number of US Supreme Court decisions, quite a few exceptions have arisen. So, even the most powerful nation on earth cannot issue a written guarantee that holds true in every situation, no matter what. As a legal commentator so eloquently put it:

> ...despite the more humble intent of the Framers, the Clause has evolved into a normative constitutional provision with corresponding mandates for the interstate effect of a state's "judicial Proceedings," or judgments, and a state's "public Acts," or statutes. While judgments traditionally receive nationwide [enforcement]..., statutes are given effect only if they do not contravene the public policy of the [enforcing state][28].

In other words, the US government cannot guarantee that a statute enacted in Alabama will be enforced in California when it involves an issue of enforcement of the public policy of Alabama in a California court – or vice versa. How can we have confidence in any so-called ironclad guarantee if the one given by the United States government – written into the constitution - has exceptions and conditions?

I dare to think that any guarantee given by any person or entity is able to withstand history and circumstance. I am reminded of the story of the wise old King and his request for an ironclad guarantee

---

[28] Between Judgment and Law: Full Faith ac Credit, Public Policy, and State Records. Elizabeth Redpath, Emory Law Journal, Vol. 62, Issue 3

that would remain inviolate in every circumstance and for all time. The occasion that caused the king to seek the guarantee happened during the planning process concerning the construction of a monument that was to mark his fortieth anniversary as the ruler of his country. To begin this process, he called together his wisest and most trusted advisors. The king brought together an esteemed group of theologians, professors, lawyers, judges, engineers, scientists, and politicians. He assembled this prestigious group to give them an important task. With his queen, princes, and princesses, generals, ministers, and inner-circle in attendance, the king gave the commission to this highly respected advisory council. It was thus:

> *I want you design the cornerstone of this great monument celebrating the fortieth year of my reign and chisel into its base a phrase that is to stand the test of time. The words that you place there must be true for all time (now and into the future) and correct in every circumstance (good or bad).*

Upon hearing the King's challenge, the committee of advisors nodded their assent to the task at hand and were whisked away to begin their work. These advisors were taken to a mountain retreat and provided every creature comfort in a sanctuary setting. The king hoped that this environment would stimulate great conversation and debate on the challenge assigned to them by the king. Every morning they would begin their discussions and would use their collective store of knowledge and wisdom to try and find the right answer that would give the king the guarantee he wished. They thought, prayed, discussed, and debated for over three months. At last, they sent word to the king that their task had been accomplished.

The following week the king called for a great celebration and holiday to announce to the kingdom that the task had been successfully completed. He planned an official unveiling of the cornerstone. It would take place at the stroke of noon the following week in the great courtyard of the castle. A multitude of subjects arrived at the appointed time and filled the garden of the palace with great anticipation. The king's banners and flag were flying and his royal band was playing as the king and queen took their place on the throne. There, before the assembled court and the people of his kingdom, was a raised dais upon which was placed a large square object covered by a sumptuous royal purple drape. Behind the drape-covered object stood all of the King's wisest advisors, grinning ear-to-ear.

After the band finished its triumphant song and the wild applause died down, the king motioned to the crowd to sit as he addressed the assembled counsel. "Wise men and women of the kingdom, have you completed the task I have commanded of you?"

With a humble bow, the advisors said in union "Yes, your majesty."

The king went on; "Did you craft a phrase that is guaranteed to stand the test of time?"

Again, bowing to show their respect, they answered, "Yes, your majesty."

"Are the words that you have placed upon this cornerstone for my greatest monument guaranteed true for all time?" the king inquired.

"They are, your royal highness" was the response.

The King inquired further. "Are these words true now and will they be true into the future?"

"Yes, our mighty king" was the reply by each of the assembled experts.

And, the king pressed, "Are these words that have been chiseled into the cornerstone guaranteed to be true and fitting in *every* circumstance – in bad times and in good?"

Without hesitation they said, in one voice, "They are!"

The whole assembly was then holding its collective breath as the king said, "Sound the trumpets and clang the symbols" and motioned to his knights to remove the velvet drape to reveal the cornerstone. It seemed like time stood still as the knights gently and slowly removed the covering to expose the beautiful, polished block of gleaming granite. There, etched into the stone, was a phrase that was placed into the face of the rock upon which the monument was to be positioned. The words read, "*This Too Shall Pass.*"

The only guarantee that the greatest minds could give the king was that nothing will last forever. Nothing can withstand the vagaries of what will happen to each of us. In good times or bad, this too shall pass. Now and into the future, whatever we are going through, happy or sad, shall pass. Is this sobering thought the end of the discussion? I hope not, or all my work on this book is finished. No, not everything shall pass into nothingness. There *is* a guarantee given by an impeccable source – a source that can issue the guarantee with the ultimate authority. The guarantor that gives this guarantee has all the power, all the knowledge, and all the authority. His guarantee has no expiration date. And this one has no exceptions or conditions. This guarantee shall never pass!

But before we can understand the guarantee we have to get our heads around why God would give us such a thing. After all, each and every one of us are sinners undeserving of a guarantee from the Ruler of the Universe. As sinners, we are separated from God. None of us (all sinners) can seek a guarantee, can we? It would be similar to purchasing a rusted-out 1970 VW Beatle without a properly functioning engine, and asking the car dealer to give you a two-year warranty that this car will operate properly and without problems. And if problems do occur, the car will be repaired – parts and labor included. The dealer would respond to such a request with laughter and point to the "As Is" sticker on the side window. Andy Stanley put it this way:

> Jesus, along with a host of others, makes it pretty clear that we were goners, hopelessly separated from God. But God had mercy and gave us exactly what we did not deserve: forgiveness. The price? His Son. The truth is, we owed God a debt we couldn't pay ...[29]

What he is saying, I believe, is that even though our old VW Bug is broken down and lacking a functioning engine, God will issue us a lifetime guarantee to get each of us home to Him. And we don't have to pay a thing for this guarantee. The warranty that comes with this vintage VW is included in the price. This is so because someone has already paid the price for us.

A. Created in His Likeness

The universal truth is that we have all sinned and will continue to sin. We will do so despite our best intentions and to the exclusion of our most fervent promises. In fact, if you are as I am, you will continue to commit the same sin, day after day in a never-ending cycle. If we are created in God's image why is this so? The Apostle Paul gives us a peek into the type of people God created... and chose. He said that "...God chose the foolish things of the world to shame the wise; God chose the weak things of the world to shame the strong. He chose the lowly things of this world and the despised things — and the things that are not — to nullify the things that are, so that

---

[29] Enemies of the Heart, Multnoma Books. P. 236 (iBook)

no one may boast before him" (1 Cor. 1: 27-30 NIV). Basically, God chose all of us no matter our outward or inward defects or appearances.

There is no greater example of this than the famed *Elephant Man*. This man was discovered and put on display at carnivals and side shows because of his disfigured body. People paid ten cents to view a creature that they saw as lowly. Carnival operators considered him weak. But God viewed him as beloved. To understand why God would accept a sinner like us (who must seem disfigured to God because we are sinful people), the Elephant Man teaches us a very valuable lesson. A lesson about God and His guarantee of salvation. Was this lowly, weak and disfigured person created by God? Was the Elephant Man a person who God created his own image?

Philip Yancey in his book, *Rumors of Another World*, gives us a glimpse into God's character through the retelling of the story of the Elephant Man. He ends his description of the life of this "despised person" this way:

> God himself assured the prophet Samuel, "The Lord does not look at the things man looks at. Man looks at the outward appearance, but the Lord looks at the heart." Everyone who met the Elephant Man went away marveling that such a pure and gentle soul — such a heart — could live inside that monstrous exterior.

> ...I must consciously call to mind the apostle Paul's advice, "Set your minds on things above, not on earthly things."

Dr. Frederick Treves found treasure hidden in the misshapen disguise of the Elephant Man. These are his final words about the patient who became his friend: "As a specimen of humanity, Merrick was ignoble and repulsive; but the spirit of Merrick, if it could be seen in the form of the living, would assume the figure of an upstanding and heroic man, smooth browed and clean of limb, with eyes that flashed undaunted courage."[30]

We are as the Elephant Man because of our sinful nature. An almighty and blameless God must look past our sinful exterior and see something deep within us that He created in his own image. Something that is heroic, smooth-browed, and clean of limb, with eyes that flash undaunted courage.

As I will try to discuss in this book, I believe that God sees us this way because His grace poured out through our belief in His Son, who wiped our sins away and allows us to be seen in a way that is free of the grotesque stain of sin. God, after all, made us in His likeness and even when we reject Him, God reaches out to us and gives us a guarantee that we can have fellowship with Him.

The beloved author, C. S. Lewis, found love late in life. And when he found the love of his life he fell headlong into marriage. She changed everything in his life and he wanted to be by her side every moment. They tried to spend every waking minute together. He was never so happy. After a brief time, however, his love and his best friend was diagnosed with cancer. He had to watch as she suffered a long, drawn-out, downward spiral that ended in a painful death. Lewis was overcome by grief. This pillar of Christianity began

---

[30] Chapter 12, iBooks

to crumble, to doubt his faith. He questioned how a God who created this wonderful woman could let cancer ravage her body and take away his only love in such a terrible way.

It took a long time to come to grips with this tragedy but out of it Lewis had a renewed faith and spirit. In his book about the experience he said this about God's creation of people: "And then, of her, and of every created thing I praise, I should say, in some way, in its unique way, like Him who made it...Thus, up from the garden to the Gardener, from the sword to the Smith. To the life-giving Life and the Beauty that makes beautiful."[31]

God finds treasure in our broken, sinful souls and allows us to enter eternity as upstanding women and men with our sins washed clean. This He has guaranteed. As God revealed to the prophet, He will look beyond our sins and find beneath our gentle souls a beauty that is acceptable to a Holy God. Therefore, even though we are "repeat offender" sinners, we have been created in His image and are made acceptable to God by the blood of His son who paid the price to get the guarantee for us.

E. The Authority to Grant the Guarantee

The guarantee of salvation that is given by God has been codified throughout the history of God's interaction with His creation. God first revealed it directly to a small number of people. Thereafter, it was revealed to a wider audience through His prophets.[32] Finally, God's guarantee of salvation became known to the whole world through His son, Jesus.

---

[31] A Grief Observed. Chap. 4, P. __

[32] "All the prophets testify about him that everyone who believes in him receives forgiveness of sins through his name." Acts 10:43 (NIV)

It is natural to be skeptical of the guarantee because fallible humans have recorded and passed on through time the terms of the promised salvation. You cannot help but ask if there is proof that Jesus had the *authority* to issue such a guarantee to the whole world? The best way to determine that is through Jesus's own words. Here is what Jesus said, "Father, the time has come. Glorify your Son, that your Son may glorify you. For you granted him authority over all people that he might give eternal life to all those you have given him" (John 17:1-2, NIV). Jesus said that He had the authority to issue the guarantee to ALL people. He said that this guarantee will give each of us eternal life – and eternal life means fellowship with God for all time.

But some will ask, *Isn't this proclamation by Jesus just words?* How do we know that Jesus had the *actual* authority to say such things? The answer to this question calls my legal training and experience into play. In a civil trial, the person testifying may make a statement about themselves and their position of authority. This is called a self-serving statement or self-serving testimony. Such a statement is viewed by the courts with a healthy dose of skepticism because such a proclamation is just that; a statement of authority made by the person who professes to have that power. However, when such a statement of authority is confirmed by someone else, it is bolstered in such a way as to make it credible.

The Bible provides proof of Jesus's authority through the testimony of someone who had His own vested authority. And by someone who would be viewed in a court of law as having an adversarial relationship to Jesus. In a trial, if someone who is a recognized authority provides testimony about the authority of another, this testimony can form the basis for the self-serving statement to be deemed credible. For instance, if a professional society has deemed a person an expert in her field, then the testimony by that person, although self-serving, is given greater weight[33]. If an adversary testifies regarding the authority of his opponent, this would naturally give credibility to the person who made the self-serving statement. This is so because the adversary has a natural interest in testifying against the authority of an opponent. On many occasions, I would get the opposing expert in a case to testify that my expert is a recognized expert in the field he or she is testifying about. Usually, I would stipulate in a trial to the expertise of an opposing expert to forgo that expert's self-serving testimony about his many accomplishments.[34]

When someone or a recognized organization confirms the authority of a witness in trial, the weight to be given to their testimony is viewed by the jury based on whether the attesting witness has any bias in favor or is opposed to the person issuing the self-serving statement. For instance, if the person that is making the self-serving statement is related to the person affirming the authority "by blood or marriage," the jury would look skeptically on that person because the blood relative would tend to be biased in favor of the person giving the self-serving statement.

However, if the person who is affirming the authority has an adverse relationship, their testimony will be weighted in favor of the self-serving person. For example, if the expert for the plaintiff in a civil case affirms the authority of the witness giving testimony for the defendant, the adverse witness's testimony would be viewed more favorably by the jury. This is so because it would be in the best interest of the plaintiff for their expert to discredit the

---

[33] An example of this is where a surgeon has attained her "Board Certification" from a National Board in a specific area of surgery - such as "Plastic Surgery"

[34] I am using this only as an example or analogy – because if Jesus says He has His father's authority that is the end of the story as far as I am concerned and, therefore, should be unquestioned

defense witness, not bolster that witness's self-serving statement of authority to speak.

In the book of Matthew, there is documentation of an inter-action between Jesus and a Roman figure of authority – a centu-rion. In the Roman Empire, a centurion held absolute authority over his men[35]. This soldier was vested with authority by the Roman military – a force that reported directly to the emperor. In chapter eight of the book of Matthew, he deals with a grieving centurion who was greatly troubled over an injured servant who was para-lyzed. The Roman military officer humbled himself before Jesus and said his house was not worthy to host Jesus. He pleaded with Jesus to just "say the word" and his servant would be healed. He spoke these words to our Lord with the assurance in his heart that Jesus had the authority to heal his servant. Think of it! An officer of an occupying army who held unquestioned authority over 100 men to carry out the orders of an emperor of Rome, was attesting to the authority of Jesus to heal a broken man. Read Matthew 8:6-9 (NIV). This centurion most decidedly was in an adverse relationship to this Jewish rabbi. This was graphically borne out through the torture, humiliation, and crucifixion of Jesus. The centurion was assuredly an adverse witness attesting to the authority of Jesus.

Max Lucado phrased it this way:

> [Jesus] marveled, and said to those who followed, "Assuredly, I say to you, I have not found such great faith, not even in Israel!...Go your way; and as you have believed, so let it be done for you." And his servant was healed that same hour. (vv. 8, 10,

---

[35] Centurion, the principal professional officer in the armies of ancient Rome and its empire. The centurion was the commander of a centuria (about 100 men), which was the unit of a Roman legion. www.britannica.com

13) The centurion's confidence in Jesus ran deep. Jesus could handle the request long distance. Just a word from Jesus would suffice. Jesus was stunned. Finally, his response implies, someone understands my authority! Do we? Jesus has unimpeachable authority. "He sustains everything by the mighty power of his command" (Heb. 1:3 NLT). "God exalted him to the highest place and gave him the name that is above every name" (Phil. 2:9 NIV). The Roman government tried to intimidate him. False religion tried to silence him. The devil tried to kill him. All failed. Even "death was no match for him" (Acts 2:24 MSG). [36]

He was not kidding when he declared, "All authority in heaven and on earth has been given to me" (Matt. 28:18 NIV).

The authority of Jesus was thus confirmed by an adverse witness. A commander of an occupying force that eventually would carry out the death sentence imposed by the Sanhedrin. Hardly a friendly witness. In a civil trial, such a witness would be viewed as a very credible witness to the self-serving statement made by Jesus as to his authority to give the guarantee.

John MacArthur says this about the authority of Jesus in his book, *One Perfect Life*, "He will judge the world in righteousness by the Man whom He has ordained. He has given *assurance* of this to all by raising Him from the dead." (Emphasis added.) MacArthur affirms, I believe, that God has given us a guarantee (assurance) that

---

[36] Before Amen. P. 96-97

Jesus had the authority to forgive our sins as evidenced by His death on the cross and resurrection on Easter Sunday.

Eugene Peterson put it this way:

> When mountain climbers are in dangerous terrain, on the face of a cliff or the slopes of a glacier, they rope themselves together. Sometimes one of them slips and falls—backslides. But not everyone falls at once, and so those who are still on their feet are able to keep the backslider from falling away completely. And of course, in any group of climbers, there is a veteran climber in the lead, identified for us in the letter to the Hebrews as "Jesus, who both began and finished this race we're in" (Heb 12:2).[37]

A. The Dying Declaration

Another credibility tool used for the admission of evidence at trial is the *dying declaration*. It is often used in movies as a "death bed confession." In law, it is "... a statement made by a declarant, who is unavailable to testify in court (typically because of the declarant's death), who made the statement under a belief of certain or impending death."[38] The law gives special credibility and admissibility to such a statement because it is made under circumstances where the person making the statement (the declarant) firmly believes he or she is going to die within a short period of time. This rule originated in the 1200s. In Medieval English courts,

---

[37] "A Long Obedience in the Same Direction". InterVarsity Press, IBooks, P. 134

[38] Legal Information Institute, Cornell Law School, Section 804 (b) (2), Federal Rules of Evidence

the principle originated of *nemo moriturus praesumitur mentiri* — "no-one on the point of death should be presumed to be lying." An incident in which a dying declaration was admitted as evidence has been found in a 1202 case[39]. It was founded on the principle that a person will not utter a lie when they believe they are "going to meet their maker."

What does this have to do with the reliability of the guarantee given by Jesus and by Jesus's authority to give such a guarantee? As a lawyer, I was required to provide foundational proof to the judge before he or she would allow admission into evidence of some types of testimony. In the case of a dying declaration, this foundational proof would require testimony that the declarant (Jesus) made the statement under a belief of certain or impending death. In the case of Jesus that proof would, unfortunately, be very easy to prove. It is without dispute that death through the means of crucifixion was certain to occur. In fact, in the case of Jesus, he was savagely scourged by a whip designed to tear His flesh in the hours before He was crucified. He was then forced to carry the cross He was to be hung on for almost a mile, without any hydration. By the time he was nailed to the cross he was already near death.

Therefore, the foundational proof that Jesus was "under a belief of certain impending death" at the time He made certain statements would be without question. Therefore, the dying declarations of Jesus would be admissible in evidence in a criminal or civil trial and would form credible evidence of the truth of the matters contained in those statements.

If we apply this dying declaration rule to Jesus, we can see that one of the last things Jesus said related to the guarantee. The Bible records it this way. When Jesus was led to the cross two other men,

---

[39] En.wikipedia.org/wiki/Dying_declaration

criminals, were led out with him. They were also crucified with Jesus, one on his right and one on his left. In Luke 23: 32-34 (NIV), Luke goes on to describe this scene as follows:

> One of the criminals who hung there hurled insults at him: "Aren't you the Christ? Save yourself and us!"

> But the other criminal rebuked him "Don't you fear God" he said "since you are under the same sentence? We are punished justly, for we are getting what our deeds deserve. But this man has done nothing wrong."

> Then he said, "Jesus, remember me when you come into your kingdom."

> Jesus answered him "I tell you the truth, today you will be with me in paradise." Luke 23:39-43 (NIV)

Jesus' dying declaration stated, without equivocation, that he had the authority to guarantee eternal life. One of His last statements before He "committed his spirit" to God was that the sinner (the criminal) who confessed his sin and asked for forgiveness from Jesus would be in heaven upon his death. This powerful evidence proved that (1) Jesus had the authority to give the guarantee; (2) the guarantee was available to any sinner; (3) the guarantee could be claimed by professing your belief in Jesus as your savior, confessing that you are a sinner and relying on Jesus to forgive you of your sin. Once the criminal did these fundamental and important things, Jesus guaranteed him forgiveness and, as a result of that cleansing of his sin, promised him eternal life with Jesus in heaven upon his death. Jesus even punctuated this fact by saying in his dying declaration, "I tell you the truth..."

These are only some of the ways that the source of the guarantee could be proven in a court of law. Once I began examining the origins of the guarantee of salvation it became obvious to me that God not only provided written evidence of the terms of his guarantee of salvation, but He did so over a long period of time. As I read the Old and New Testaments, I was amazed at the consistency of God's plan of salvation. It began with the way God showed Abraham how He would provide a *substitute sacrifice* for the expected death of Abraham's only son. It then developed into the use of a scapegoat which the Israelites heaped their sins upon and drove out of the encampment as a method for the nomadic Jewish people who wandered in the desert to atone for their sin. God gave His people methods of sacrificing animals without blemish to atone for sins.

God provided priests who would offer these atoning sacrifices on behalf of everyone as a way to ask for forgiveness from a holy Creator. And this process was completed when God sent His only Son into the world to live among His creation and teach God's love and understanding. God planned that Jesus would be the ultimate substitutional sacrifice for the sins of mankind. For God so loved the world that He allowed Jesus, without the blemish of sin, to die for the sins of us all.

In succeeding chapters, I will attempt to examine the guarantee of salvation in such a way as to provide you with some sense of assurance that the guarantee is real and is obtainable by anyone. I will also examine and offer proof that the Bible is a reliable historical account worthy of belief that it is an authentic document.

Chapter Four:

Why Do We Need the Guarantee?

O ne of the primary things I focused on when preparing for a jury trial was trying to foretell and comprehend questions the jury may have about my case. I would ask myself, *If I were hearing this case, what proof would I need to decide the issues presented?* Once I thought I had a feel for these questions, I would endeavor to craft my case so that the questions the jury may have would be answered as the case was presented to them. In this way, I would have a greater chance of convincing the jury of the justness of my client's case.

In this book, I have sought to do the same regarding questions you may have relative to the guarantee of salvation and how that relates to you. Therefore, this chapter will focus on one of the primary questions I would ask myself if I were considering the case of a guarantee from God. Namely, what good is a guarantee if it is not needed?

I am a good person. I am not a habitual liar or a cheat. I study the Bible every day. I pay my taxes and have never been arrested. I have been married to the same wonderful woman for over forty-five years. I am a pretty good dad and attend church (almost) every Sunday. Heck, I have even led a men's Bible study for over ten years. I give to the church and to charities regularly. I give of my time by mentoring a young man who is without a dad. I don't have any bad vices although I watch football almost every Saturday and Sunday afternoon in the fall.

If you add up every good thing I have done in my life I think it would outweigh the bad. Isn't that enough to get me into heaven? Aren't the scales tipped, even if ever so slightly, in favor of me entering the pearly gates when I die? Certainly, St. Peter will check my naughty and nice list and welcome me into heaven...*won't he?*

Living a good life is not enough for God to allow you into His presence. You must, as I have said before, be perfect. You must be without sin.

This standard reminds me of the dilemma my clients often faced when one of their products was involved in an injury. During my years as a trial lawyer defending manufacturers in product liability lawsuits, I have found that some plaintiffs' lawyers basically present such a notion to the jury. They blame the product for causing their client's injuries even though this product has been on the market for ten years, over three million units have been sold and this type of accident has only occurred five times before. This amounts to a "failure rate" of .00000167%. Despite this excellent track record of safe operation, the lawyers claim the product's manufacturer was responsible for the injury to their client.

The Plaintiff's lawyer expects perfection. He or she still claims that the person who misused this product and caused his own injuries is entitled to compensation. It seems as though the manufacturer must make a perfect product. That is an impossible standard to use when judging a man-made object.

Even the most well-built and expertly maintained pieces of equipment fail. My former partner, Andy, who went on to become a respected judge, used the analogy of a fine race car when he tried a product's liability case. He told the jury of gleaming machines, driven by daredevil drivers as they race the clock and each other at speeds unimaginable. These cars, costing millions of dollars, are designed by the best engineers, using the best equipment and materials in the most modern facilities in the country. Major car manufactures lend their expertise in the design and build stages as the cars go from the drawing board to the test track. They are tested to the limit, refined, and redesigned to make them the most perfect machines to grace a race track.

What's more, the racing teams have dozens of mechanics whose only job is to make subtle changes to the car and to keep it running at peak performance. Months go into road-testing and time trials. Then the best drivers in the world are selected and teamed up with the engineers and mechanics. Expert drivers put these marvelous machines to the test and learn to drive the car in such a way as to enhance its endurance and speed. Everything culminates in racing events that take place before thousands and in some cases, hundreds of thousands of race fans. As Andy made his case for an analogy to the product on trial in his case, he told the jury, "and what do fans see during each race? Blown engines, shredded transmissions, busted pinion rods and shattered dreams." He pointed out that even the most carefully built and expertly tested machines, made with the best and most expensive materials, still fail. Failure is part of racing. Failure occurs despite every care being taken to make the machine perfect.

Sin is like this. Despite all our best efforts, sin is a part of every life. No matter how we are trained and how strong our will is, sin invades our lives. So, if failure and sin are an unmistakable and inexorable part of life, why not simply throw up our hands and give up? There is no way we can be perfect. Perfection in anything simply does not exist. It's as if we were in a situation where we lived for eighty years but we only sinned .00000167% of the time. This would be an incredible (and unattainable) accomplishment for any person. However, by God's standard, we would not be *good enough*. "Christ sets an unattainable standard. This sums up what the law itself demanded" (James 2:10). Christ was the only being to walk the face of the earth without sin.

Though this standard is impossible to meet, God could not lower it without compromising His own perfection. "He who is perfect could not set an imperfect standard of righteousness." However, we should not lose heart because "[t]he marvelous truth of the gospel is that Christ has met this standard on our behalf (2 Cor. 5:21)."[40]

In the days that Jesus walked among us, there was a group of people who were the most "religious" people of the Jewish faith. They took pride in following all the rules and thus not sinning. They were called Pharisees. They "religiously" followed all of God's rules and were very devout in following those prescriptions, laws, and commands. For example, in order to follow the commandment that they shall not work on the Sabbath, they would refrain from even walking up a flight of stairs for fear that this would be considered work. In order to follow the rule of tithing ten percent of their wealth, they would set aside ten percent of everything they had for God – ten percent of their salt, their flour, their grain, their clothes, etc. They were the closest example of doing what God said they should do - so much so that they were revered in Jewish society.

Do you know what Jesus said of them? "For I tell you that unless your righteousness <u>surpasses</u> that of the Pharisees and the teachers of the law (the Scribes), you will certainly not enter the kingdom of heaven" (Matt. 5:20 NIV), emphasis added. How can someone

---

[40] John F. MacArthur, One Perfect Life, Chapter 51. The Sermon on the Mount: True Righteousness and External Morality

surpass them? It looks like my idea of my good outweighing the bad just went out the window. I am NEVER getting into heaven!

John MacArthur in his book *One Perfect Life* put it this way:

> On the one hand Jesus was calling His disciples to a deeper, more radical holiness than that of the Pharisees. Pharisaism had a tendency to soften the law's demands by focusing only on external obedience. In the verses that follow, Jesus unpacks the full moral significance of the law and shows that the righteousness the law calls for actually involves an internal conformity to the spirit of the law, rather than mere external compliance to the letter.

This sets an impossible barrier to works--salvation. Scripture teaches repeatedly that sinners are capable of nothing but flawed and imperfect righteousness (e.g., Isa. 64:6). Therefore, the only righteousness by which sinners may be justified is the perfect righteousness of God that is imputed to those who believe (Gen. 15:6; Rom. 4:5).[41] Not only that we should conform to all of God's commandments, but that we should be conformed internally so that, for example, if we give ten percent of everything we have we should do so with a spirit of generosity and joy.

Now I am really getting apprehensive. I can't do better than the people who followed the law and commands of God with a religious fervor. And, according to Jesus, I can never enter heaven unless I am *perfectly* righteous – totally without sin; inside and out! How did we get here? Isn't America built on those who *worked* their way to

---

[41] One Perfect Life, Part Five, Notes

the top? Don't we get ahead by the sweat of our brow and the determination of our will?

Why can't I be good enough to get my final reward and gain admittance to heaven? What can I do? How does the guarantee enter into the equation of *what we must do to be perfect enough for God?* I hope to present the answer to this very question. My desire is that you will be presented with proof that will, in turn, lead you to answer this question for yourself.

A. How Can I be Good Enough?

The tension between perfection and forgiveness is resolved by grace. God, knowing that we can never be perfect (free of sin) sent grace in the form of His Son, Jesus so that all who believe in Him will be purified by and through God's grace. This tension is felt by most, if not all, of God's children.

One of the world's greatest authors tackled the notion of perfection and grace in his novels. Russian writer Fyodor Dostoevsky had his own way of meeting these seemingly divergent issues head-on. Author Philip Yancey gives us an overview of the tension that occurs when God's perfect standard - His "high ideals" - meets with our urgent need for forgiveness and redemption.

> Dostoevsky lived a tortured life but he got one thing right: his novels communicate grace and forgiveness with beautiful stories. He spent ten years in exile poring over the New Testament and emerged with unshakable Christian convictions. In prison he came to believe that only through being loved is a human being capable of love. He went on to write about grace in his novels.

From Dostoevsky I learned the full extent of grace. Not only is the kingdom of God within me, Christ himself dwells there. There is only one way for us to resolve the tension between the high ideals of the gospel and the grim reality of ourselves. We must accept that we will never measure up and also understand that we do not have to. We are judged by the righteousness of the Christ who lives within, not our own. Why did Jesus give us the Sermon on the Mount? Not to burden us but to tell us what God is like. He gave us God's ideal to teach us that we should never stop striving yet also to show us that none of us will ever reach that ideal.[42]

I don't know about you, but I am relieved to find out that I can never measure up to the standards God expects of His children. I have company in my sinfulness – the entire world! But "my fears are released" by the very same person who revealed God's standard of perfection, Jesus. Because of the indwelling of Christ and His ever-present love for me, my burden of perfection is lifted. The sweat of our brows cannot provide the moral authority or avenue to get us to heaven. Only God and our faith in Him will be able to bridge the chasm that is created by our sin.

B. The Human Need for God

I have noticed that the catch-phrase "You can't buy happiness" has been borne out by today's headlines. Powerful business people

---

[42] Philip Yancey & Brenda Quinn. "Meet the Bible." Pages 1454-55. Zondervan. iBooks.

– multimillionnaires – are constantly trying to find happiness in extramarital affairs, drugs, thrill-seeking behavior, and other dangerous undertakings that eventually lead to destruction. Famous actors and musicians who have money, power, and the adoration of millions of fans end up in the same boat. They are lonely, self-absorbed, broken, and unloved.

These people who seem to have everything still can have difficulty finding happiness. Perhaps people with wealth and power focus on what they have accumulated and the pleasure these things can bring rather than putting their trust in God. This may be why they are so unfulfilled and unhappy. They often end up empty-handed when they go searching for something that brings them true meaning. How can these people with seemingly everything remain so empty?

One of the richest and most powerful people who ever walked the face of this earth was King Solomon. Living in the period of time between approximately 970 to 930 BC, he ruled the Middle East with impressive power and authority. He built great buildings and cities and was probably the most educated man of his time. He was fabulously wealthy and is reputed to have been the richest person of that age. He had property across a vast region of the world, commanded the largest army, and had a horde of servants who attended to his every wish. He excelled in every aspect of life. This man had *everything* a person could ever want or dream of attaining. He was the poster boy of having it all.

Yet, when he was getting old and taking stock of his life, he famously said, "Meaningless! Meaningless! Utterly Meaningless! Everything is meaningless!" (Eccles. 1:2 NIV). The person who owned everything his heart could possibly desire, the man who conquered most of the known world at the time, the all-powerful king; he summed it all up as... meaningless. The wisest, most educated person of his day said "for with much wisdom comes much sorrow, the more knowledge the more grief" (Eccles. 1:18 NIV). Seems the more things change, the more they stay the same. Everything old is new again.

The Reverend Billy Graham put it this way:

> The heart cannot be satisfied with computers and sophisticated video equipment. We were created "a little lower than the angels" (Hebrews 2:7), and our souls can never subsist on the husks of this plea-sure-seeking world. Our deeper yearnings and long-ings can be met only by a renewed fellowship with the One in whose image we were created: God. As St. Augustine said, "Thou hast made us for Thyself, and our hearts are restless till they find their rest in Thee."[43]

King Solomon's heart was restless and yearned to find answers for his conclusion that everything was utterly meaningless. Despite all of the buildings he built, the powerful army he commanded, the people who attended to his every want or need, yet, nothing satis-fied his heart. It was restless.

As the song on the Urban Cowboy soundtrack put it, he was "looking for love in all the wrong places." In the end, after all of his hand wringing and spewing forth gloom, doom, and laments, Solomon finally came to a realization. Without God at the center of his life, he could find no pleasure or meaning in anything he built, controlled, enjoyed, or achieved. The answer was not more wisdom, more possessions, or more experiences. Fellowship with God was

---

[43] The Secret of Happiness, Billy Graham, Chapter 5

the answer to everything for him. He realized that the "whole duty of man" was to seek fellowship with God. With God at the center of his life, everything made sense. C.S. Lewis describes this as the human need for God. He uses an analogy to make this plain:

> God made us: invented us as a man invents an engine. A car is made to run on petrol, and it would not run properly on anything else. Now God designed the human machine to run on Himself. He Himself is the fuel our spirits were designed to burn, or the food our spirits were designed to feed on. There is no other. That is why it is just no good asking God to make us happy in our own way without bothering about religion. God cannot give us a happiness and peace apart from Himself, because it is not there. There is no such thing. (Excerpt from Mere Christianity)[44]

Human beings, made in the image of God, need to be in His presence. They need to be in fellowship with the Creator, lest they be forever lonesome and unfulfilled. Children need to be in close fellowship with their parents lest they be forever lonesome and unfulfilled. The Library of Congress is filled with books that describe this hunger for meaning, happiness, and fulfillment. Authors go to great lengths to describe the yearning people have for love and acceptance. Beautiful stories are crafted to help the reader understand the anguish and frustration people feel when their search for meaning winds its way through the material things of this world. Great songs are sung about finding true love and acceptance, only

---

[44] "A Year with C. S. Lewis." P. 93. HarperCollins. iBooks.

to have those hopes dashed on the altars of idolatry, drugs, sex, and consumption. These books and songs reflect a longing in the human heart that only God can meet.

As I have mentioned before, Philip Yancey has a way of sharing unexpected sources that resonate with me. He offers this example to describe what I have been trying to say:

> I went looking for spirit and found alcohol; I went looking for soul, and I bought some style; I wanted to meet God, but they sold me religion, the rock star Bono sometimes shouts at concerts. In Yahweh, a song I heard him perform in a packed arena, he offered God his hands, which clench into fists, his mouth "so quick to criticize," and finally his heart: "Take this heart, and make it break." [45] By the end of the concert he had twenty thousand fans joining him in the chorus to Leonard Cohen's *Hallelujah*. [46]

Yancey says that Bono was describing the anguish he felt as an artist of world-wide fame desperately trying to fill an unmet longing deep inside of him. Bono was a lost soul looking for meaning in a material world of meaningless "things." In the end, the answer given in his concert and particularly in this song was the same answer arrived at by the "wisest man who ever lived." Putting God at the center of your life is the only way to find true meaning. But how can we put God at the center of our lives when we are polluted by sin?

---

[45] See also: Chapter nine, the power of a broken heart, which Bono describes in this beautiful lyric.

[46] *Vanishing Grace*, Philip Yancey, chapter 4, p. 54, iBooks

The reason that putting God at the center of everything is so very difficult is because our free will tempts us to do otherwise. Since we realize that we are lost, we often feel unworthy. Perhaps we feel unworthy of a holy and perfect God who desires fellowship with us. We are unworthy because we are unable to cleanse the stain of sin from our lives. An author who describes his quest for fellowship with God as a form of separation from his Creator couched this feeling as shame or unworthiness.

> I would learn something about that kind of shame: it is exactly that feeling, exactly that sense of unworthiness that forms the fertile ground from which most spiritual troubles sprout. Trite as it may sound, the fact is that the Being that created us loves us, approves of us, expects the best from us – to steal a phrase from a fellow named Walt Whitman. So often, in the whirl of earth, amidst the complexities of family life and our professional ambitions, we lose sight of that existential approval. We turn away from that love. And after that, well... no place to go but down.[47]

Billy Graham described what my early relationship with my Creator looked like. A hunger for God with an inability to satisfy that need.

What do we make of the person who lacks the hunger for God? If God is our creator, can't God simply will or command us to hunger for Him, to love Him? As the character God (played by

---

[47] Golfing With God, Roland Merullo. P. 42. Algonquin Books of Chapel Hill. 2007

Morgan Freeman) described to Bruce Almighty in the movie of the same name, Bruce (endowed with God's powers) cannot force or will someone to love him. Even though Bruce had God's powers, he was unable to make the love of his life, Grace (played by Jennifer Aniston) actually love him. Bruce used all the powers that God gave him, yet he was powerless in the arena of love. At long last, out of desperation and anguish, Bruce prays that God grant the prayerful request of Grace, even if that meant that she will find happiness apart from Bruce.

Bruce came to realize that God loves us so much that he gave us the gift of free will – even though that gift allows us to turn away from God. Imagine that paradox! The very gift that God gives us allows us to turn away from Him. It gives us the power to alienate ourselves from fellowship with God. Billy Graham said, "[i]t is possible through sin to harden our hearts against God so long that we lose all desire for God."[48] People, by turning away from God through sin, develop hearts of stone. In doing so they lose the hunger for God.

C. Why Do We Need to Be Sin-Free to be in Fellowship with God?

God is fully righteous. He is without fault or sin. Jesus said that "[t]here is only One who is good" (Matt. 19:17, NIV). C.S. Lewis tries to explain this concept in his book, *The Great Divorce*. He looks at the separation of God from woman and man, through sin, as akin to divorce – a separation that splits us from God's presence. "There is but one good; that is God. Everything else is good when it looks to Him and bad when it turns from Him." Sin is a turning away from God. God, being fully righteous and good, cannot allow

---

[48] The Secret of Happiness, Billy Graham, Chapter 5

anything sinful to be in fellowship with Him. This seems like a cruel joke. God gives us free will to do as we please – all the while knowing that we will sin. Yet He desires to be in fellowship with us. And we cannot be in fellowship with Him when we sin.

There has got to be an answer for this conundrum because God loves us and desires to have fellowship with us. Perhaps the answer can be found in the life and times of King David's son, Solomon. David, the man who slew Goliath and saved the Israelite army with his heroics was a world-class sinner! He famously lusted after a woman he saw bathing on a rooftop adjacent to his castle and wanted her so badly that he had her husband killed.

After the deed was done, David was overcome with grief, knowing that he had sinned against God. Such a sin, he believed, surely would forever lead to a divorce from God. In Psalm 51, David cried out to God in distress, knowing that he would forever be banished from fellowship with God. David also realized that no ritual or spiritual sacrifices will work to assuage his sin or remove his guilt. Yet, David pleaded for God not to "cast me from your presence" (Ps. 51:11 NIV).

David realized that being cast away from God is the worst thing that could ever happen to anyone. In his grief David realized that "[t]he sacrifices of God are a broken spirit and a contrite heart..." and he prays that God will forgive and "will not despise" him (Ps. 51:17 NIV). To restore his fellowship with God, David sought redemption and forgiveness.

Bono clearly knew that King David's plea for forgiveness was coming from his broken heart. Bono understood this when he penned his song. Bono understood the value to God of a broken heart and spirit. Broken hearts and spirits lead to an urgent and fervent need for repentance. King David and Bono know that without a cry to God for forgiveness they would forever be divorced from a righteous God. And repentance leads to redemption.

If this is true we need to answer a further question. How do we know that God will forgive us if we come to Him with a broken heart and spirit? Just because God forgave David doesn't mean He will forgive us, will He? After all, God chose David to be King over his chosen people. I have no "in" with God as David enjoyed. What about my assurance of forgiveness? Yancey in his book, *The Question That Never Goes Away*, notes that

> The entire Bible is a story of redemption. Adam got a second chance, along with his murderous son Cain. Blessings were offered to the likes of Abraham and Jacob despite their lapses and lies. Joseph and Daniel were triumphant after false imprisonment. Balky Moses and lusty David and whiny Jeremiah received forgiveness along with the entire motley assortment of murderers, adulterers, and rotten kings tucked into Matthew's list of Jesus's ancestors. Jesus himself laid down his life for the sake of others. As novelist Marilynne Robinson puts it, 'The great recurring theme of biblical narrative is always rescue, whether of Noah and his family, the people of Israel, or Christ's redeemed.'[49]

We need to be rescued from our free will, from our desire to put ourselves first. We are all in need of this guarantee of redemption whether we are Moses, David, Bono, or you and me.

---

[49] Philip Yancey. iBooks, p. 100

D. The Seven Deadly Sins

When I was young, I was taught that there were seven sins that are classified as *deadly*. However, the more I learned about God's Word, the more I understood that all sins are deadly. The wages of sin are death. They are deadly because *any* sin separates us from God. So, who came up with only seven sins being deadly? They were originated by Pope Gregory the First in the sixth century and were later elaborated upon by Saint Thomas Aquinas. The list was supposed to be a guide or a shorthand way of categorizing sin so that if a person memorized the seven they could more readily understand what was "sinful."

The seven categories of sin were also taught along with seven counterbalancing virtues that were viewed as practices that one could follow to "lead you not into temptation." The seven deadly sins, with the countering virtues[50], were:

1. Pride/Humility
2. Greed[51]/Charity
3. Lust/Chastity
4. Envy/Gratitude
5. Gluttony[52]/Temperance
6. Anger[53]/Patience
7. Sloth/Diligence

---

[50] www.britannica.com

[51] Or covetousness

[52] which included eating too much and drunkenness

[53] or wrath

The Encyclopedia Britannica says: "[t]he seven deadly sins can be thought of as dispositions toward sin and separation from God." It seems as if the Pope wanted the sixth-century church to have them as a guide or tool to help avoid those "near occasions of sin". If everyone was able to always stay true to this list and practice these seven virtues at all times, there would be no need for the guarantee. However, no one can. Free will shall always get in the way.

So, what are we to do? How can we be free of sin? When Jesus was asked this very question, He said that what God wants most from us is summed up in the first two commandments. The first; to love God with all our heart and soul. And the second; to love others as we love ourselves. "All the Law and the Prophets hang on these two commandments" (Mark 22:37-40). But what does the world tell us every day? Just the opposite. Sin freely! Dress provocatively and immodestly so you can attract a sexual partner. All-you-can-eat buffets in every section of town. Single's nights at bars – ladies drink free! Buy a house with no money down. Greed is good.

Jimmy Carter was, in my opinion, probably the most religious of the modern American presidents. Whatever your political views, he was thought of by the vast majority of the American public as a good, virtuous man. He taught Sunday school before and after he held the most powerful position on the planet. He was an evangelical Christian his entire life and has supported important causes, such as Habitat for Humanity, with his money and muscles. President Carter was a role model. If ever there was a "Mother Teresa" of American Presidents, it was Jimmy Carter. He was unabashed, certain, and steadfast regarding his faith. So much so that he agreed to an interview with Playboy magazine when he was running for president.

As mentioned previously, when asked about one of the seven deadly sins, this is what then-candidate Carter said: "I've looked on a lot of women with lust. I've committed adultery in my heart many times." What? Lust by looking? President Carter was a student of the Bible. He remembered what Jesus said in the Sermon on the Mount. "… anyone who looks at a woman lustfully has already committed adultery with her in his heart" (Matt. 5:28 NIV). Looking at someone with lust is the same as adultery? How can we not commit the sin of lust? According to Pope Gregory, only with chastity. According to Jesus, just don't look!

This standard is impossible to meet. C.S. Lewis analogizes it this way, "…there were things too hot to touch with your finger but you could drink them all right? Shame is like that. If you will accept it— if you will drink the cup to the bottom—you will find it very nourishing: but try to do anything else with it and it scalds."[54] Sin is an affront to God. Sin is the wedge that we drive between God and us. If sin separates us from fellowship with God, it only seems logical that we must go to God to find the way back. We must find what it is we can do to mend the relationship we desire with a Holy God.

As I began writing this book I had so many questions. More questions than answers at first. Where do we go to find what we need? What penance should we make? What penalty do we need to pay? Where do we make the payment? Do we need to serve time in prayer to atone for our sins? If so, how long? And what about the degree of fault? Is looking upon a person with lust as big a sin as actually having an extramarital affair? Is wanting a bigger house as large an affront to God as cheating on a business deal to get more profit? I had so many questions! How about you?

---

[54] The Great Divorce, Chapt. 7

E. Degrees of Sin

God does not punish based on our fault. That is both the good and the bad news. Since He views all sin the same, He grants the same grace to all. A great example of this comes from the book of Luke. In chapter eight, Jesus tells a parable in answer to an accusation leveled at Him by Simon, a Pharisee who invited Jesus to dinner. Simon was trying to get Jesus to "grade" sin. This happened when a woman who had lived a sinful life showed up at Simon's house with a jar of perfume and proceeded to pour the perfume on Jesus's feet. Upon seeing this Simon exclaimed that such a sinful woman should not be allowed to even touch Jesus. And, what's more, Jesus should know this if he was actually a prophet. In response, Jesus told Simon and all who were there a parable.

The story dealt with two men who owed money to a lender. One owed 500 denarii and the other 50 denarii. Neither of the men had any money to repay their loan. Upon learning this the lender decided to cancel both debts. After telling this story Jesus turned to Simon and asked him which debtor would love the money lender more. Thinking for just a moment Simon replied. "The man who owed 500." Jesus said, "Simon answered correctly." However, Jesus added, the woman who had sinned "more" was not forgiven less but was forgiven just the same as the person who sinned less, implying that Simon the Pharisee was this other person. "Therefore, I tell you, her many sins have been forgiven - for she loved much. But he who has been forgiven little loves little" (Luke 7:36-48).

Jesus shamed the Pharisee Simon, who thought he was better than the sinful woman because he followed God's laws and therefore sinned less. But Jesus turned this attitude on its head by pointing out to the prideful Simon that the "sinful woman," who humbled herself before Jesus by weeping tears (thus acknowledging her sinfulness) and by making a desperate plea for forgiveness (by pouring out perfume on Jesus's feet) actually loved Jesus more. Nevertheless, each received the same grace: complete forgiveness.

God does not grade sin. And He does not grant forgiveness in proportion to a person's sinfulness. In fact, God's grace is enough to cover or wash away any and every sin. It is enough to cover what man views as a big sin (adultery) or as a little (venial) sin (lust). This is because all sin separates us from God. Philip Yancey said this on the subject:

> ...I do know that singling out one behavior as "sin" and emphasizing it over others provides a convenient way of dodging our own need for grace. High-minded moralism and shrill pronouncements of judgment may help fundraising, but they undermine a gospel of grace.
>
> In the Sermon on the Mount Jesus raises the ideals so high that none of us can reach them. I have not committed adultery — have I ever lusted? I have not murdered — have I ever hated? Do I love my enemies? Do I give to everyone who asks? What sounds at first like bad news, a moral standard that no one can reach, takes a dramatic shift, for in the same sermon Jesus lowers the safety net of grace.[55]

Every affront to God - regardless of whether man views it as large or small - will drive us away from God. A so-called "white lie" is still a lie to God – it doesn't matter how we intended it, it is a sin.

---

[55] Vanishing Grace, P. 228-29, iBooks

And, because of this impossible standard, God loves us so much that He gives us a way to wipe away the stain of all sin. This is the guarantee, God's grace is at the center of it all. Grace does not discriminate. Grace does not grade (not even on a curve). Grace is enough - no matter the sin or the sinner. Grace is guaranteed!

F. The Dangers of Life Without the Guarantee

If we try to navigate the perils of life without God at the center, we will be caught up in a whirlwind of uncertainty, doubt, and frustration. The world will try to tell us that the key to security is a bank account, a home in a safe neighborhood, sending our kids to the best schools, and a big 401-K retirement account. While all of these things bring us a sense of security, bad things and things we cannot control will still happen. Some will try to tell you that this is proof that there is no God and that if he was a loving God, bad things would not happen.

This is the propaganda that communist nations tried to feed their population. Their citizens should rely upon the state and if they rely on the communist party, it will take care of them. All will be treated the same and commodities (and security) will be available to everyone, no matter their station in life.

Vaclav Havel lived under the communist Soviet Union in his native Czechoslovakia. When the USSR fell and the Czech Republic gained freedom, Havel became its president. When asked about the loss of God during communist rule and how it affected his life, he said that "...with the loss of God, man has lost a kind of absolute and universal system of coordinates, to which he could always relate everything, chiefly himself."

Havel understood that without God at the center of his decision-making, his life was rudderless. And certainty (the guarantee) was an important part of making sense of the world. "Hope is not the conviction that something will turn out well," he said, "but the certainty that something makes sense, regardless of how it turns out." Putting his trust in God allowed him to be certain that he had that moral gyroscope at the center of his character that enabled all of his decisions to make sense. He also knew that the guarantee that God gave of forgiveness did not mean that everything in life would turn out well. Only that God would be with him through the trials that he would experience in life.

A God-centered life provides a measuring stick for each decision that you make. It does not let your envy, your lust, or your gluttony make the decisions. As Ravi Zacharias once said, "...setting life's purpose first and then measuring each moment by this purpose is so important." Conviction, he said, "is something rooted so deeply in the conscience that to change a conviction would be to change the very essence of who you are."[56] Zacharias and Havel knew that sailing the seas of life without a compass and rudder allows one to drift in stormy seas so that you are in danger of being dashed on the rocks.

G. The Things That Lead Us Away From God

There are many things in this world that lead us away from God. There are dangers that loom in a life without God at the center. False gods can allow you to drift onto dangerous shoals. The gods of ambition, prosperity, pride, greed, and avarice can cause us to alter our direction and lose our way. By replacing the one true God with these false gods we give ourselves over to the seductions of the world. These false gods cause us to change the very essence of who we are.

---

[56] The Grand Weaver, p. 181, iBooks

So much so that you can wake up one morning and not recognize the person staring back at you in the mirror

1. Ambition

What's wrong with ambition? It is an admired trait in American business. Sports stars are brimming with ambition. The most successful writers and artists have this trait. It drives us to be better, to get ahead, to succeed. The famous theologian Eugene Peterson described it this way, "Our culture encourages and rewards ambition without qualification. We are surrounded by a way of life in which betterment is understood as expansion, as acquisition, as fame. Everyone wants to get more. To be on top, no matter what it is the top of, is admired."[57]

But ambition is what got Adam and Eve kicked out of the best gig ever - living in the Garden of Eden. In that idyllic paradise, there was no pollution, disease, stress, or want for anything. Everything was provided. The lucky couple got to stroll in the peaceful, lush surroundings, and actually have fellowship and converse with God. But, as I have pointed out before, God loved them so much that He gave them free will. He only asked one thing of them. One simple command (no Ten Commandments). While he told them they could eat whatever they wanted in the garden (there were no poisonous plants or species) they were to refrain from eating from the tree of knowledge of good and evil. God even warned them that if they ate from this tree they would die. Prior to that pronouncement, they were going to live forever.

Ambition crept into the minds of the pair. They were convinced that if they ate from this tree they would be like God! They wanted

---

[57] A Long Obedience in the Same Direction. InterVarsity Press, p. 223, iBooks

more, they were ambitious. They wanted it all. They ate from the tree and were cast out of the presence of God. No more would they be allowed to have fellowship with their Maker. No longer would they have the idyllic life. They were now destined to grow old and die. They lost everything. They were cast out of the garden – and divorced from God.

Ambition, however, is not the problem. The key is to find a God-centered ambition. Peterson said that "if we take the energies that make for aspiration and remove God from the picture, replacing him with our own crudely sketched self-portrait, we end up with ugly arrogance." Robert Browning's fine line on aspiration, "A man's reach should exceed his grasp, or what's a heaven for?" has been distorted to become *Reach for the skies and grab everything that isn't nailed down.* Ambition is aspiration gone crazy. Aspiration is the channeled, creative energy that moves us to grow in Christ, shaping goals in the Spirit. Blind ambition takes these same energies for growth and development and uses them to make something tawdry and cheap."[58]

2. Success

The sweet smell of success. When we work hard and keep our nose to the old grindstone, along with a little luck, we can succeed in whatever we put our mind to achieving. Success is the reward for diligently pursuing a goal. But success can also lead to a prideful attitude. When a person has achieved a long-sought goal they have the natural tendency to look back and say "Look what I have done. See what I have accomplished?"

---

[58] Supra., P. 226-27

Success can be fertile ground for the growth of a prideful attitude. A great example of this was the Israelite people who were led out of captivity and toward the promised land. God had provided for their freedom, parted the sea and destroyed Pharaoh's army in one bold move. He gave them a simple, straightforward set of rules to govern their new society so that they could live in harmony with God and each other. He even gave them manna from heaven to eat and a column of fire to protect them when they slept. And God gave them a leader, Moses, to look after them and guide them to the land of milk and honey. Moses, knowing human nature (free will) and God's will, said to them:

> When you have eaten and are satisfied, praise the Lord your God for the good land he has given you. Be careful that you do not forget the Lord your God, failing to observe his commands, his laws and his decrees that I am giving you this day. Otherwise, when you eat and are satisfied, when you build fine houses and settle down, and when your herds and flocks grow large and your silver and gold increase and all you have is multiplied, then your heart will become proud and you will forget the Lord your God.... Deuteronomy 8:10-13

> You may say to yourself, "My power and the strength of my hands have produced this wealth for me." But remember the Lord your God, for it is he who gives you the ability to produce wealth, and so confirms his covenant. Deuteronomy 8:17-18

Moses knew the people would have success. He knew that they would credit that success to their own sweat, desire, and drive. They, like we, need a constant reminder that everything we have and everything we need must be credited to and come through God. In the parable of the sower (Luke 8: 1-15, NIV), Jesus explains how the lure of riches can choke out our trust and hope in God. In verse 14, Jesus says that when the seed (God's Word) is sown in and among thorns (the trapping of riches and pleasures) this will distance us from the fellowship we so desperately need with God. "Not only can money and material possessions not satisfy the desires of the heart or bring the lasting happiness they deceptively promise, but they also blind those who pursue them to eternal, spiritual concerns (1 Tim. 6:9–10)."[59]

When we fool ourselves into believing that "we did it all" when we achieve success, we believe we are independent. When people pull themselves up by their own bootstraps to gain wealth and fame they are called "independently wealthy". But such self-centered attainment of prosperity and fame deludes us into believing that we are the source of our own achievement. To really succeed in a life with God at the center, all boastful and prideful attitudes must be set aside. Easier said than done. "In modern society that means rejecting the false gods of independence, success, and pleasure and replacing them with love for God and neighbor."[60]

C.S. Lewis, in *The Screwtape Letters,* describes how the devil wants us to look at prosperity:

> Prosperity knits a man to the World. He feels
> that he is 'finding his place in it', while really it is

---

[59] John MacArthur, One Perfect Life, Part 5, Notes, iBooks

[60] Philip Yancey, Vanishing Grace, P. 125, iBooks

finding its place in him. His increasing reputation, his widening circle of acquaintances, his sense of importance, the growing pressure of absorbing and agreeable work, build up in him a sense of being really at home in earth, which is just what we [the devil's minions] want[61].

Success can either bring us to the realization that we owe all to God, or it can distance us from the relationship we so urgently need. God's guarantee of forgiveness and redemption is there to rescue us from our own success.

3. Greed & Pride

In the 1987 movie, *Wall Street*, the protagonist Gordon Gekko was famously quoted as proclaiming that "greed is good." Jesus, however, said that greed and the love of money are the root of all evil. Why is that so? Because the love of money makes money the god which we worship. Once money and the accumulation of wealth become our god, we can have no other gods than these. Jesus addressed this problem head-on when a rich young ruler asked him what he could do to live with God in eternity.

Jesus, knowing this man's heart, got straight to the center of his soul. He knew this man had accumulated wealth and power and that he was esteemed for both. Jesus told this man that he must give up every trapping of his success and follow Him if he wanted everlasting life. Jesus knew that this rich ruler was worshiping the gods of money and power and that he must humble himself to gain

---

[61] P. 202-03. From the Screwtape Letters. "A Year with C. S. Lewis." HarperCollins. iBooks.

forgiveness of his sins. Upon hearing this recipe for redemption, the rich ruler "became very sad, because he was a man of great wealth."

Then Jesus uttered a seemingly obtuse statement. He said "[h]ow hard it is for the rich to enter the kingdom of God! Indeed it is easier for a camel to go through the eye of a needle than for a rich man to enter the kingdom of God." (Luke 18: 18-25. Matt. 19:24, NIV). What in the world was Jesus trying to say?

The eye of the needle was a section of the great wall that surrounded the city of Jerusalem. It was used at night when the main gate into the city was closed so the capital could be secured. At night this small side entry was used to tightly control anyone or anything that needed to get into the walled city after sunset. This way, the guardians of the city could screen each person individually to make sure no enemies were able to gain admittance.

If a person with a camel tried to come in this gate, all baggage from the camel had to be removed and the camel had to kneel down to pass through the needle gate. Jesus was telling the rich man – and all who were present that day – that he (we) would need to jettison the baggage that wealth and power hold over our lives if he wanted to gain entrance into the kingdom of God. In doing so he had to humble himself (kneel) and bow to an almighty God, his creator[62].

Greed is not good. The love of money hardens our hearts. As Bono found out, God wants a broken heart for Him. When we humble ourselves, He finds us where we are and offers us the "keys to the kingdom"; forgiveness of our sins and everlasting life. "A man's life does not consist in the abundance of his possessions," Jesus said in Luke 12:15. His words offer loving insight that we as believers can take to heart. What we have has nothing to do with who we

---

[62] I want to acknowledge my bible study buddy Doug for pointing me toward the origin of the eye of the needle

are. Solomon, the wisest man of all time (and one of the wealthiest), said, "Whoever loves wealth is never satisfied" (Eccles. 5:10). God has made it clear. Money won't give us what we truly need. Only He can do that."[63]

Pride goes before the fall - a truism we see throughout history – the world's and our own. Why do you think that is so? Pride says, *Look at me and see all I have accomplished.* Humility responds with, *Others have helped me achieve. And without their help, love, and support I would not be the person I am today.* True humility says, *Without God I am nothing, have nothing and I am going nowhere.*

4. Anger

Anger is another reason we are separated from God, and another reason we need the guarantee. Anger hardens our hearts and blinds us to the needs of others. It clouds our ability to speak kindly and makes us say things we would not normally say. It also incites violence and hatred. Anger also builds walls against forgiveness. It *allows* the hurt person to have the *strength* to resist an offered apology. In sum, it separates us from the love of others and from God.

When I harken back to my days as a trial lawyer, one of the things I always did was take adequate time to prepare my clients for their depositions. I explained that my job in preparing them was to help them be sure that their testimony was both truthful and accurate. I explained that the opposing lawyer would try to elicit testimony from them that helped the opposing lawyer's case and, as such, would damage our case. I explained that everything they said – and the way they testified – would be taken down by the court reporter.

---

[63] Philip Yancey & Brenda Quinn. "Meet the Bible." P. 2108 Zondervan. iBooks.

This made every part of their testimony significant and subject to being repeated in court when their case was called.

I warned them that the opposing lawyer would try to *trip them up* with the questions that he or she asked. The opposing counsel would also use the manner and rhythm of questions to throw off the witness. When this method was used, the witness may not understand or fully grasp the nature of the information they were giving. One of the primary things that prevented witnesses from testifying truthfully and accurately, I would say, was anger. Opposing lawyers would annoy, needle and provoke a witness to get them agitated. Do it enough times and witnesses might lose their cool and get angry. When this occurs, a witness may blurt out in anger something they may not ever say when calm and cool. If this happens during a deposition under oath, the person is stuck with their testimony.

If this happens when two friends argue, the offending party may later say, "Sorry, I only said that in anger. I didn't mean it." In a deposition or in court you don't have that luxury. Once you say something on the record and under oath your testimony is now documented in black and white and in the case of a video deposition, in full color for the jury to see and hear.

Therefore, when I prepared people for their depositions or trial testimony I told them not to get angry – even when the opposing lawyer tried to provoke them and get under their skin. I explained that anger leads to a diminished ability to think clearly and testify truthfully and accurately.[64]

---

[64] "Probably the most insidious harm of anger is that it simply serves as a barrier between a witness and the kind of focus and attention needed in order to effectively process questions and contemplate responses. As psychologists have noted, anger and other forms of anxiety in witnesses 'tend to impair perceptual efficiency by creating 'blind' spots, blurring impressions, and increasing the likelihood of blocks and distortions' (Lezak, 1993)." Persuasive Litigator, Defuse Your Angry Witness, January 17, 2013. Dr. Ken Broda-Bahm.

Anger also is a trigger that causes us to lose our moral compass and therefore leads people into other sinful behavior. "What's true of anger is also true of guilt, greed, and jealousy. All four reduce our resolve against sexual temptation. They tilt us off balance emotionally, leaving us vulnerable to lust. They're like out-of-control viruses weakening our spiritual immune system[65]." "...[A] healthy heart puts us in a stronger position to ward off temptation of all kinds. Confessing, forgiving, celebrating, and giving are habits that strengthen our resolve and remove the enemy's base of operation in our lives. The healthier our hearts, the easier it will be for us to keep this God-given appetite properly focused and under control."[66]

H. What Makes Us Seek the Guarantee?

In this chapter, we have explored the things that lead us away from God and how we can navigate life's problems and crises with God as our compass and rudder. However, we also know that even with God at the center of our lives we still face difficulties, pain, and inevitably, death. So what good is it that we have faith in a God who allows bad things to happen to good people?

First of all, not one of us is "good" as that term is used by God. We are all sinners – every one of us. Read Romans 3:23, NIV. Second, sin was invited into the world by our own free will, not by God. Therefore, we have no one to blame but ourselves.

As Flip Wilson (a comedian from the 1970s) so wrongfully claimed every time he was caught doing something bad, "The

---

[65] As I am editing this chapter in December 2020 the Coronavirus is wreaking havoc in our lives, just like anger can do to us physically, emotionally and economically

[66] Andy Stanley. "Enemies of the Heart." Multnomah Books, 2011-06-21. iBooks. Pps. 271-72

Devil made me do it!" Pain, disease, hardship, calamity, and loss have occurred in the life of all of God's people. As you read the Bible, you can see that it is filled with bad things happening to God's people. These things occur in the lives of His representatives and the leaders he put in place to guide His people. Even his own Son was subjected to ridicule, poverty, treason, torture, and the most painful, slow death known to mankind at the time. God (and Jesus himself) had the power to prevent any such harm or pain from ever occurring to God's Son – but did not.

Why would God do anything differently with us? However, as I will try to demonstrate in these next chapters, God reaches out to us to bring us back to Him. As we sin and separate ourselves from God, He reaches out to us to forgive our sins and restore us to the fellowship we rejected.

I trust that I have given you the facts needed to answer the question of why we need the guarantee. To put it simply, we need it because we are habitual sinners who cannot overcome our own desires and our free will. We need it because we desperately want to know our Maker. We have a desire to be back in His presence. Without God's promise of salvation, we cannot overcome our sin. Without being cleansed of our sin, we have no possibility of being in fellowship with God.

CHAPTER FIVE

FOCUS ON THE IMPORTANT THINGS

God has a way of helping you focus on Him when the world seeks to distract you. John Lennon wrote a love song to his son that touched on this subject. He called it *Beautiful Boy*. To me, one lyric in that poignant song stands out. In an attempt to show the paradox of our lives Lennon sings some words of advice to his infant son. He says that "[l]ife is what happens when you are busy making other plans." John reminded his son Sean that no matter how you plan and prepare, the world deals you cards that you have not anticipated and, if you were able to choose, you would discard.

Lennon perhaps foretold, without realizing it, that his life would end tragically and without warning. In a single instant on December 8, 1980, his life was taken by a shot that rang out as he entered his apartment complex in New York City. He was just forty years old. Little did Lennon realize that one of the Beatles' "fans" (shorthand for a fanatical person) made the decision to end Lennon's life, purportedly because of an offhanded facetious remark Lennon made that the Beatles were more popular than Jesus. Lennon was one of the most popular persons on the planet in December of 1980 who, undoubtedly was busy making other plans. We do not always get to choose how to live our lives and do not get to select how long we will inhabit this earth.

C.S. Lewis was an avowed Atheist most of his young life. A renowned professor at Cambridge and Oxford he was the consummate academic. To him, being an atheist and an academic went hand-in-hand. But God put people in his world who would trigger within him a stirring that caused his intellectual curiosity to lead him in a direction that was unplanned.

One of those persons was the acclaimed author J.R.R. Tolkien. Tolkien became one of Lewis' best friends. They often debated and talked on the subject of God and faith for hours on end. They shared countless conversations on this subject – often in pubs and on their many walks in the woods. Lewis, ever the pedantic inquisitor, did not want to accept Christianity out of blind faith. He did not want an emotional conversion. Instead, as he was prodded by Tolkien, he chose to logically sort through the Bible to come to his own conclusions, much the way a lawyer sorts through the facts of a case to come to a logical resolution and outcome.

After reading the Old and New Testaments, both in Greek and English, with a discerning eye and constant questioning of God's words with his academic skepticism, Lewis indeed arrived at his own conclusion. When he completed his thorough interrogation of God and the claims made by Jesus in the New Testament, Lewis concluded that Jesus was who He said he really was – God incarnate. He came to the realization that logic dictates that either Jesus was just a good man saying good things or He was something more. "I am trying here," he was quoted as saying, "to prevent anyone saying the really foolish thing that people often say about Him, 'I'm ready to accept Jesus as a great moral teacher, but I don't accept his claim to be God. That is the one thing we must not say.'"

Lewis, ever the intellectual and logical thinker, explained that a man who said the things that Jesus said would not be a great moral teacher. "He would either be a lunatic – on the level with the man who says he is a poached egg – or else he would be the devil of hell. You must make your choice. Either this man was, and is, the Son of God, or else a madman or something worse." Lewis made his choice and, in doing so, changed the course of modern Christian writing.

But Lewis, as any person, was human. And as a human, he was subject to doubts and lapses of faith. As I referenced in chapter three, Lewis' faith was tested by the world. When his wife suffered and later succumbed to cancer, Lewis' faith was shaken. As such he went through a period of great emotional turmoil and doubt. How could he, a born-again believer who sought God with his whole mind and soul, be given the one true love of his life, only to have that person snatched away with such brutality?

Why did God force him to watch helplessly as his darling partner withered away in agony? How could a holy and perfect God allow such a sweet, kind, and loving person to contract and suffer through such a terrible disease? Her faith was strong and she lived a good life. Why her? Why him? His strong faith did not spare him from this cruel and heartbreaking ordeal. He asked, therefore, how good is God after all? All his prayers seemed to go unanswered. Lewis's view of a kind and benevolent God was shaken to its core. He reached a point in his life when he went from the highest highs of meeting and marrying this wonderful woman to the depths of depression as he sat at her bedside watching as she painfully slipped away from him. He was broken.

But God did not turn his back on C.S. Lewis. God used that experience to remind him that a holy and righteous God let his own Son die a painful and humiliating death. God listened as his Son prayed in a garden the night He was betrayed by one of His closest confidants. God heard the anguished prayers of Jesus pleading with His own father to spare Him from the ordeal He knew he was about to face. God heard these prayers and saw His son so overcome by grief and emotion that Jesus cried tears of blood. God watched as His one and only Son was arrested on false charges, convicted by God's own chosen people, and handed over to an invading army for the sentence of death to be carried out. God allowed his Son – part of the triune God – to be mocked and scorned by the very people who only a week before showered Jesus with praise, palm branches waving as he processed into Jerusalem. Lewis, no doubt, was sure that God wept as his Son was beaten with such ferocity that His skin was torn from His back. God "allowed" his Son, Jesus, to carry a heavy wooden cross – the very implement of His own death – to a place of public execution. God stood by as they nailed His Son to a cross – a form of execution reserved for slaves and criminals and a form of execution that was one of the cruelest deaths ever imagined by man.

God saw from on high as His Son cried out in pain and anguish appealing for this form of death to pass him by. And God witnessed His frail and bleeding Son breathe His last breath. Lewis realized that God allowed this to happen to his Son so that His creation could be cleansed of their sin and become one again, with God. Lewis realized that God was with him as he watched the love of his life, breathe her last. I have no doubt that God wept with a broken C.S. Lewis.

That experience, however, caused a strengthening of C.S. Lewis's beliefs and drew into sharper focus Lewis's understanding about how God works in our lives and His plan of salvation. Lewis had the answers to his question of how a holy and perfect God could watch as a loved one suffered and died.

In October of 2007, my life was turned upside down. A year previously I saw my internal medicine doctor about a small growth on my right shoulder that wouldn't go away. After examining it, my doctor of over fifteen years assured me it was nothing. *Don't worry*, he told me, *it's only a harmless purpura*. Assured by my doctor, I ignored this harmless bump and continued to live my life as usual.

One of my favorite leisure activities is tennis. At that time I played in a men's tennis group every Tuesday evening. About two months after the visit to my doctor, I noticed that the *purpura* would bleed after my tennis matches. However, as instructed, I didn't pay much attention to it except to apply a Band-Aid and spot treat my tennis shirt before washing.

Nevertheless, over the successive twelve months, the bleeding became routine and I became concerned. Almost a year to the day of getting the "all clear" from my doctor I asked one of my very good friends, Jim (a skilled surgeon and the godparent of my son) what he thought I should do about the growth. The answer came swiftly and directly. The next day I was in his office and it was removed. A few days later Jim called. He had received the pathological report. "Lewis, you have a stage 4 malignant melanoma".

I was in a state of shock. What just hit me? My life was going as planned and this was not part of the plan. I thanked him and hung up the phone. As I furiously typed the search terms into my computer my head spun. What was Mary Alice, the love of my life, going to do? How would my son react? He was only nine at the time. What about my two grown daughters – one living in LA and the other in Dallas – how do I tell them? I was in the prime of my legal career. I was a senior partner in a growing firm. I had three associates, four paralegals, and two legal secretaries working in my department. They all depended on me. How am I going to continue to practice law? How could God let this happen to me?

That day, at the urging of Jim, I called Moffitt Cancer Center, located in Tampa. Three days later I was consulting a surgeon who specialized in skin cancer. My cancer specialist gave me the straight story. My expected survival rate for stage four melanoma was 30%. He explained that the tumor would be removed, along with a significant amount of the surrounding tissue and adjacent lymph nodes. The samples would be sent to pathology and he would have a more definitive diagnosis in a few days. Thereafter, the tissue specimens would be sent off for genetic testing – which would take a month. The pathology results confirmed the diagnosis. My surgeon confirmed his prognosis and the words sank deep into my psyche: I had a thirty percent chance of surviving the next five years. In the meantime, I waited and began to come to terms with my *new* life. Life with cancer and chemotherapy. Life with a death sentence hanging over me. Suddenly the fragility of life hit me like a sucker punch. And I, like C.S. Lewis, began to question my faith.

My wife and I lay in bed that night, held each other, and cried. How were we going to deal with this? We talked and prayed and she eventually drifted off to a fitful sleep. I stayed awake with my mind racing as my wife slept at my side. I simply placed this at God's feet and I prayed. I asked God to remove this cup from me. I asked that my holy and perfect God take the death sentence I received away. I asked for help. How do I prepare my family for the news? God, are you there? Are you listening to my urgent prayers? Say something, do something!

In the month that passed after my surgery, my physical wounds healed and I began the process of rehabilitating the muscles in my shoulder, arm, and chest. I also began to get a perspective on my life. I had spent fifty-four years on this earth and lived a full and rewarding life. My thirty-one years of marriage had been the best of those fifty-four years and my three children were the delight of my heart. I had a job – a profession – that I enjoyed immensely. It challenged me daily and I thought that I was a pretty darned good lawyer. Most of all, my faith became something more than what I did on Sunday. It became the bedrock of my life.

Instead of questioning *where* God was I slowly began to realize that I knew exactly where to find Him. He was *within me*. I actually felt a strength that only God can provide. I had entrusted my life to Jesus and depended on Him to free me from the chains of sin. I began to realize that no matter what, I *WAS* saved and *ASSURED* that my many and frequent sins *WERE* forgiven. It wasn't a situation of *IF* I was forgiven. I *WAS*.

The realization of this fact (not a theory) gave me a strange sense of courage. I realized that I was not afraid of dying because I knew what I had in store for me when I did. The words came to me, as I had read them many times in my Bible study. Every tear shall be wiped away and there shall be no more pain. Revelation 21:4, NIV. I knew this as surely as I knew who I was. This, Jesus had promised me. This He guaranteed me.

Instead of being afraid of death, I felt calm. Sure, I was heart-broken that I would leave my children without a dad and my wife without her best friend. There was also no getting away from the anxiety of the economic consequences of my death to my family. All of this came into sharp focus now. However, I had planned for this eventuality. I knew that I would die at some point in my future. I had life insurance in place, a retirement plan that was funded, and a sum of money put away so that my family would be taken care of. My two girls had completed their education and my son had suffi-cient money in place to fund his college expenses. But I knew that death had no hold on me. I knew that cancer would not beat me – even if it took my life. This diagnosis had caused me to focus on the important things in life – my faith and my family.

As I thought of my circumstance, I was reminded of three brave people that God chose to undergo an ordeal that could lead to their deaths. These men were taken captive when an invading army overran the territory that God gave His chosen people after leading them out of slavery in Egypt. These men were now slaves, just as their ancestors were in Egypt. They were ordered by the ruler holding them captive that they must not worship their God. They were to bow down to their captor's god – an image of gold. They knew if they refused they would be put to death. Despite these threats, the men were faithful and would not worship something other than the one true God. By doing so, they would be writing their own death sentences. The form of death chosen by the king was cruel and painful. They were to be thrown into a blazing furnace and burned alive!

However, they were given a way out of the flames. All they had to do was simply renounce God and worship the king's god: an idol of gold. In response they boldly proclaimed "[i]f we are thrown into the blazing furnace, the God we serve is able to save us…". Notice the words *"able* to save us." They knew that an all-knowing and all-powerful God *could* save them – not *would* save them from the furnace and certain death. This distinction was important and they further elucidated this by the words that followed. They said that "even if [God] does not, we want you to know, O king, that we will not serve your gods or worship the image of gold you have set up" (Dan. 3: 17-18).

Shadrach, Meshach, and Abednego reminded me that my fervent prayers would be answered by God… but the answer may be "no." I knew that God would be with me every step of the way during my ordeal. However, even though God *could* save me from the death sentence of cancer, he *may* not.

As I hope I will be able to show you in this book, I also knew something else. I knew that God would never leave me and would never break His promise to me. He guaranteed my salvation. That is why I was not afraid of death. I knew that I would be with God after my death and that I would never again have to experience pain, rejection, doubt, stress, loneliness, or any of the hurt that we all have to endure during our lives on earth. I also learned another lesson that God was teaching me.

Not long after my shocking diagnosis, I was driving to work early in the morning, as I usually did. As I made my way down Bayshore Boulevard I heard a song by Tim McGraw that caught my attention. After hearing those haunting lyrics, I tried to find out more about the song that I felt he sang just for me that morning. Those lyrics spoke directly to what I was going through at that time. I discovered that the words were written by Tim Nichols and Craig Wiseman[67]. After they proposed this song to McGraw, it immediately struck a chord (no pun intended) with him. You see, McGraw's father, former major league baseball player Tug, had recently passed away (in early 2004) after a battle with brain cancer. The songwriting duo, however, had written the song based on the experience of a friend of theirs who had been misdiagnosed with cancer. As they told Parade magazine, the song was their observation of how their friend dealt with his cancer diagnosis.

This friend who received the cancer diagnosis said: "Wow, it's time to get busy." The songwriting duo thought that their friend would instead say "I'm going to go lay down in my bed and freak out." The lyrics confirmed in me how I was going to respond to the prognosis given by my doctors. The changes I would try to make in my life were bolstered by my faith, my wife's and children's love, and strengthened by the guarantee God gave me. The lyrics talked about cancer causing a person to do daring things, such as riding a bull and

---

[67] and after listening to the lyrics, I thought he was indeed a wise man

skydiving. The person also climbed a high mountain and challenged himself to do things he never would have done, but for his death sentence. But the song talked about much more important things. The person pledged to love deeper, speak to others with a kinder and more gentle tone and to forgive those who he had refused to forgive in the past. This song, *Live Like You Were Dyin'*, was an answer from God to my prayers.

Although I was given only a 30% chance of survival, I was also given a new perspective on life. With my salvation assured, I was going to look at the remaining time I had on earth in a different way. I was going to slow down as I drove. I was going to spend more time with my wife and children. Giving forgiveness – even when an apology was not given first – was something I was going to try my best to do. I was going to try to love deeper and speak sweeter. I was given the chance by God to live as he told me I should. I was going to try to live like I was dyin'.

After a month of waiting, my wife and I went together to receive the results of the genetic testing. We promised each other that we were not going to cry but I knew my tender wife couldn't keep that pledge. We were going to take in the news with a sense of calmness. We convinced each other that we were at peace with the prospect of what this type of cancer could bring to bear on or lives[68]. As we waited in his office we held hands and silently prayed.

My heart was in my throat as he opened his file and told us the results of the testing. He began by describing the genetic testing that the lab put my samples through. Samples were taken from the tumor itself, the tissue surrounding the lesion, and the lymph nodes that were removed from my armpit. Moffitt Cancer Center was working

---

[68] Melanoma is usually curable when detected and treated early. Once melanoma has spread deeper into the skin or other parts of the body, it becomes more difficult to treat and can be deadly. Source: The Skin Cancer Foundation

with this lab on a long-term study of skin cancer. The doctors and researchers at Moffitt comprise one of the top skin cancer treatment and research centers in the world. Located in Florida placed them at one of the epicenters of skin cancer exposure. We were so very fortunate to have this expertise in the city where we lived.

He told us that the original pathological diagnosis of stage four cancer was wrong. The cancer had not spread into my lymph nodes and was contained in the tissue removed during the surgery. Because the tumor was malignant, I would need constant monitoring for the rest of my life. However, since the spread was contained, my chance of survival was 70%. My head was spinning as I tried to process this news. How could my prognosis change so dramatically? How could my life expectancy flip this way? My doctor explained that this new genetic testing was more accurate and he was confident in the results. The same physician who just a month before was describing how a stent would be implanted in my chest for the easy administration of poisonous chemotherapy was now telling me that while I would require continual monitoring, no further treatment was indicated.

As we left the cancer center we held hands and tried to hide our tears of joy. However, as we walked out of the lobby, I think we both were aware of those patients still battling the second leading cause of death in the U.S. I was given, that day, a temporary reprieve. I was also given the gift of perspective. My faith was put to the test and I stared death in the face. This experience, however, caused me to focus on the important things, my faith and my family. Cancer did not shatter my faith, it strengthened and deepened my blessed assurance. It caused me to focus on what was important. It reminded me that I am held in God's embrace and will always be in fellowship with Him. I was temporarily "cured" of this malignant melanoma[69]. But I was not (and will never be) cured of the stain of sin. I must turn, each day, back to God and ask His forgiveness from an endless list of the sins I committed that day and every day. This experience, however, has galvanized my belief that God has guaranteed that if we ask His forgiveness and claim His Son's death as the basis for our request, that God *will* forgive all of us for those sins.

A. The Greatness of Faith

Philip Yancey, in his book, *The Question That Never Goes Away*, relates the story of a Scottish woman stricken with throat cancer who responded to the many well-meaning visitors who came to see her in the hospital. She responded as follows: "This is not the worst thing to ever happen! Cancer is so limited. It cannot cripple love, shatter hope, corrode faith, eat away peace, destroy confidence, kill friendship, shut out memories, silence courage, quench the Spirit or lessen the power of Jesus."[70] She had placed her cancer in its proper perspective. Cancer was not going to define her, not with God at the center of her life.

Cancer had caused me to focus on the important things and strengthened my faith that was initially shaken when I received the diagnosis. However, much to my surprise, my faith was not strengthened when the genetic test results came back. No, my faith was reinforced by the test that God put me through in the thirty days that I waited on the results of the genetic testing. The courage

---

[69] This form of cancer can "pop up" again in many different locations - hence the continual monitoring that was required. As of the writing of this chapter I have been free of this form of skin cancer for 12 years!

[70] Part 3: When God Overslept, p. 104 , iBooks

I found during this waiting period came during the time that a 70% chance of death was hanging over my head.

God, I believe, was plumbing the depths of my heart. He was testing my faith through a broken spirit. He was finding out what type of a man he created. This, I realized, was part of God's way of dealing with all of his children. We all turn our backs on Him, time and time again, through sin.

Deuteronomy tells the story of the Israelites in the wilderness after they are led from their slavery in Egypt. This story of their wilderness experience is emblematic of a biblical pattern that often repeats itself. "Remember how the Lord your God led you all the way in the desert these forty years, to humble you and to test you in order to know what was in your heart" (Deut. 8:2).[71] As C.S. Lewis was reminded, God even followed this pattern with His own Son.

On the night of Jesus's betrayal, as He was pouring His heart out to His Father, Jesus was tested. He was in pain and distress because He knew what lay before Him. He was distraught to the point of tears of blood flowing from his anguished body. He pleaded with His Father to release Him from the duty He was destined to fulfill. But God would not take away the scorn, ridicule, agonizing torture and the excruciating death that awaited Jesus. God so loved each of us that He gave up His son, Jesus, to this form of death because all who believe in Him and all who put their faith in Him **will** be saved from their sins and forgiven. John 3:16. This is God's promise, this is His guarantee.

Søren Kierkegaard, who lived a Job-like existence of inner torment, ultimately concluded that the purest faith, refined as gold,

---

[71] Yancey, Philip. "The Bible Jesus Read." P. 91 Zondervan, 2017-03-01. iBooks.

emerges from just such a state of paradox, or suspension of what we might expect from God.[72]

No matter how hard we try, we cannot purge ourselves of sin. No matter how good we try to be, sin always seems to creep into our lives. The famed author of the Reformation, Martin Luther, spent many torturous years trying to rid himself of sin. He was focused on being "good enough" for God. He tried and failed in this endeavor many times. He began his life as a Catholic monk and priest. Ordained in 1507, he was said to have been terrified at the prospect of officiating daily Mass. His single-minded attempts to rid himself of sin led him to take extraordinary measures.

As a young monk, Luther was obsessed with atoning for his sins and went to ridiculous lengths to punish himself for the sins he committed each day. This ranged from extreme self-denial to physical and mental tests and even self-flagellation. One such punishment consisted of lying in the snow, through the night at the height of winter.[73] His self-penal measures were extreme... and futile. He soon began to realize that nothing *he* could do would rid him of sin. Distraught, he plunged into the study of the Bible to quench his thirst for repentance. He began to realize that the whole purpose of Jesus coming into this world was to act as the sacrificial lamb for our sins. We could never be good enough to meet God's standards. This all came into sharp focus for Luther. Jesus, in His *Sermon on the Mount*, details both hope and the impossible standard of unadulterated goodness. He said that the poor in spirit were "blessed" but also said that we need to be without sin to be "good enough" for God.

In the very last sentence in the Beatitudes portion of the sermon, Jesus said, "Be perfect, therefore, as your heavenly Father is perfect"

---

[72] Supra. P. 93

[73] Martin Luther, The Reluctant Revolutionary. PBS.org

(Matt. 5:48 NIV). This was the standard that Luther was holding himself to, an absolutely unattainable standard. *If this is God's standard*, thought Luther, *we might as well give up because no one can attain this level of "goodness."* Luther, like us, realized that he could never be good enough to meet this standard of perfection. But Luther also came to realize that he could never be bad enough to be denied forgiveness. This revelation changed everything. He came to understand that forgiveness of sins was the answer – not purging oneself of the scourge of sin. Grace became the center of his reformation movement – because grace was at the heart of the gospels. Grace was enough!

Martin Luther's faith was restored by this grand revelation. My test of faith was minuscule compared to many of God's chosen people. As previously mentioned in chapter two, one of the greatest tests of faith was given by God to Abraham. Abraham was chosen by God as the seed of the tribe of Israel and the father of His chosen people. But before he could be given this mantle, God had to test Abraham's faith.

Abraham's entire adult life was focused on longing for a son. Yet, his wife was barren. Even though Abraham had given up on God, God did not give up on him. Shortly after Abraham was 100 years old, Isaac was born. Abraham was overjoyed and Isaac was the apple of his eye. Abraham loved his son with all his heart and did everything to teach him about the goodness of God. Abraham's life was now complete. That is, however, until God spoke to Abraham and told him to take his son with him on a journey. A journey that would end in God commanding Abraham to offer his only son – his pride and joy – up as a sacrifice to God. As we know, Abraham obeyed God and tied his son to the makeshift altar they had built. With a heavy but obedient heart, Abraham pulled out his knife to plunge it into Issac's chest. At that moment of obedience, he was interrupted by an angel of the Lord calling from heaven who said, "because you have not withheld from me your son, your only son," Abraham would be provided a substitute sacrifice, a "ram caught in a thicket by his horns." The angel told Abraham to sacrifice the ram instead of his son. Isaac was spared and Abraham was placed by God as the head of a new nation, Israel. Abraham's descendants were to be as numerous as the stars in the sky. He would have abundant prosperity. Genesis 22:1-14 NIV.

Søren Kierkegaard in his ground-breaking book, *Fear and Trembling*, said that "[t]he dialectic of faith is the finest and most remarkable of all; it possesses an elevation, of which indeed I can form a conception, but nothing more. I cannot perform the miraculous, but can only be astonished by it." Such faith is indeed astonishing. But faith must have a firm foundation. Faith reveals the utter hopelessness we have if we depend on our own acts to obtain everlasting life.

As Luther realized, he lacked the power to control sin. Nothing he tried could ever be good enough for God. God requires a perfect soul without the stain of sin to gain salvation. That standard of perfection is unattainable by anyone. That is why we need the guarantee of forgiveness.

The Apostle Paul, in his letter to the Roman church, taught this young congregation of first-century Christians the difference between *earning* fellowship with God through good works (the law as set forth in the Old Testament) and redemption through belief. He acknowledged that only the righteous can obtain salvation. However, attaining righteousness cannot be accomplished by following the law. He said, in no uncertain terms, that "... righteousness from God comes through faith in Jesus Christ to all who believe. There is no difference, for all have sinned and fall short of the glory of God, and are justified freely by his grace through the redemption that came by Christ Jesus. God presented him as a sacrifice of atonement, through faith in his blood. ...Therefore no one will be declared righteous in his sight by observing the law; rather, through the law we become conscious of sin" (Rom. 3:10–31, NIV).

B. Honing of Character

The apostle Paul wrote much of the New Testament. This giant of faith was converted through a direct visit from Jesus while he was walking along a dusty road in the Roman Empire. He was on his way to persecute more Christians. After his conversion, he spread the word of redemption of sins through faith in the risen Christ, for he had seen Jesus in his resurrected form. God's favor was surely placed on Paul. You may expect, this favor would protect him from harm and provide him a sense of freedom from injury, disease, imprisonment, and harm. But God had different plans for Paul – as He does for us.

God put a series of obstacles in Paul's path. These included beatings at the hands of the Roman and Jewish authorities, being shipwrecked, abandoned at sea, imprisoned in Roman jails, scorned, and tortured. In fact, after his conversion, he developed some sort of malady that was constantly with him, despite his prayers that it be taken away. He described it as a thorn in his side.

Through all of this suffering and injury, Paul realized that his character was being refined by way of these trials. God developed in him a strengthened spirit. In fact, Paul realized that he would not have been able to serve God if it not for these ordeals. A point in fact is Paul's imprisonment in a Roman jail. Through this ordeal, he was given access to his jailer who, through Paul's preaching and teaching, converted to Christianity. This led to the conversion of many more

Roman authorities and the eventual conversion, some 300 years after the crucifixion of Christ, of the Roman Emperor Constantine.

Paul, in the book of Romans, reflected on the tragedies of his life in the service to God. He concluded that his suffering produced perseverance in him. This perseverance in the face of trials, in turn, produced character. And with his honed character, he was given the gift of hope. Such suffering and pain "...can bring us closer to God and make us better, more mature people. Mysteriously, God brings lasting good from what at first seems utter despair. Regardless of where we go or what we encounter, his love looms greater, letting nothing come between us and God's grace. And in the midst of our pain, Jesus prays continually, holding us in the center of God's presence."[74]

The endowment of perseverance that I received from having cancer was a strengthening of my faith. I realized that faith provides a guarantee that a death sentence cannot overcome. Cancer had taught me a valuable lesson. I learned that cancer is what happens when you are busy making other plans. However, the *gift* that cancer gave me was a reminder to focus on the important things in life: my faith and family. I learned that there was nothing *I could do* to change the hold that sin had over me. No matter how hard I tried, sin kept creeping back into my soul. But God taught me that sin is no match for faith. Cancer may have altered the plans I made for my life but it did nothing to touch the plan God had for me. A plan to save me and change me from the inside out.

---

[74] Philip Yancey & Brenda Quinn. "Meet the Bible." P. 1983. Zondervan. iBooks.

Chapter Six

How Solid is the Guarantee?

Now that we have explored what a guarantee looks like, why I believe a lawyer's view is important, and why we so urgently need God's guarantee of salvation, you may be asking yourself some questions.

- Is this guarantee really something I can count on?
- Is it given by a source in whom I can place my trust?
- Is the source reliable?
- What is the track record of the guarantee?
- How did this guarantee come about?
- Where did it come from?
- How can I assure myself that this guarantee will be there when I need it?

We would ask these same questions when a business, a governmental entity, or a person provides the guarantee or assurance. Is the insurance company that issues the policy solid and "A" rated? What is the track record of the automobile manufacturer in standing behind its products? Is the insurance that backs my savings account sufficient if the bank goes under? These, among others, are questions that logically flow from the claims made by the guarantor of a product, service or financial instrument. Can we dare ask the same questions of God? Are there reliable sources of information available to answer these areas of uncertainty?

I will try to identify and answer some of these questions so that you can comprehend the strength of the promise of eternal life. When I think of strength and something that is solid, I think of the many products that are advertised as "indestructible." Really? Can you run over a flashlight with a Hummer and do no damage? In his article of July 30, 2014, Mike Brown attempts to list *Ten Products That are Indestructible.* In the preface to his article, Mr. Brown says that "[i]f only we could bid for a Clark Kent-esque supersuit on eBay – life would be pretty awesome if we were invincible. Ridiculous daydreams aside, some people are hard at work developing indestructible materials...*No one has succeeded yet* but while we're waiting there are a few things you can get your hands on today that come pretty close." (Emphasis added)[75] Man has not invented any material or product that even comes close to being indestructible – not even Superman's suit and cape (kryptonite anyone?). But Jesus said that the Word of God - the Bible - is indestructible. Here are some examples:

1. "I tell you the truth, until heaven and earth disappear, not the smallest letter, not the least stroke of a pen, will *by any means* disappear" (Matt. 5:18); emphasis added.
2. it is infallible [completely reliable and authoritative] or "unbreakable" (see John 10:35).
3. it has final and decisive authority (Matt. 4:4, 7, 10).

---

[75] https://www.toptenz.net/10-indestructible-things-known-man.php

4. it is sufficient for faith and practice. Jesus spoke of the sufficiency of the Jewish Scriptures: "If they do not listen to Moses and the Prophets, they will not be convinced even if someone rises from the dead" (Luke 16:31).[76]

As mentioned before, C.S. Lewis said that unless you think Jesus was a madman, you must believe what He proclaimed. Jesus told us that the Bible is indestructible – God's word is perdurable. But I think we need more proof than the four passages above to establish the foundational question: can we rely on the Bible which tells us that the guarantee is real? In other words, we need more evidence, more proof.

A. Signs of God's Presence

The first book of the Bible, Genesis, packs a long period of time into a condensed fifty-chapter narrative. It begins with the creation story and ends with the life and times of Joseph, one of the sons of a man named Jacob, later called Israel. Joseph was the youngest of his brothers but he was favored by his father. You may be familiar with the multi-colored coat his father gave him.

Because he was the father's most cherished child, his brothers were jealous of Joseph. They were so very envious that they plotted to kill him. They decided to throw him in a deserted well and leave him for dead. They planned to tell their father that a wild animal killed their brother. After taking his coat and throwing him down the well Joseph's siblings changed their minds and decided to profit from this brother instead of killing him. They did this because they saw, in the distance, a caravan on its way to Egypt. Instead of leaving

---

[76] Ravi Zacharias, Who made God?

Joseph to die, they decided to sell him to the merchants as a slave and make some money out of the situation. After giving over their sibling to slavery, they set off for home with his coat. The deceitful brothers smeared animal blood on Joseph's coat and mournfully presented it to their father with the false narrative (fake news?) of Joseph's demise. Upon hearing the fate of his beloved son, the father became inconsolable.

Meanwhile, upon arrival in Egypt, the traveling merchants re-sold Joseph, this time to an official of the Pharaoh. That person, Potiphar, decided to use him as one of his house slaves.

Joseph was discarded by his own brothers and doomed to live a life of slavery in Egypt. While enslaved to the official, Joseph was falsely accused of making an advance on the official's wife. Despite his protestations to the contrary, Joseph was convicted and thrown into an Egyptian jail. You could say that Joseph probably thought that God had turned His back on him and was not present in his life. But Genesis tells us that "while Joseph was in the prison, the Lord was with him..." (Gen. 39:20 NIV).

How so? Was God with Joseph when he was accosted by his own brothers and thrown into the well to die? Was God there when Joseph was sold to the merchants and then to an official of the Pharaoh? How about when he was unjustly accused and thrown into jail? Seems like God turned His back on Joseph, doesn't it? But this passage says God was with Him! We find out that this was not the end of Joseph's story, it was just the beginning. God gave Joseph the ability to correctly interpret dreams just at the time when the Pharaoh was having troubling nightmares. The jailor remembered that Joseph was able to interpret dreams and upon telling the Pharaoh's officials, it was arranged for Joseph to be taken before Pharaoh.

The Pharaoh was greatly troubled by his nightly dreams and called together his advisors and mystics to interpret these nightmares. However, not one of the Pharaoh's magicians or advisors were able to interpret the troubling dreams of Pharaoh. Joseph, the imprisoned slave, was able to perfectly and precisely interpret his dreams and, as a result, he was released from prison to become one of the Pharaoh's trusted counselors.

Max Lucado poignantly describes how a seemingly absent God takes Joseph's life and reveals to him what God had in store for Joseph all along.

> The brothers had every intention to harm Joseph. But God, in His providence, used their intended evil for ultimate good. He never robbed the brothers of their free will. He never imposed His nature upon them. But neither did He allow their sin and their sinful nature to rule the day. He rerouted evil into good. God uses all things to bring about his purpose. He will not be deterred in his plan to sustain and carry creation to its intended glory.[77]

Joseph, by virtue of the gift that God gave him of interpreting dreams, was appointed as the Pharaoh's right-hand man. Joseph was the second highest ranking person in all of Egypt. In this position, he was instrumental in saving his family (and the initial core of God's chosen people) from the drought and famine that had engulfed them in their native land. Joseph's brothers and all of their relatives and friends would have perished had Joseph not brought them to Egypt during the depths of a killing drought.

---

[77] *Anxious for Nothing*, P. 57

God indeed was with Joseph every step of the way. Although Joseph did not feel God's presence at the lowest ebbs of his life, God was there nonetheless.

Lucado explains that "[t]he ultimate proof of providence is the death of Christ on the cross. No deed was more evil. No other day was so dark. Yet God not only knew of the crucifixion, he ordained it. As Peter told the murderers, 'This man was handed over to you by God's deliberate plan and foreknowledge; and you, with the help of wicked men, put him to death by nailing him to the cross. But God raised him from the dead, freeing him from the agony of death, because it was impossible for death to keep its hold on him'" (See also Acts 2:23–24 NIV). Jesus was dead and buried and his disciples turned and ran. They trembled with fear, not wanting to be found out and treated the same as Jesus. They hid behind locked doors as terror engulfed each one. The disciples must have thought that God had turned his back in His Son and them.

Wouldn't we have had the same mindset as Joseph had when he is thrown down the well and left to die of starvation and dehydration by his brothers? Wouldn't we think that God had deserted us? Just before He died, Jesus cried out in a tormented voice "My God, My God, why have you forsaken me." Upon hearing this, the few remaining disciples must have thought that all was lost. If we were there at the foot of the cross and listened to Jesus's cry, wouldn't we have felt the same? We surely would have thought that Jesus had been abandoned by His Father. How did his eleven remaining disciples feel? Just a week prior they were with Jesus as he triumphantly entered Jerusalem on Palm Sunday, yet now they saw him hanging on a cross, with criminals on each side and solders shooting dice, gambling to divide up his garments.

However, just when we think God has gone "on vacation" we realize that He was there with Jesus and Joseph all along. Similarly,

God is present and with us through the darkest hours of our lives. Joseph finally realized God's presence and providence were with him when he was elevated to his position of power in the vast Egyptian empire.

When we think that God has turned his back on us we fail to understand that He is right there with us. God showed His love to all of us by raising Jesus from the grave. He used the suffering and death of His Son as proof that He wants to forgive us. Even though our sin distances us from God, He found a way to bring us back into fellowship with Him.

It is when we are in our darkest places, when we are in physical or emotional pain – when all seems lost, that is when we fall to our knees and pray our most fervent prayers. Aren't those lowest ebbs the times where we most desperately seek God?

C.S. Lewis, remarking of the opportunity pain has to get our attention, said, "[b]ut pain insists upon being attended to. God whispers to us in our pleasures, speaks in our conscience, but shouts in our pains: it is His megaphone to rouse a deaf world." That tells me that God wants our most fervent prayers. He wants us to desperately long for Him. He wants us to love Him above all.

Someone once said that God drives us to our knees, because that's where we should be. When we are in pain, when life sends a punch right to our gut, when we reach the end of our emotional rope, when we receive that cancer diagnosis; that is when we seek the lifeline of the guarantee. We need the guarantee to be indestructible because the times of trouble call for such a durable promise of salvation. When our health or wealth or security are shaken and called into doubt we fervently want something we can rely on as our rock. We need a sign of God's presence when we feel that He "seems" most distant. But we find instead, that God was there all along. I realized this after my cancer diagnosis. Joseph found this out and so must we.

B. All True Moral Teachings Come From God

In the opening paragraph, I asked these questions: Is the guarantee given by a source in whom I can place my trust? Is the source reliable? If God is the author of all great moral teachings, He is speaking the truth. Moral teachings are bedrock principals. They help us navigate our lives. As such, they should serve as a reminder that God is ever-present in our lives. These moral teachings are not meant to control our lives, rather they are guard rails that are meant to protect us from the freewheeling use of our free will. Every theory exposed by the great philosophers have their roots in God's moral laws. As C.S. Lewis described in *The Screwtape Letters*; God sends us the great moralists "not to inform men but to remind them, to restate the primeval moral platitudes against our continual concealment of them"[78]

We attempt to control our lives by the sweat of our brow and the determination of our will. However, we do so not to sustain ourselves but to accumulate more and obtain the greatest amount of pleasure as a *reward* for our hard work. We can only seek to control our lives in this way if we *conceal* God – or rip Him from the center of our lives. If we succeed in doing so, we will tear down the very guard rails He has erected to protect us.

One of the great moral lessons God has given us is that the love of money is the root of all evil. We have heard this a million times, but those words seem to roll off our backs like water on a duck. However, if we place money at the center of our lives (and therefore

---

[78] Letter 23

displace God) we become workaholics and strive to obtain more money with each rung of the corporate ladder we climb. In doing so we become like Ebenezer Scrooge in Dickens' *A Christmas Carol,* a cold-hearted miser who values work and money more than anything.

The guardrail that God has erected warned Scrooge that the love of money was the root of all evil. This safety device, however, was demolished by the greed and avarice of this miserly old man. The only way Scrooge was successful in tearing down this protective guard rail was by continuously concealing God's moral law. Scrooge became blind to His moral directive. As Scrooge learned, once he let money become his god, he lost everything. Scrooge lost the chance to experience love, humility, friendship, and caring. Scrooge (and his love of money) was in total control of his life. Without God at the center, he lost the important guard rail that God had erected to protect Scrooge.

But, on the darkest and most painful night of his life, Scrooge was brought to his knees (a place he needed to be all along) and his cold and hardened heart was broken. He was forced to face the man he had become and was yet to become. On that night he replaced the god of money with the God of love. The one true God of the universe. And his life was forever changed. He was saved from the false god he created and his painful plea for forgiveness was heard. He had seen the signs of God's presence and he was freed from the chains of sin that doomed his deceased partner, Jacob Marley.

This wonderful story shows, in a fictional way, the indestructible guarantee that God provides to everyone – even someone as despicable as Scrooge. Even someone as detestable as a slave ship captain.

In the days of slave trading in the British Empire, slave ships would anchor off the coast of Africa in search of the commodities that were most needed in the cocoa, sugar, and cotton plantations of the West Indies and the Caribbean.

African tribesman were viewed as nothing more than *goods*. Hundreds of men and women were taken from their families and stored in tiny pigeon-holed bunks, below deck. They were stacked like firewood. The maritime transportation of these articles of commerce from Central and Western Africa arrived in the South Atlantic and the Caribbean to be sold. These harrowing voyages often resulted in 30-50% of the "cargo" being lost to all forms of disease and malnutrition. Current estimates are that about 12-13 *million* people were shipped across the Atlantic over a span of 400 years.

How could God let this happen? Where was He during this grave time in the world? He was watching as his creation abused their free will to work unfathomable evil. But through this dark and shameful time, He was there. He took one of the most hated slave ship captains, John Newton, and broke his hardened heart. He would use this man to bring Great Britain to its knees and begin the slow and tortuous process of abolishing slavery and the slave trade. Newton had an *Ebenezer Scrooge* transformation.

After being morally convicted of his misdeeds as the captain of this human trafficking ship, God began a transformation of Newton's life. God broke his hardened heart. Newton responded by giving up his livelihood and entering into God's service. He enrolled in divinity school and became an ordained evangelical Anglican cleric. In this position, he took up the moral mantle of the human beings he so cruelly and callously treated. Newton became a leader of the abolitionist movement in England. With God at the center of his life, he was able to speak God's morality to the governing authority of the greatest military power on Earth at that time. And he did so with boldness!

Newton would describe to the political and business leaders, in a horrifyingly detailed fashion, how the slaves were mistreated aboard the slaving ships. He made England's commerce and political leaders face the brutality and moral bankruptcy that was the slave-trading business. In doing so, he inspired a young member of Parliament by the name of William Wilberforce. Wilberforce joined with Newton to lead a twenty-year battle to outlaw the slave trade in England.

But you may remember this remarkable man for something else. This grizzled ship captain was transformed from the inside out. The man who perpetrated such misery was responsible for writing one of the most beloved hymns of all time. He wrote about God saving a "wretch like me." The man who had placed avarice and greed at the center of his unworthy life wrote a song about being lost. Newton found God and, when placing Him at the rightful place in his life, his fears were relieved. This slave ship captain was not abandoned by God, because, as Newton writes, *God had a plan for him all along.* This plan was for him to do good and not evil. Newton realized that God's guarantee of grace was cherished – more valued than the gold he'd collected for his misdeeds.

"How precious did that grace appear, the hour I first believed!" The song, *Amazing Grace*, published in 1779, has become one of the most sung and beloved hymns of all time. God had not turned His back on the detestable Newton, neither did He turn away from the slaves who'd been taken from their native homes.

The Creator was not finished with this slave ship captain. God used Newton's evil for good. The Lord had promised good to this hard-hearted man. As Newton writes in his evocative song, once God was rightfully at the center of his life, God remained there as long as Newton's life endured.

C. A Blood Oath

How can I assure myself that this guarantee will be there when I need it? When you were a kid, did your friends ever ask you to promise to do something? Did you have to "pinky swear"? And did you have to seal that promise by interlocking your pinky finger with theirs to confirm that promise? Did you ever become a "blood brother" (or sister) with your best friend? I did. If so, you (like me) braved a pin prick of your finger to seal the commitment to your friend as your blood drops mingled in pressed thumbs. The Urban Dictionary[79] defines a blood oath in a similar fashion.

> Traditionally a blood oath was when one would shed his own blood and offer it onto an altar, swearing to uphold a certain task, **no matter what.** Sometimes persons would shed blood, usually by cutting their hands and then shake hands in agreement to a task they swore to uphold.

> More modernly it just means you swear to do something **no matter what**...thus 'blood' oath, meaning blood would be shed in promise. (Emphasis added)

A blood oath is, therefore like a guarantee. In the case of God, that is exactly what it was. God, through His Son Jesus, shed blood to seal the promise of forgiveness of our sins. Jesus shed his blood in order to uphold God's promise of salvation. *No matter what* you do or fail to do, you have the guarantee. *No matter what* number of sins you commit, God's grace is sufficient to guarantee your salvation. So, if Jesus is God, then God's promise of eternal life was sealed with His blood oath. The blood was an outward sign of the covenant (agreement) that God made with His creation.

---

[79] www.urbandictionary.com

John the Baptist said, "For the one whom God has sent speaks the words of God, for God gives the spirit without limit. The father loves the Son and has placed everything in his hands. Whoever believes in the Son **has** eternal life, but whoever rejects the Son will not see life, for God's wrath remains on him" (John 3:34-36. Emphasis added).

The night before Jesus was betrayed and offered up to the religious leaders to be put on trial in the Sanhedrin, He tried to teach his disciples the meaning of the blood oath that he was swearing to uphold. As Jesus broke bread and poured wine, He tried to get his disciples to visualize what He was going to endure for them (and all of us). Keep in mind the importance of the timing of this demonstration. This occurred during the Passover feast and, unbeknownst to the disciples, was the last time they would eat together.

The disciples thought they were going to the upper room to celebrate the feast of the Passover. The Feast of the Unleavened Bread was a remembrance of the time when the people of God were slaves in Egypt. This Passover Feast was a remembrance of the night when God asked the Israelites to place the blood of a lamb over their doorways so that death would pass them by and would not take the lives of their firstborn sons. God was going to force the Egyptian Pharoah to "let his people go" by causing all of the eldest sons of Egypt to die – including the Pharaoh's own son.

On this Passover celebration in the upper room, however, Jesus was the Pascal Lamb. He was giving wine and bread to His disciples to help them remember that He was now becoming the sacrificial lamb for not only the Jews but for all people. In speaking to the gathered men, Jesus told them that His blood was an <u>agreement</u> that He was sealing with all of creation. His blood would be shed to guarantee forgiveness of sins. Mark 14:12, 22-24, NIV. Jesus was swearing a blood oath. On the night where the Jews celebrated the sacrificing of the Passover lamb, Jesus was teaching his disciples and all of us that He was now the sacrificial lamb. He promised that His blood was about to be shed as a blood oath guarantee. If we place our faith in Him as God's Son and confess our sins, He promised, they will be forgiven and we will be cleansed of the stain of sin.

> "I am the Living One," Christ said to the awestruck apostle John in a vision. "I was dead, and behold I am alive forever and ever!" (Rev. 1:18). The Lord's Supper sums up all three tenses: the life that was and died for us, the life that is and lives in us, and the life that will be and will come for us[80]. Christ is no mere example of living; he is life itself.[81]

> Jesus spoke as he did not to offend, but to effect a radical transformation in the symbol. God had said to Noah, if you drink the blood of a lamb, the life of the lamb enters you — don't do it. Jesus said, in effect, if you drink my blood, my life will enter you — do it![82]

> Just as blood cleanses the body of harmful metabolites, forgiveness through Christ's blood cleanses away the waste products, sins, that impede true health.[83]

---

[80] Perhaps this inspired Dickins to conjure up the ghosts of Christmas past, present and future who visited Scrooge

[81] In His Image, Philip Yancey & Dr. Paul Brand, Chapter 8, Zondervan, iBooks

[82] Supra, Chapter 5

[83] Supra, Chapter 6

Yancey and one of his mentors, Dr. Brand, showed us in their book how God made us wonderfully in His image. God designed our bodies with systems that sustain us and keep us healthy. As the above description so perfectly illustrates, our circulatory system is designed in a way that utilizes our blood to clean the impurities and toxins from our bodies. Jesus's blood oath will cleanse our souls of the contamination of sin. The way we exercise our free will can act as a cancer that can rob us of our very lives. But God had devised a plan for our rescue from the cancer of sin. He determined that on a specific Passover feast in an upper room in the city of Jerusalem, His son would pledge a blood oath which guarantees that the cancer of sin would be cleansed from our soul.

That blood oath was finalized by Jesus's blood being spilled and resulting in the death of God's Son on a cross. That oath was then sealed by the unsealing of the tomb. And the guarantee agreement was fulfilled by the resurrection of Jesus on Easter morning. "Easter, the day that gives a sneak preview of how all history will look from the vantage point of eternity, when every scar, every hurt, every disappointment will be seen in a different light. Our faith begins where it might have seemed to end. Between the cross and the empty tomb however is the promise of history: hope for the world, and hope for each one of us who lives in it."[84]

D. The Guarantee of His Word

Just like a blood oath, the hallmark of a pledge to do something is the dependence on a promise made by a trustworthy source. "My word is my bond" is a common phrase used to portray this concept. While the true source of that phrase is unknown, it is believed to

---

[84] The Jesus I Never Knew, Philip Yancey, P. 274

have originated in 16th century Scotland. This saying may have originated from the Scottish idiom "O kingis word shuld be o kingis bonde." "My word is my bond" was so ingrained in English culture that it was adopted as the motto of the London Stock Exchange.

When it is used, it is meant to portray the same thing as a blood oath. The person issuing such a message is saying that "you can depend on what I am saying" and "you can bank on the promise I am making." When uttered, it is basically an oral guarantee. To rely on such a promise, the person to whom this pledge is made must rely on not only the terms of the statement but the person making the claim. In legal parlance, it is sometimes called an oral contract. A contract consists of an offer, an acceptance, and valid consideration (i.e., money or something of value) that is exchanged or that must be exchanged. If the terms of a contract are agreed upon, the person to whom the pledge is made can act on the agreement.

Another legal term that comes into play on occasion when considering oral contracts is detrimental reliance. This occurs when the person seeking to impose the promise (the promisee) tries to show that he or she relied on the oral promise made by the person making that promise (the promisor). In so relying, something bad happened and the promisee was damaged. In such a situation, the promisee must prove two primary things. First, that the promise made was something the promisee could reasonably rely on. And second, that the promisee relied on that promise to their detriment – their harm.

For instance, what if I said that if you allowed me to sprinkle on you some of the fairy dust I had in my hand you would then have the ability to fly. You agreed. With a flourish, I took some glittery particles of dust from my hand and dusted you with them. Relying on my promise you then jumped off a two-story balcony and broke your ankle. Would this oral promise of mine be enforceable?

When you were released from the hospital you brought me to court in an effort to make me pay for your medical bills. Your legal theory was that you "detrimentally relied" on my oral pledge and that this reliance caused you to spend a great deal of money on medical bills. In this scenario, you would be able to prove the second element. The medical bills you incurred for your broken ankle were a direct result of the promise I made to you. However, you could not prove the first element, that you "reasonably" relied on the promise. There is no way a person in their right mind can reasonably rely on the promise that fairy dust would make them fly!

Using the legal principle of detrimental reliance can we prove our case that both of the elements of an oral agreement of salvation have been proven? The Gospel of John recounts the cross-examination of Jesus by a Pharisee named Nicodemus. This Pharisee was a very sharp lawyer in his day and a member of the Jewish ruling council. Nicodemus had to admit that the miracles Jesus performed indicated that Jesus had some connection to God[85]. But Nicodemus was pressing Jesus on the claim that a person had to believe in Him and to be "born again" to see heaven. When pressed further in the cross-examination, Jesus got straight to the point.

> "No one," He explained, "has ever gone into heaven
> except the one who came from heaven – the Son
> of Man." Jesus went on, explaining "that everyone
> who believes in Him may have eternal life." Jesus
> closes by saying that "God so loved the world that
> he gave his one and only Son, that whoever believes

---

[85] By recognizing the acts performed by Jesus as true miracles this member of the Jewish ruling counsel confirmed that they did indeed take place. They were historical facts confirmed by the ruling body of the Jews. More about this in Chapter Eight - where we will explore how History Proves the Guarantee

in him shall have eternal life. For God did not send
his Son into this world to condemn the world, but
to save the world through him." John 3:13-17, NIV

This promise is real and not fairy dust. Reliance on this promise
can be the most important gift you have ever been given. Not relying
on the promise of salvation is detrimental. Not relying on this claim
has damages associated with it – damages that last for all eternity.
These damages relate to a person's estrangement from their Creator.
Relying on the oral promise guarantees eternal life.

But what does all of this have to do with the guarantee? And
does this answer the question posed of how solid is this guarantee?
To answer these questions, I have borrowed again from my legal
training. Since this promise of salvation was made by Jesus we must
determine whether you can reasonably rely on such a promised
guarantee. To prove whether the promise was reasonably reliable
you should also ask yourself if the person making the promise is
credible. When someone testifies in court the jury must determine
if that witness is telling the truth. Are they a credible witness?

One of the ways to establish the credibility of a person making
a statement is to see if the words spoken are "recent fabrications" or
if prior words and conduct are consistent with the testimony now
given in court. To show that the statements made in court are true,
lawyers will attempt to show the jurors that the testimony is either
consistent or inconsistent with prior statements made by that witness. The inference is that if someone said that something was going
to occur or that something was true in the past and that witness is
now telling the same story or voicing the same opinions in court,
the witness tends to be more credible. If the prior statements support the current statement, now made under oath, this witness's

statements are more worthy of belief. Such statements, therefore, have credibility.

Of course, the opposite is true. If a witness says something in the past that either did not come true or was inconsistent with what the witness was testifying to in court, the witness's credibility is weakened and juries tend to disregard their courtroom testimony. For example, suppose an expert witness writes an article in a scientific journal. In this article, the author concludes that if a specific chemical additive is used in the processing of canned tuna, the consumption of that brand of tuna would likely cause gastric ulcers.

Five years after the article was published this same expert appears in a court to testify in a case involving a thirty-six-year-old man who ate a brand of tuna that contained this chemical additive and developed, over a six-month period, gastric ulcers. In court, the expert testified for the manufacturer of that chemical. In his testimony, the expert said that he examined the medical records of the man making the claim of gastric ulcers and found no link between his ulcer and the canned tuna. The lawyer for the injured man then cross-examined the expert in court. The lawyer had the expert identify the scientific study that was published five years ago and got him to admit that he was the author of that article. The lawyer for the injured man asked the expert if the chemical additive referenced in the article was the same chemical used in the canned tuna that his client consumed. When the expert answered that it was, the lawyer then asked him if he was lying in the article he wrote five years ago, or if he was lying in court for the tuna manufacturer that hired him. The lawyer has thus obtained the testimony that either the expert's predictions set forth in his article were wrong or his recent testimony was fabricated. In such an instance the jury would most likely doubt the expert's credibility - and may determine that the $600 per hour that he was being paid by the manufacturer to testify may have had something to do with his changed courtroom opinions.

The Gospels of Matthew, Mark, Luke, and John are rife with recorded statements made by Jesus to his disciples well in advance of the Last Supper. These statements foretold the betrayal of Jesus, the denial by Peter, Jesus's torture, death, and resurrection. Even though His disciples failed to comprehend the words Jesus spoke, He clearly told them what was going to happen to him – how his disciples would scatter after his arrest, who was going to betray Him, how he was going to be handed over and that He was going to die and rise from the dead three days thereafter.[86]

In fact, as will be discussed in Chapter Eight, there are many references in the Old Testament as to the coming of Jesus, where He was to be born, and who would be His mother. The Old Testament accounts, made thousands of years before Jesus's birth also forecast in detail his death and resurrection. If Jesus's credibility was judged by this judicial standard, and if the things He said indeed happened, then Jesus could be viewed as a truthful and credible witness. The statements Jesus made about the guarantee may be viewed with more credibility[87] if His prior statements of what would happen in His final days on earth actually came to pass.

Prior recorded statements that Jesus made in the days and hours before his death also came to pass, just as He predicted they would. During the Last Supper, Jesus told the "rock upon which he would

---

[86] See e.g.: Matthew 12:40, 16:13-17, 21; 17:12; 20:18-19; 26:2, 23, 31, 34, 45, 56, 75. Mark 8:27-30; 9: 9-2; 10:33-34; 14:8, 18, 27-30, 41-42, 50, 71-72. Luke 9:18-21, 35-36, 44; 11-30; 17:25; 18:31; 22:15-16, 21-22, 34, 37, 47-48, 61-62; 13:18-27, 36-38; 18:3-6, 26-27. NIV

[87] Please understand that I am NOT questioning the credibility of Jesus. I am just providing this analysis as viewed from the perspective of a non-believer who might be trying to assess the credibility Jesus's statements

build his church" (Peter) that he would deny him - three times. Not only this, Jesus actually said *when* this would happen. "This very night, before the rooster crows, you will disown me three times." Upon hearing this, Peter said there was no way he would ever do such a thing. "Even if I have to die with you, I will never disown you," Peter retorted.

Later that night, after Jesus's arrest and while He was being interrogated by the Sanhedrin, Peter was sitting outside and a servant girl recognized him as one of the men "with Jesus of Galilee." Without blinking an eye, Peter said, "I don't know what you are talking about." *One down.* Peter then left the courtyard and went further away from the building where the Sanhedrin was conducting the trial of Jesus. He went all the way to the entry gate. Again, another young lady saw him and shouted out for all to hear "This fellow was with Jesus of Nazareth." This time Peter swore, "I don't know the man!" *Two down.* As Peter tried to retreat to the shadows, the onlookers pressed him saying, "Surely you are one of them for your accent gives you away." In response, Peter, one of Jesus's closest disciples, tried to distance himself from his Savior. He adamantly told the crowd that if he was lying then he would call down curses on himself. I imagine he said something like "If I am lying may I be struck down by a bolt of lightning." In his most confident and belligerent tone, he testified to the whole crowd, again, that he "did not know *this man!*" not even daring to say Jesus's name. "Immediately a rooster crowed." *Three strikes!*

Upon hearing the rooster, Peter knew that he had done exactly what Jesus said he would do – something he *swore* he would not do. He'd disowned his Savior to save his own hide. Upon this realization, he broke down and "wept bitterly." Just as Jesus predicted, Peter turned his back on Him. Peter realized that he had fulfilled the awful testimony of Jesus. Peter had disavowed the man he idolized and followed. Peter had witnessed Jesus's miracles. He had seen Jesus walk on water. Peter was there when the blind regained their sight and when a dead man walked out of the grave. And yet Peter renounced the Son of Man. Matthew 26:31-15 and 69-75.

Also, during the Last Supper, Jesus looked straight into Judas's eyes and said, "The one who dipped his hand into the bowl with me will betray me." Remember, Jesus had told His disciples on many occasions before this Passover dinner that He would be handed over to be killed, buried, and on the third day would be resurrected.[88] Despite all of this, none of His disciples apparently believed these things would come to pass. And Judas, after hearing that his betrayal was known by Jesus, looked right back at Jesus and denied this revelation. "Surely not I, Rabbi?" Judas denied what he had just done the day before. He had met with the Jewish chief priests and offered to turn Jesus over to them – for a price. He was willing to betray Jesus for thirty silver coins. In response, Jesus answered "Yes, it is you"[89]

If I had been there (if I were one of the twelve) I would have leapt to my feet and grabbed the traitor. If not that, I would surely have done *something*. Instead of worrying much about the betrayal announced by Jesus, the disciples devolved into an argument about who was the greatest of all of them. Which one of them would sit at the right hand of Jesus when they went to heaven! Were they deaf? Were they drunk? What? Matthew 26:17-25 and Luke 2:24-32, NIV.

Again, precise predictions and testimony by Jesus before events occurred show the credibility of the promisor when He tells the disciples of the blood oath He was going carry out to save them from their sins.

---

[88] Supra.

[89] Matthew 26:14-16, NIV

Matthew's gospel recounts what happened on Easter morning. The women arrived at the tomb to properly prepare Jesus's body for burial. Instead of having to roll back the rock and break the seal on the tomb, they encountered an open tomb with an angel standing by. The astonished women trembled with fear, but the angel said to them, "Do not be afraid, for I know that you are looking for Jesus, who was crucified. He is not here; he has risen, *just as he said*." (Matt. 18:1-8, NIV, emphasis added).

Mark recounted what the women were told next. "Go tell his disciples and Peter[90], He is going ahead of you into Galilee. There you will see him, *just as he told you*" (Mark 16:7, NIV, emphasis added). And Luke continued the discussions between the angel and the women. "Remember *how he told to you*, while he was still with you in Galilee: 'The Son of Man must be delivered into the hands of sinful men, be crucified, and the third day be raised again' **Then they remembered his words**" (Luke 24:6-8, NIV, emphasis added). The angel had to remind them that Jesus's predictions about His death and resurrection had come true, just as Jesus said they would. The past testimony of Jesus was perfectly aligned with the present reality of His resurrection from the dead.

The words Jesus spoke and recorded in the months and days before the Last Supper were all precise and truthful. Jesus's past testimony was exactly what happened. Jesus spoke about His betrayal by Judas, how Peter would disown him and how He would die and be resurrected from the dead three days later. Jesus was indeed as good as His word! A guarantee of salvation based on the word of Jesus is a solid as it gets!

---

[90] Notice here that Peter is again singled out for special treatment as one of Jesus' closest followers and disciples

E. The Security of the Guarantee

The framers of the constitution called upon the notion of trusting God many times in the debates over the wording of this historic document. It was such a central notion to our democracy that the dollar bill would proudly proclaim "In God We Trust." While this motto was not added to the dollar bill until 1956, it appeared on US coins as far back as 1864. It was used as a declaration of the great need to trust God in times of despair and trouble. In fact, the Civil War caused a great awakening of faith during a very dark period of strife in the United States.

In 1956, President Dwight D. Eisenhower signed into law a bill declaring "In God We Trust" as the nation's official motto. During a speech he gave in 1954, Eisenhower said "[i]n this way we are reaffirming the transcendence of religious faith in America's heritage and future; in this way we shall constantly strengthen those spiritual weapons which forever will be our country's most powerful resource in peace and war."[91] The president was tying the debate over the constitution and the religious fervor of the Civil War to the bedrock of American values – faith in God as the centerpiece of U.S. freedom. *Trust in God* is therefore officially sanctioned by the U.S. government. If God can be trusted in some things, He can be trusted in all things. It was so important that it has been ordained as America's motto.

If you are able to place your trust in God, the guarantee takes on a higher level of importance. When trust is used in this way (as an intransitive verb) it also takes on a deeper meaning. "If you trust

---

[91] www.eisenhowerlibrary.gov

in someone or something, you believe strongly in them, and do not doubt their powers or their good intentions."[92]

Wow, if we are able to hold in our mind that level of trust – having no doubt in either God's power to grant this guarantee or God's good intentions in providing this assurance of salvation – how would this change our outlook on life? No matter what you do or how bad things seem at any moment in your life, you will absolutely be assured that you will be with God in eternity when your days on earth are done. You have His Son's blood oath on it!

"We are secure not because we are sure of ourselves but because we trust that God is sure of us. The opening phrase of the psalm is 'Those who trust in God' – not those who trust in their performance, in their morals, in their righteousness, in their health, in their pastor, in their doctor, in their president, in their economy, or in their nation – 'those who trust in God.' Those who decide that God is for us and will make us whole eternally."[93] That is what the apostle Peter, the priest Martin Luther, the slave ship captain John Newton, and the singer Bono all came to realize. That is what this retired lawyer determined after I completed my investigation. And that is what I hope that you, ladies and gentleman of the jury, will conclude. The trust that you place in God will yield a guarantee of eternity.

When Mary was pregnant with our Savior she went to visit her cousin Elizabeth, who was pregnant with John the Baptist. This occurred shortly after an angel appeared to Mary to tell her that she would give birth to the long-awaited Savior of the world. She was told that her child to be born will be the "Son of God."

---

[92] The Collins Dictionary. https://www.collinsdictionary.com/us/dictionary/english/trust

[93] Eugene H. Peterson. "A Long Obedience in the Same Direction." InterVarsity Press, 2012-04-25. iBooks. P. 132

As Luke described in his gospel, the two ladies were overcome with joy over the coming births of their children. Elizabeth told Mary that she was blessed because Mary "believed that what the Lord has said ... will be accomplished." Notice the usage of words. Mary was told by her cousin that the Son of God she will bear *will be* the Savior of the world! Mary placed her trust in God.[94] Therefore, if we place our trust in God we have every right to expect that God will give us what He said he would.

F. Should We Expect a Direct Promise from God?

God has never appeared to me in person or through an angel as He did with Mary. He has never appeared to me in a burning bush. I have never wrestled with God in the wilderness. The Almighty has never laid out plans for me to build a great ship to save all mankind from a flood. I have never even heard an Old Testament prophet speak of fire and brimstone should I not turn from my sinful ways. Quite simply, God has never told me directly that He is granting a guarantee of salvation.

So, if I have never heard those words directly from God, how am I to know that they apply to me? In fact, has the Bible ever recorded a direct statement from God to anyone on earth that they have the guarantee of salvation? Or are all statements made concerning the guarantee made to apply to the world at large?

These may be valid points. Hearing with our own ears is sometimes the final proof that convinces a person to believe in the guarantee. These questions were answered for me by Philip Yancey in his book *Finding God in Unexpected Places*. In chapter 42, he talks

---

[94] Luke 1:26-45

about this same dilemma and answers this question in a way that hits the mark for me.

> And, listen – only one person in the Bible receives a direct promise of Heaven. It's a thief who lived a life of crime, who did not get baptized, and who probably never went to church. He died within hours after accepting Christ. Yet that thief lives in Heaven today. Jesus *guaranteed* it. (Emphasis mine)

This gives me great assurance. This account is consistent with all the other evidence that I have discovered about the strong and unwavering promise that God gives to anyone who confesses their need for Jesus and a desire for the forgiveness of their sin. If a convicted felon who is sentenced to death for his crimes can get the guarantee of heaven just before he dies, then I have supreme confidence that I can as well.

This guarantee came directly from the lips of God's own Son. But this guarantee was only finalized in death: death on a cross by the giver of the guarantee. And death was the final act that triggered the acceptance and performance of the guarantee. Remember what we learned in this chapter about oral agreements. In order for such agreements to be valid, they must have some form of consideration paid. The consideration was paid by Christ when he died for the sins of all mankind. But the oral promise was not yet fulfilled.

Easter morning brought forth the final element of the agreement to fruition. Christ died and then, as He said he would, rose from the grave to seal the contract. Max Lucado wrote in his study guide, *The Gospel of John*, as follows: "The basis of forgiveness takes us back to Christ's death, but **the guarantee** of all the promises and the hope we live by depends on the truth of the empty tomb.

Authentic believers are forever overwhelmed by two conclusions: Jesus died for me and Jesus rose again for me. In those two statements rests a hope large enough for life and stronger than death."[95]

G. The Guarantee Rests in Jesus and All Who Believe in Him

Jesus is either who he says he is or a madman. Either you have to believe what He says or declare that He was not in His right mind. Logic dictates this is true. Jesus said that He was sent by God to save the world. Jesus said he was God's Son. Jesus said he was divine. Jesus said he was God incarnate. Either you believe what he said or you believe He was deranged.

John MacArthur in *One Perfect Life* explained the sovereignty of Jesus and the guarantee of salvation that God imbued in His Son as follows:

> The absolute sovereignty of God is the basis of Jesus's **certainty** that His mission will be successful (cf. Phil. 1:6). The security of salvation rests in the sovereignty of God, for God is the **guarantee** that 'all' He has chosen will come to Him for salvation...This saving purpose is the Father's will that the Son will not fail to do perfectly [what God has ordained] (John 6:38; cf. 4:34; 10:28, 29[...] ...everyone who sees the Son and believes in Him may have everlasting life...[96] (Emphasis added)

---

[95] Lesson 7, pg. 109. Emphasis added

[96] One Perfect Life, Part VI notes, 78-80. iBooks

Jesus said that it was God's intention that everyone who looks to Him for forgiveness of sin and places their trust in Jesus "shall have eternal life" (John 6:39-40 NIV). We must be mindful of the words Jesus used in this proclamation. Jesus used *shall*, not *can* or *might*. When these types of words are used in legal documents or laws they are given special meaning. Jesus is making a declaration, for all time.

The promise Jesus made of salvation to all who believe in Him and rely on His power to forgive sins is a contract (covenant) that He has made with people of faith. This agreement is offered to anyone who seeks to claim the terms of the guarantee. Furthermore, the agreement that God, through Jesus, made with those who believe in Jesus and His powers of forgiveness is "unbreachable," something that God will never violate or break. Philip Yancey said that

> God's covenant with his people is everlasting. Nothing can cancel it. As the decades, even centuries, pass, empires such as Babylon, Persia, Egypt, Greece, Syria and Rome rise and fall, their armies chasing each other across the plains of Palestine. Each new empire subjugates the Jews with ease. Sometimes the entire race verges on extinction. Four centuries separate the last words of the prophets in the Old Testament and the first words of Matthew in the New Testament—"the four hundred silent years," they are called. Does God care? Is he even alive? In desperation the common people wait for a Messiah; they have no other hope.[97]

---

[97] Philip Yancey & Brenda Quinn. "Meet the Bible." Zondervan. iBooks. P. 1290

They had no other hope – until the Messiah arrived to seal the deal. Jesus, the Messiah, provided the payment on the contract that God made with the Jews when he led them out of Egypt and into the promised land. And, more so, Jesus offered to all who believe the opportunity to be signatories on the contract. Anyone can become a party to the agreement by accepting the payment made by Jesus as the sole means of forgiveness of their sins – and thus the only way back to fellowship with a Holy God. The one and only way to obtain the guarantee of salvation is, therefore, available to everyone and not limited just to God's chosen people, the Jews. As Brenda Quinn observed, in *Meet the Bible*, "Belonging to a Christian community can be nerve-racking. Believing, it seems, opens up a whole new world of voices telling us what to do, how to act, who to vote for, how to worship, what to buy or not buy, and more. Gaining a grasp of the Bible and getting to know God is merely the beginning, we're often led to believe. Then comes the indoctrination into what a *Christian* must look like. These pressures are hardly new." However, Ms. Quinn reminds us that none of this is of concern. "The only thing that matters is God's preeminent grace in the form of his son, Jesus...Since the days of the early church God has had to remind believers that only one thing matters for salvation: faith in Christ. One who believes in Jesus, Paul declared, is saved from sin. Period. Nothing else factors into the equation."[98]

H. Certification of Testimony as True

John the Baptist was born approximately six months before Jesus. His purpose was to prepare the way for Jesus by proclaiming the arrival of the expected Messiah. The promised Messiah was

---

[98] Philip Yancey & Brenda Quinn. "Meet the Bible." P. 1854-55. Zondervan.

long-awaited by the Jewish people. John, through his preaching about the coming Savior and by baptizing people with water, had his own following and disciples. As the time came near for the beginning of Jesus's ministry, John and his disciples got into an argument with one of the leaders of the Jews. This Jewish religious leader said that "someone else" is now baptizing people and noted that John's own disciples were now following Jesus. This, the Jewish leader posited, put John in an awkward position. In response, John pointed to Jesus as the Son of God and affirmed His divinity.

> The one who comes from heaven is above all; the one who is from the earth belongs to the earth and speaks as one from the earth. The one who comes from heaven is above all. He *testified* to what he has seen and heard, but no one accepts his testimony. The man who has accepted it has *certified that God is truthful.* For the one whom God has sent speaks the words of God, for God gives the Spirit without limit. The Father loves the Son, and has placed everything in his hands. Whomever believes in the Son **has** eternal life, but whomever rejects the Son will not see life, for God's wrath remains on him. John 3:31-36, NIV, emphasis added

John was thus testifying to the fact that *Jesus is the Messiah*, the One who his followers and the Jews were waiting for, the One who would liberate them from their sinful ways. John *certified* through his testimony that Jesus is God and is speaking the words of God. John's words, most importantly, affirmed Jesus's authority to forgive sins and in doing so, guaranteed eternity for the person forgiven. If Jesus had the authority to forgive sins He must be God, because, as will be shown below, only the one sinned against has the right and authority to forgive the sinner. John said Jesus was this person. This testimony was later affirmed by Jesus himself. Jesus declared that He had the right, power, and authority to forgive sins. Theologian Max Lucado described this authority as "unimpeachable"[99].

When a witness takes the stand in court, the witness is first "sworn in." By taking the oath the witness swears to tell the truth "so help me God."[100] In this way the jury can assess whether that witness's testimony is worthy of belief. After the witness provides her testimony, the opposing counsel can try to discredit that testimony by what has been described as the single best device, invented by man, for determining the truth. No, not a lie detector. A skilled advocate can, through the art of cross-examination, seek to reveal the truth. As I mentioned previously, "Cross-examination is the greatest legal engine ever invented for the discovery of truth." So declared the author of American evidentiary procedure, John H. Wigmore.

In law school, I studied his treatise on evidence. The first edition of this well-known legal treatise was published in 1904. In fact, this quote from Wigmore's book on the Anglo-American System of Evidence in Trials at Common Law—usually referred to as Wigmore on Evidence, has been relied on by courts as "authoritative law" since the early 1900s. One more recent example of this reliance is found in the US Supreme Court case of *Lilly v. Virginia*, 527 U.S. 116 (1999).

When a lawyer, during cross-examination of a witness, suspects that the witness is not being wholly truthful, the witness is subjected

---

[99] Before Amen, iBooks, p. 95

[100]This phrase has recently been changed (in our "modern" society) to "under penalty of perjury" - meaning instead of God's judgment being laid on the witness for telling a lie, the witness would be subjected to man's law of perjury and the criminal penalties that would attach to untruthful testimony

to pointed questions probing the truthfulness of their testimony. These specifically designed questions can be based on many different sources. One of the most common relates to a prior statement made by or attributed to the witness that differs with their sworn testimony given in court. This method is called "impeachment." In this circumstance the witness is confronted with their *contrary* prior statement. This usually comes with a predicate question such as: "Were you telling the jury the truth then, or are you telling the truth now?" If the statements are truly contradictory, the witness is boxed into a corner from which they cannot escape. The jury is left doubting the witness's truthfulness and the credibility of the witness is diminished – if not destroyed. The term *impeachment*, therefore in legal parlance, means that a lawyer has proven that the statement made by the witness under examination has been proven as false. Thus, an *unimpeachable* statement is incapable of being anything other than true. When a witness withstands rigorous cross-examination she is said to be "unimpeachable."

It is in this context that the phrase used by Lucado above is so pivotal. If Jesus and His statements about His ability to forgive sins are "unimpeachable," then His credibility is unquestioned. "He sustains everything by the mighty power of his command" (Heb. 1:3 NLT). "God exalted him to the highest place and gave him the name that is above every name" (Phil. 2:9 NIV). The Roman government tried to intimidate him. False religion tried to silence him. The devil tried to kill him. All failed. Even "death was no match for him" (Acts 2:24 MSG). Jesus was providing unimpeachable testimony when he declared, "All authority in heaven and on earth has been given to me" (Matt. 28:18 NIV).[101]

---

[101] Before Amen, iBooks, p. 95-96

As laypeople, we are encouraged by God to "cross-examine" His words and look over His contract. Some question the authenticity of Jesus's proclamations without even giving the Bible a thoughtful reading. As I previously pointed out, Eugene Peterson observed "[t] he reason many of us do not ardently believe in the gospel is that we have never given it a rigorous testing, thrown our hard questions at it, faced it with our most prickly doubts."[102] This type of rigorous testing is the same method used in the art of cross-examination employed by trial lawyers in the courtroom. It is precisely what Wigmore cites as the most powerful truth-finding device ever created.

In law school, students were taught by the use of an educational system called the Socratic Method. This form of teaching came from the great philosopher Socrates. "The Socratic Method requires cooperative argumentative dialogue between individuals, asking and answering questions that stimulate critical thinking and draw out underlying presumptions."[103] Law professors taught us by asking a series of questions that would lead their students to the right answer. They did not simply lecture us.

The Bible has an account of Jesus being cross-examined by means of the Socratic method about His authority and divinity. He was cross-examined specifically about the guarantee of salvation. The Gospel of Luke details a day in Jesus's ministry when He was confronted by a Jewish lawyer. This lawyer tried to trap Jesus through the use of a series of questions coupled with the art of cross-examination. The Socratic confrontation starts out with the lawyer asking Jesus a question. "What must I do to inherit eternal life?" A seemingly simple question but one packed with tremendous implications.

---

[102] Eugene H. Peterson. "A Long Obedience in the Same Direction." InterVarsity Press, 2012-04-25. iBooks. P. 108

[103] https://www.teachhub.com/teaching-strategies-about-socratic-method

In response, Jesus asked the lawyer His own question. "What is written in the law?" This question pointed the Jewish lawyer back to the Torah and the Ten Commandments. The lawyer correctly answered the question by reciting the first two commandments. The first, that he should love God with all his heart and soul and the second, that he was to love his neighbor as himself. Then, the clever lawyer pressed on with his cross-exam. He asked, "and who is my neighbor?" Jesus's reply came through a parable – the story of the good Samaritan. In this parable, Jesus showed the Jewish lawyer that to love others as ourselves includes showing love to an enemy. (As a postscript, you should know that the Samaritan people of Jesus's day were despised by the Jews.)

The parable begins with Jesus telling the lawyer (and all who were near) about a man who was robbed and beaten by thieves. The robbers took everything from this victim and left him for dead along the side of the road. The first person to come along and see the beaten man was a Jewish priest. He saw the bloodied and battered man but didn't do anything to help him. Instead, he crossed the road and avoided him altogether. Then a Levite[104] happened along and does the same – ignoring the man and crossing the road to avoid an encounter with this poor soul. Finally, a hated Samaritan saw the man and showed him kindness. The Samaritan bandaged his wounds, put the man on the Samaritan's donkey, and took him to a nearby inn. That night the Samaritan feeds the stranger and takes care of him. The next day the Samaritan gives the inn's owner some money and asks the innkeeper to take care of this poor soul. What's more, the Samaritan promises to come back and reimburse

---

[104]Levites' principal roles in the Jewish religion included singing Psalms during Temple services, performing construction and maintenance of the Temple, serving as guards, and performing other services at the Temple. Levites also served as teachers and judges, maintaining cities of refuge in biblical times

the innkeeper for any further expense incurred in nursing the man back to full health. Luke 10:25-35, NIV.

After answering the lawyer in this way, Jesus turned to him and asks, "[w]hich of these three do you think was a neighbor to the man who fell into the hands of the robbers?" The lawyer was humbled by this parable and the pointed questions asked by Jesus. Now, defeated by Jesus's cross-examination, the Jewish lawyer knew the answer to his own question. Through this Socratic exercise the lawyer was taught the true meaning of the second commandment. The lawyer, his eyes lowered, answered Jesus's question: "[t]he one who had mercy on him." Jesus's cross-examination was concluded. The lawyer hoped for a successful impeachment of Jesus but was instead shown who Jesus was – God incarnate. The lawyer's plan to tarnish the credibility of Jesus failed and he was the one who was taught a lesson by THE unimpeachable source.

H. Only the One Sinned Against Can Forgive

It is only logical that if someone wrongs you, only you can grant true forgiveness. In this chapter, I have been exploring, from a trial lawyer's point of view, whether the guarantee is given by a source in which we can place our trust. I promised that I would address the origins of the guarantee and the source of the promise of eternity.

All sin is a turning away from God. If a person has an affair they are, of course, wronging their spouse but at the same time they are turning away from God by violating His commands. Therefore, while the wronged spouse must be the one to grant forgiveness, true forgiveness must come from the one who created the command of fidelity to one's spouse. By way of analogy, one who robs a bank must account to the bank for the money taken, but it is the state that holds the person accountable and must mete out the punishment for the robbery. If we lie we are committing a wrong against the person we are lying to or telling a falsehood about. Thusly, we must ask for forgiveness from that person. However, if the same lie is told to an investigating police officer we are also committing a wrong against society (i.e. obstruction of justice). And if that same lie is told, under oath in court, we have committed perjury. Obstruction of justice and perjury are punished by the state. The basis of lying, at its very root, is a sin. Lying is a sin because it violates one of God's commands. The ninth Commandment is God's prohibition against lying. It is therefore a sin against God, not just a wrong against a police officer or a judge.

The same holds true for all wrongs -- they are the breaking of God's commands. These are contained not only in the Ten Commandments but throughout the Bible. Some would say that the primary purpose of the Bible is to illuminate sin. God has proscribed ways that He wants us to live. These proscriptions protect us and please the Creator. As I have discussed above and will highlight further in this book, no matter how hard we try, no one has been able to purge sin from their lives. That is the very point of the guarantee. God does not give the guarantee to only those who manage to avoid "most" of their sins. It is given to everyone. That is why we can never be *good enough* to gain entrance into the heavenly realm.

However, the opposite is also true, we can never be *bad enough* to prevent the promise of salvation from protecting us from eternal separation from God. Nothing can separate us from the guarantee of forgiveness. Nothing, however, except our own willful rejection of that guarantee. "Often our mistakes bring difficult consequences. But as we look at how tenderly God cares for us, we can echo David's words in Psalm 103: 'He does not treat us as our sins deserve or repay us according to our iniquities' (v. 10). The price we pay for sin does not even approach the price we owe God for the grace he so willingly provides to us. We have this grace because of the price Jesus paid for our sin."[105]

That grace, which God so freely gives, provides us total forgiveness. This grace is enough to wipe out the sin we have committed because those who place their trust in Jesus are extended the guarantee. This guarantee can only be given by God: the one against whom we sin, just as the only person who has been found guilty of a crime can only have that conviction wiped out through a pardon by the head of state (a governor or president).

I. As Good as the Paper it is Written on

As you might expect, any guarantee is as good as the issuer of that guarantee. If the issuer of the guarantee does not stand behind the promises made, the guarantee is of little value. Fine print in many contracts of assurance often provides ways for the issuer to void (or avoid) the guarantee. Money is as good as the paper it is printed upon. When the issuer goes bankrupt the guarantee becomes worthless. But God's guarantee of forgiveness is unbreakable. When the "one sinned against" is God, His guaranteed forgiveness is good forever -- throughout your lifetime.

During Jesus's ministry, He was often challenged by the Jewish authorities over how He had the ability and authority to heal or cleanse people. This is so because Jesus linked the healing of people's illnesses or deformities to the gift of forgiveness of sins. When people approached Jesus, they asked for their sins to be wiped away. Upon hearing the honest plea of a sinner asking for forgiveness, Jesus would forgive their sins through the blessing of God's grace.

---

[105]Philip Yancey & Brenda Quinn. "Meet the Bible." P. 705. Zondervan. iBooks.

Jewish Scribes[106], however, took exception with Jesus having the right or authority to forgive sins against God. In response, Jesus said that He *was* God and therefore had this authority. Matthew 9:1-8, NIV. "...[F]or only the One who has been sinned against has the prerogative to forgive. Jesus's words to the man were therefore an unequivocal claim of divine authority. The scribes were correct in saying that only God can forgive sins (cf. Isa. 43:25), but incorrect in saying Jesus blasphemed. They refused to recognize Jesus's power as coming from God, much less that He Himself was God."[107] The scribes, therefore, claimed that Jesus had used the name of God in vain and that He himself was a sinner. However, Jesus proved that He was God and thus had the right and power to forgive sins.

C.S. Lewis, in *The Screwtape Letters*, talks about how grace has given us the confidence (through the guarantee) to know that we are forgiven. This he describes is a sort of smugness or arrogance that believers have. It is the sort of arrogance that Michael Jordan displayed when launching a jumper and then turning to go down court during the arc of the ball and before its descent to the rim. Jordan knew the shot was good as soon as he let it fly!

In Letter #2, the devil's soldier on earth is receiving words of advice from his superior about how a new Christian is behaving. The soldier is seeking to turn his subject away from God. The devil's agent on earth listens in on the subject while he is in fervent prayer.

---

[106]Scribes had knowledge of the law and could draft legal documents (contracts for marriage, divorce, loans, inheritance, mortgages, the sale of land, and the like). Every village had at least one scribe. Pharisees were members of a party that believed in resurrection and in following legal traditions that were ascribed not to the Bible but to "the traditions of the fathers." Like the scribes, they were also well-known legal experts: hence the partial overlap of membership of the two groups. https://www.britannica.com/biography/Jesus/Scribes-and-Pharisees

[107]John F. MacArthur, One Perfect Life, Chapt. IV, notes, iBooks.

As the devil's representative listens he hears his subject admitting to God (a/k/a "his Enemy") that he is a sinner and is asking God for forgiveness. The man in prayer is relying on the contractual guarantee of God's grace. Here is the advice the devil's soldier on earth is given by his superior:

> What he says, even on his knees, about his own sinfulness is all parrot talk. At the bottom, he still believes he has run up a very favorable credit-balance in the Enemy's ledger by allowing himself to be converted and thinks that he is showing great humility and condescension in going to church with these smug, commonplace neighbors at all. Keep him in that state of mind as long as you can.

The devil's supervisor is telling his soldier on earth to let the man believe he is merely "racking up points" with God as he prays. The devil wants the man to believe that as long as his ledger of sin vs. good deeds balances out to more good than evil; he is good with God. However, as the reader finds out at the end of *The Screwtape Letters*, much to the ultimate consternation of the devil's soldier, he has mistaken the smugness of this Christian man for the arrogance of forgiveness.

The devil is unable to claim the man's soul because the man fervently relies on God's grace to forgive his sins, not on his own good deeds. The man relies on God's forgiveness when he humbles himself before God. He does so by admitting that he is a sinner and in need of forgiveness and asks God for grace. When he does this he knows that he *will be* forgiven. The man, who has claimed the guarantee, *knows* that God will forgive his sins! That is the arrogance of forgiveness. This is a guarantee that is as good as the paper it is written on – as good as the Giver of the guarantee.

J. Faith Alone?

As can be seen above, I do not believe that God is asking us to take a blind leap of faith. The guarantee is written as part of His covenant contract with us, His people. However, God does expect us to put our faith in Him as a result of that guarantee. Jesus tells us that we have the guarantee by believing in Him with all our heart, mind, and soul. But how do we know that we truly believe? If only God knows our hearts, what outward sign can we see or know to confirm that we have truly accepted that covenant guarantee?

If you want evidence, look to these words from James:

> Do you want evidence that faith without deeds is useless? Was not our ancestor Abraham considered righteous for what he did when he offered his son Isaac on the altar? You see that his faith and his actions were working together, and his faith was made complete by what he did. James 2:20-22, NIV.

As mentioned in chapters two and five, to make complete the acceptance by Abraham of God's covenant, Abraham was asked by God to do the unthinkable. He was asked to kill his only son as an outward sign of his acceptance of God's covenant promise. Even though God spared Abraham from having to go through with this terrible command, God, nevertheless, asked Abraham to show his faith by doing God's will.

In the book of James, he points to Abraham as an example that God's guarantee has been accepted and confirmed in each of us.

We can look to our own fulfillment of God's commands as an outward sign of acceptance. Søren Kierkegaard in his book, *Fear and Trembling*, says:

> By faith I make renunciation of nothing, on the contrary, by faith I acquire everything, precisely in the sense in which it is said that he who has faith like a grain of mustard can remove mountains. A purely human courage is required to renounce the whole of the temporal to gain the eternal; but this I gain, and to all eternity I cannot renounce it, that is a self-contradiction; but a paradox enters in and a humble courage is required to grasp the whole of the temporal by virtue of the absurd, and this is the courage of faith. By faith Abraham did not renounce his claim upon Isaac, but by faith he got Isaac.[108]

Kierkegaard, I believe, was telling us that we need faith to fully grasp and accept the guarantee of salvation. But only the faith that moves us to action shows us that the guarantee is real and unbreakable.

> The picture of faith that emerges from [chapter 11 of Hebrews] does not fit into an easy formula. Sometimes faith leads to victory and triumph. Sometimes it requires a gritty determination to 'hang on at any cost'. Hebrews 11 does not hold up one kind of faith as superior to the other. Both rest on the belief that God is in ultimate control and

---

[108]Chapter 2: Preliminary Expectoration

will indeed keep promises – whether that happens in this life or the next. For such people, Hebrews says, "God is not ashamed to be called their God, for He has prepared a city for them."[109]

So is faith revealed in action? Are good works required before we can claim the guarantee? As will be explained in this book, no matter how hard you work to earn God's favor, it is never enough. Good works, without faith, are wholly insufficient to *earn* you God's guarantee. Abraham had to first show his faith so that his acceptance of God's covenant could be completed. It is similar to the legal concepts we explored when examining how a contract can become legally binding.

Take for example, this simple set of facts. Diane desires to sell her vintage 1964 Chevy Corvette. She takes the first step by placing an ad in the local newspaper. The car is listed as an immaculate one-owner vehicle with original equipment. Paul sees the ad and decides to take a look at the car. He spends two hours going over the car from the inside out. Diane even lets him take the car on a test drive. Diane asks Paul if he likes the car.

Paul says, "Yes, very much." Paul asks Diane what she wants for the car and Diane tells him $70,000. Paul offers $65,000.

Diane says "Okay, we have a deal." Everything about the car is exactly what Paul was looking for and he tells Diane that he will "take the car" and wants to accept delivery the following day. She agrees. When Paul shows up the next day with a cashier's check for $65,000, Diane tells him the car was sold last night for the full

---

[109]Philip Yancey and Brenda Quinn. "Meet the Bible " P. 646-47. Zondervan. iBooks

asking price of $70,000. Has Diane breached the contract? Can Paul successfully sue to force her to sell him his dream car?

The answer to both questions, unfortunately for Paul, is no. A contract has not been formed because there was one missing element: consideration. Had Paul made a down payment on the $65,000 agreed-upon price, Diane would not have been able to sell the car to someone else. Without the payment of consideration, the oral agreement to sell the Corvette was incomplete. There was no contract.

Once God extends the promise of the guarantee we know that the covenant is confirmed when we act on the faith we have accepted because the payment of the consideration for that covenant agreement has been made.

As James says,

> What good is it, my brothers, if someone says he has faith but does not have works? Can that faith save him? If a brother or sister is poorly clothed and lacking in daily food, and one of you says to them, 'Go in peace, be warmed and filled,' without giving them the things needed for the body, what good is that? So also faith by itself, if it does not have works, is dead. James 2: 14-17, NIV.

James, the author of this letter, was probably one of Jesus's brothers – the oldest and a prominent leader in the early church. He teaches, as Jesus did, that how we live reveals the sincerity of our faith. "Certainly, good works do not bring us salvation, but if our salvation has not changed who we are and how we live, we might rightly question whether we've really given our life to Christ." [110]

So is James telling us that good works are required for salvation? Some people may say that James is saying just that. However, the apostle Paul in Ephesians explains (and James agrees) that God's forgiveness, through the sacrifice of Jesus's atoning death, is not earned through good works.

> For it is by grace you have been saved, through faith
> – and this is not from yourselves, it is the gift of God
> – not by works, so that no one can boast. For we
> are God's handiwork, created in Christ Jesus to do
> good works, which God prepared in advance for us
> to do. Ephesians 2: 8-10, NIV.

Paul thus explains that there is nothing we can do to merit God's forgiveness through penance or good works. However, he reminds us, that if we love God and His son, Jesus, one of the things we were created to do is good works. Therefore, a tug-of-war in the minds of people of faith is created. On one hand, they accept Jesus's sacrificial death as the payment for their sins, and on the other, they struggle with the *need* to do good works in His name. Philip Yancey put it this way, "I will not attempt to resolve the tension between grace and works because the New Testament does not. We must not try to solve the contradiction by reducing the force of either grace or morality. Grace presents a 'Yes and,' not a 'Yes but.' Ephesians pulls the two strands neatly together..." [111]

---

[110] Philip Yancey & Brenda Quinn. "Meet the Bible." P. 2169. Zondervan. iBooks.

[111] Philip Yancey & Brenda Quinn. "Meet the Bible." P. 2184. Zondervan. iBooks.

So grace and good works are two sides of the same coin. One goes with the other – like peanut butter and jelly. If you have accepted Christ into your life and have been forgiven of your sins through confession, you will show that truth by following God's commands. If you follow God's commands, you will be doing good works. You will feed the poor, take care of God's people and love your neighbor just as the Samaritan did.

God, through his son Jesus, provided each of us the guarantee of forgiveness. This guarantee is documented. It has no exceptions and has been issued by an impeccable and unimpeachable source. It is a guarantee that this world cannot take away from us. One that the world can never match in scope, power, and value. This guarantee is a solid as it can get! We know we have the guarantee by the fruit it bears in our lives. Our faith in the guarantee is confirmed when we show God the love we have for Him and each other. This love is depicted in the way we live our lives. We live out our faith, knowing that we have the guarantee, by doing the things Jesus asks of us. We feed his sheep, clothe those in need and live our lives as changed people.

CHAPTER SEVEN

HOW DO YOU KNOW YOU HAVE THE GUARANTEE?

When you purchase a car or buy insurance, you know you have a guarantee associated with that purchase because you get a warranty booklet or policy documents. These rather large and hard-to-read agreements spell out the terms and conditions of the guarantee that you receive with your purchase. You know you have the warranty because it is set forth in black and white (albeit in legal-ese). The document allows you to determine when the warranty begins and ends.

You can ascertain the scope of the warranty: the parts covered, the risks included, the dollar value or scope of the agreement. The assurance you receive is set forth in detail including any exclusions, limitations, and preconditions. You should be able to determine the answer to questions such as:

- Is normal wear and tear is covered?
- Do I need to conduct routine maintenance in order for the warranty to remain in effect?
- Are there are any deductibles that apply to a loss or breakdown?

The documentation of the guarantee will also indicate the way you must make a claim or seek repairs. You can find out if you have to take your car to an authorized dealer or if your insurance claim must be presented within a certain period of time. These documents can provide you with a sort of *proof of purchase* that verifies the coverage for your loss or breakdown and provides assurance that you will be made whole within specified circumstances.

But how can you have such proof if the guarantee is one of salvation that was given by God ages ago? How can you determine that the guarantee given by your Creator even applies to you? Are there preconditions that you must meet? What do you need to do in order to qualify for the guarantee? Are there exceptions that apply to you? Do you need to pay premiums for this guarantee? If so, what is the cost and how do you make payment to the Almighty? If you get this guarantee, is there a booklet or policy document that spells out the terms? Once the guarantee is obtained, do you need to make periodic payments to keep it in force? How do you know that the guarantee has been issued by God? What must you do, or how should you act to keep the guarantee in effect throughout your life?

In this chapter, I will attempt to answer these questions in the same way I have done thus far. In the format of a legal brief[112] with arguments laid out in the same way I would present them to a judge or jury. Arguments that must be supported by facts and citations to authorities that support the issues involved. And, just as I would have done in making my case, I will endeavor to provide my presentation in a logical manner that will not be too technical or overly complicated. Even the most learned jurists will tell you that being pithy and to-the-point is the most effective means of passionately

---

[112]It's an interesting term, "brief" because in my legal career these documents are never short nor are they concise

conveying your premise. So, without further fanfare, let's delve into these issues to answer the question at hand: How do you know you have the guarantee?

A. The Contract That Contains the Guarantee

God has given us the assurance that there is a guarantee in the form that most humans use to solidify or confirm a bargain between two people – a contract. There are many places in the Bible that contain a reference to the contract between God (the grantor) and His creation (the grantee). These citations first appear early in the Old Testament.

The first documentation of this covenant agreement is set forth in a conversation between God and Noah. Civilization, in Noah's day, was fraught with rebellion against God. This was evidenced by murder, lying, deceit, and overall wickedness. The gift of free will had been abused by humanity in such a way that God was "grieved that he had made man on the earth and [God's] heart was filled with pain." (Gen. 6:6, NIV). As a result, God was determined to wipe humanity from the face of the earth and start anew.

So, God decided to save the one righteous and faithful man on earth (Noah) along with his family and all of the animals. As to the rest of mankind, God was determined to bring about the demise of these wicked people. He would use a great flood that would cover the entire world. We all know the story of how God instructed Noah to construct an ark to save his family and the animals. After being afloat for 150 days, the water began to subside. Forty days later Noah released a dove to determine whether there was any dry land that appeared above the floodwaters. After several attempts to find dry land, the dove finally returned with an olive branch and Noah knew it was time to start again. It was then that God provided Noah with the agreement.

This agreement is codified in Genesis 9:8-17, NIV. God agreed that "[n]ever again shall all life be cutoff by the waters of a flood; never again will there be a flood to destroy the earth" (Gen. 9:11, NIV). This agreement was also sealed by, of all things, a rainbow. The agreement set forth that God would again allow humanity to spread over the entire earth with our will free will intact. The agreement also provided that the rainbow would be a sign "of the covenant[113] between me and the earth" (Gen. 9:13, NIV).

There are many other instances of extensions or renewals of God's agreement with His creation. In prior chapters, I referenced the story of Abraham. The story of God's commands and Abraham's obedience with those commands. Once fulfilled, God provided a covenant agreement to Abraham. This contract provided that God would anoint Abraham as the foundation for the Israelite people – God's chosen people. Since Abraham had no children, the agreement also provided that his formerly barren wife would conceive a son. The agreement was sealed by Abraham's strict adherence to the instructions of God. Genesis 12:2, 15:18-21, 17:7-8; NIV.

The Old Testament also documents a covenant between God and Moses. God provided the assurance to the Hebrew people (who were enslaved in Egypt) that they would no longer be held captive. God sent his representative, Moses, to present this promise of freedom from the tyrannical rule of the Pharaoh to the Jews being held captive. Exodus 3:9-10, 9:9, NIV. Furthermore, the contract between God and His people was completed by way of a "seal" being placed on the agreement. Sealing a contract makes it official.

---

[113] A covenant was the conditional promises made to humanity by God, as revealed in Scripture. www.dictionary.com

A contract under seal is also termed as sealed contract, special contract, deed, covenant, specialty, specialty contract or common-law specialty. A contract under seal is a formal contract which does not require any consideration and has the seal of the signer attached...It is conclusive between the parties when signed, sealed, and delivered.[114]

God sealed his contract with the Hebrews when the Pharaoh rejected the last opportunity to let God's enslaved people go. As discussed earlier, Ramses was told that if he did not free the slaves, the firstborn male of every family in Egypt would die – including Ramses' own son (the heir to the Egyptian throne). When the Pharaoh refused, God acted. God sealed his promise with His people by His own form of a sealed agreement. "... [T]he Passover. That day marks the birth of a nation, when God freed his people from slavery in Egypt. In a real sense, the Passover sealed the covenant, ..."[115] Exodus chapter 12

There are many other instances of God's covenant promises (oaths) detailed in the Bible – too many to discuss in detail here. However, as I would in a legal brief, I will provide you with some other instances of God's agreements with humanity. I will do so through what is known as a "string citation." Therefore, for those of you who want to explore the foundation of this statement they are provided in this footnote[116].

---

[114]US Legal, Legal Definitions, Contract Under Seal

[115]Philip Yancey & Brenda Quinn. "Meet the Bible." P. 963. Zondervan. iBooks

[116]Exodus 19:5; Deuteronomy 7:8; 1 Chronicles 16:15-16; Job 31:1, 31. "Dozens of other passages in the Old Testament set forth the details of God's covenant, or contract, with his chosen people. (The word testament means covenant.) Genesis 15 is the first to spell out the terms of this covenant." Philip Yancey & Brenda Quinn. "Meet the Bible." P. 194. Zondervan. Apple Books.

As the Puritan scholar, Perry Miller has said, "when you have a covenant with God, you no longer have an ineffable, remote, unapproachable Deity; you have a God you can count on."[117]

The agreement between God and the Israelites is not just documented in the pages of the Old Testament but it was actually written down and then saved by the Jews as their sacred covenant with God.

The prophet Josiah railed against the Jews after one of the (many) times they rebelled against God and turned to idol worship. In their book, *Meet the Bible*, authors Brenda Quinn and Philip Yancey describe an amazing artifact that was found after Josiah went on a tirade and destroyed all the false idols the Israelites had erected in God's house of worship.

> Josiah devotes much time and energy to a favorite public works project: repairing the temple. And one busy day, as carpenters saw new joists and beams, masons carve new stones for the temple walls, and workmen haul off rubble from the idols Josiah has smashed, a priest makes an amazing discovery in the midst of that din and clutter. He finds a scroll that looks like - could it be? - the Book of the Covenant, the original record of the agreement between the Israelites and their God. (Most scholars believe the scroll contained part or all of the book of Deuteronomy.)[118] See also: 2 Kings chapter 22

[117]Philip Yancey. "The Bible Jesus Read." Zondervan, 2017-03-01. iBooks. Chapter One

[118]P. 1011. Zondervan. iBooks.

The covenant agreements given by God had one key element at the core of these contracts. They were always intended to restore the relationship between God and his people. As noted, sin was the crack that split wide the divide that separated us from God. We rebelled against our own Creator. Our sin turned us away from God. As a parent longs for a child that loves and obeys them, so God desires a loving relationship with us. God also seeks our obedience to his commands and values. God desires this not as a way of controlling us, but as a means for our protection.

Many people rebel or chafe when it comes to the discipline or commitment that obedience requires. They think that being obedient means they must be dominated or subservient. But I believe God does not seek our obedience out of the need to dominate us, He sought it as a way to lead us away from sin and toward Him. As a means to protect us from the problems and heartache that sin causes. Jesus, in his time on earth, was fully God but He also had human attributes. He felt pain in the same way as we do. Jesus also modeled obedience.

As He hung from the cross, in profound pain and anguish – his human body suffering from this crushing pain – He experienced the utter devastation of separation from God, the Father. Jesus was led to the cross so that He could bear the sin of all people. Jesus took the punishment we deserved. Jesus knew that God had to turn away from the human sin that had been placed on Him. In this way Jesus paid for our sins so we could forever be free from sin.

The last words Jesus uttered before He obediently gave up his human life, was "My God, my God, why have you forsaken me." In C.S. Lewis' book, *The Screwtape Letters*, the devil's lieutenant, Screwtape, explained the problem of obedience to Wormwood, his agent on earth. "Our cause is never more in danger than when a human, no longer desiring, but still intending, to do our Enemy's

[God's] will, looks round upon a universe from which every trace of Him seems to have vanished, and asks why he has been forsaken, and still obeys."[119]

I think that Lewis was using Jesus's obedience, even to death on the cross, as an example for us. If Jesus, fully God, can be obedient to His Father, why should we be so resistant to obeying God's commands? If obedience for us means tithing or honoring our marriage vows, how can that be so difficult when Jesus was obedient to the ultimate degree – even when that meant dying an excruciating death for us on the cross?

The only way that our relationship with God can be restored is if we are cleansed of the sin that separates us from our Creator. God's contract was thus centered and focused on the forgiveness of our sins. As God proclaimed through the prophet Jeremiah, the people of God "will know me, from the least of them to the greatest ... For I will forgive their wickedness and will remember their sins no more" (Jer. 31:34, NIV). The prophet said these words in light of the "new covenant with the house of Israel and the house of Judah[120]." 31:31. The agreement that God made with His people was predicated on a promise. *If the Israelites repented of their sin and turned away from their wicked ways, God would forgive them.*

The terms and conditions of the contract were initially accepted by God's people but, in short order, this contract was broken by the Jews time and time again. Something had to change. God's people would have to find a way to keep their part of the bargain and *sin no more.* In order for this to happen, God would provide a way for all people to break the cycle and atone, once and forever, for their sins.

[119]Excerpt From The Screwtape Letters. C. S. Lewis. "A Year with C. S. Lewis." P. 231. HarperCollins. iBooks.

[120]In the time of Jeremiah the nation of Israel was divided into two separate states: Israel and Judah

This brings us to the final chapter of the covenant contract between God and his creation: the guarantee given by God's Son directly to us. This contract came in the form of symbols and words that forever cemented the agreement that God provided to His creation. This was an agreement that had been continually broken by God's people but never breached by God. It is, even now, an agreement that is available to each of us whenever we want to accept its terms.

This covenant was voiced by God the Father and Jesus His Son during the short time that God became man and revealed the transcendent guarantee that changed the world forever. We first get a glimpse of the foundations of this covenant when Jesus began His direct ministry to the people of earth. As already referenced, John the Baptist was tasked with heralding the arrival of the Savior to the people who were drawn to his preaching. John, known for preaching repentance and absolution of sins through the symbol of baptism, was baptizing his followers in the waters of the Jordan river when Jesus appeared on the scene. One day, after all the people were baptized, Jesus appeared. He presented himself to be baptized by John. No sooner was the water running from Jesus's head than a great voice from heaven said, for all to hear: "You are my Son, whom I love; with you I am well pleased" (Luke 3:22, NKV). God had put His stamp of approval on Jesus. All those present heard that Jesus was God's Son – endowed with all the right, power, and authority of God. The foundation was thus laid for the final version of the guarantee to be issued.

As authors do when planning any great novel, the early New Testament accounts of Jesus's life *laid the foundation* for what was to come in the last days of His time on earth. Everything about Jesus's ministry points to the culmination of His mission of redemption. Jesus shows us who God is and the provisions of His plan of salvation. Jesus puts together a collection of disciples that include ordinary men (fisherman), a despised Jew (a tax collector), and men of prominence (a doctor). He brings His message of compassion to the outcasts of society. He heals lepers and engages with Gentiles, prostitutes, and Samaritans. His inner circle of followers includes many women at a time in history when women were not allowed to vote, hold property or even speak in the synagogues.

He preached a radical message of showing love to one's enemies and exercising compassionate care for prisoners, widows, and orphans. He told all who had assembled that if they look with lust on someone to whom they are not married they are committing adultery. And if they have anger toward their fellow humans they are guilty of murder. In short, Jesus turned the world upside down – much like He did when He overturned the tables of the money changers in the Temple.

This Son of God, with all the power, might, and authority of God Himself, set forth an unattainable standard for mankind to meet. He showed us, through His words and actions, how we are to live. He told us that in order to do what is necessary to enter the kingdom of God, we must sell everything we have, take up our cross and follow him[121]. In short, He informed everyone that while we should live as He instructs us, we will never be able to live up to that standard.

Then, in the culmination of the story – in the final days of His life on earth – Jesus revealed the final version of the guarantee. Our very own *get-out-of-hell-free card*. He models for us how to live and then, knowing that we can never meet that standard of perfection, He offered to take the fall for us. Jesus became the payment for our guarantee. His death was the premium for our insurance policy. He

---

[121]Matthew 19:16-22, NIV

transformed into the substitute for our sentence of death – a death we deserve because of our sin. Jesus's unimaginable criminal conviction, humiliation, berating, beating, scorn, and horrible death has become His substitutional sacrifice for our sin.

The last supper that Jesus had with his followers set the table for the guarantee. When Jesus was describing the contract that contains the guarantee, He did so in words and symbols so that his disciples (and we) could understand this most important agreement. As He broke bread and shared it with all assembled He said that the bread they consumed was a representation of His body that would be broken for all people. Then, He took a challis and filled it with wine and had all His disciples drink from the cup. In doing so, He said that the sharing of the wine was a symbol of the spilling of His blood for the complete absolution of all our sins.

Jesus specifically cast this symbol as a *new contract* between God and all humanity. Matthew 26:27-28. The culmination of Jesus's entire time on earth was the pronouncement of the final agreement between God and everyone who wants to enter into the covenant of forgiveness.

Clearly, the cup only represented the New Covenant... **Covenants were ratified with the blood of a sacrifice** (Gen. 8:20; 15:9-10; Ex. 24:5-8). Jesus's words here echo Moses's pronouncement in Exodus 24:8. The blood of the New Covenant is not an animal's blood, but Christ's own blood – shed for the remission of sins. The New Covenant has been ratified once and for all by the death of Christ. Cf. Jer. 31:31-34; Heb. 8:1-10:18; 8:6; 1 Peter 1:19.

[This shedding of blood was done] "for the benefit of many." The *many* are all who believe, both Jew and Gentile. Cf. Matt. 20:28; Luke 10:45.[122]

The Last Supper (the Passover feast) was the occasion that Jesus used to renew the contract (covenant) that God made with Abraham, Noah, and Moses. God told Abraham that if he sacrificed his son, God would take special care of his people.

Jesus said that His body would be broken and His blood would be shed to forgive our sins. Jesus, during the Last Supper, asked us to remember this new covenant. The terms of the contract were thus spelled out and Jesus made the final payment for this guarantee on Good Friday. Then, on Easter Sunday the final condition was met. Therefore, through words and symbolism, Jesus showed His followers the terms and provisions of the guarantee. He set forth the parameters of the agreement between God and His creation. The covenant that God first made with His people, the Jews, was now being offered to the rest of the world. "...salvation's truth came first to [the Jews] (cf. Luke 19:9) and through them to the world (cf. Rom. 3:2; 9:4–5)."[123] And the pages of the Bible reveal and define this contract.

God has never broken his promises, agreements, or covenants – even when we have. He wants us to understand that He has offered to all of us unconditional forgiveness and all we have to do to receive this gift of inestimable value is simply to accept the grace He is offering. "We wander like lost sheep, true; but God is a faithful shepherd who pursues us relentlessly. We have our ups and downs, zealously believing one day and gloomily doubting the next, but he is faithful. We break our promises, but He doesn't break His.

---

[122]John MacArthur. "One Perfect Life". Part IX, Notes

[123]Supra. Part IV Notes

Discipleship is not a contract in which if we break our part of the agreement, He is free to break his; it is a *covenant* in which he establishes the conditions and *guarantees* the results."[124] Emphasis added.

B. Only One Way to Get the Guarantee

God has offered a guarantee of salvation, paid in full by Jesus's death on the cross and confirmed by His resurrection from the dead. We have only to accept the terms of this contract to make it binding. As we know from Chapter One, a contract is only binding when the offeror (God) presents the offer to the offeree (us) and we accept the terms of that agreement. I will now attempt to lay out what we need to do to make sure all terms of God's offer are accepted.

The most important thing to know about the guarantee is that there is nothing we can do to *earn* this promise. As I have pointed out in earlier chapters, we can never be good enough to warrant salvation. No amount of good works can earn us the guarantee. No matter how hard we try, we cannot purge sin from our lives (see e.g. Martin Luther). "[A]ll have sinned and fallen short of the glory of God" (Rom. 3:23, NIV). Some find this disheartening. I find it comforting. I am no Mother Theresa. She was, however, a sinner just like me! Neither the Pope nor Billy Graham could earn their salvation. The Gospel of Matthew, chapters 5-7, compiles Jesus's teachings on how to live by God's standards. They show the holiness of God and the standard by which He judges us. Yet they are impossible standards to live up to and, without putting them in the context of the whole of God's message, these standards would lead the most fervent Christian to feel broken and disillusioned. In the

---

[124]Eugene H. Peterson. "A Long Obedience in the Same Direction." P. 131. InterVarsity Press, 2012-04-25. iBooks.

closing verses of Matthew chapter 7, Jesus talks about how to get the guarantee. Instead of giving us a step-by-step process, Jesus shows us the way through several analogies.

> This closing section of the Sermon on the Mount is a gospel application. Here are two gates, two ways, two destinations, and two groups of people (Matt. 7:13, 14); two kinds of trees and two kinds of fruit (Matt. 7:17–20); two groups at the judgment (Matt. 7:21–23); and two kinds of builders, building on two kinds of foundations (Matt. 7:24–28). Christ is drawing the line as clearly as possible between the way that leads to destruction and the way that leads to life.[125]

After giving the assembled crowd this impossible standard to attain, Jesus then concludes this remarkable sermon by telling them that *He* is the *only* way to eternal life. They may not have known it at the time, but Jesus would be the foundation of our salvation by traveling the narrow way that led to the cross. Belief in Jesus would be the only way to fulfill the impossible standard of a sinless life because He would be the ultimate and final sacrifice for our sins. His blood would be shed to atone for our inability to live by God's standard. In order for us to claim the guarantee, we simply need to admit that we are unable to live a sin-free life.

We, like Mother Theresa, the Pope, and Billy Graham, are sinners. No matter how hard we try, we sin each and every day and there is no way we can stop, although we try, time and time again. Each day we need to admit our need for salvation through the utter

---

[125]John MacArthur, One Perfect Life, Part V notes

surrender to, and acceptance of, Jesus as our atoning Savior. We proclaim our belief in Him as the only way to atone and pay for our sinfulness. And finally, we ask God for forgiveness for our sins. When we do so, we become grantees of the guarantee. We claim the contract of forgiveness and the consideration already paid by Jesus for us to accept the benefits of eternal salvation. Once we do so, we are now "good enough" for God. We now qualify for fellowship with our creator. We now KNOW that when we die we WILL be in heaven – where every tear will be wiped away and peace will forever be ours.

If you can't be good enough to save you, can you be bad enough to forever be denied salvation? Let's take, for example, this man: he is a Jewish religious zealot whose sole mission was to hunt down and kill Christians. Surely he was incapable of earning God's forgiveness, right? Well, what if I told you that this man became the greatest evangelist for God, proclaiming God's gospel of love. He was transformed into God's greatest preacher. Yes, Saul of Tarsus the persecutor of Christians, became the great Apostle Paul.

Paul understood the meaning of grace. On the road to Damascus, he encountered the resurrected Jesus who revealed to him the good news. As a result, Paul became a new man. Paul traveled the length of the known world, changing lives through the message of grace. Paul understood that you can't work hard enough to earn redemption. God changed Saul's life forever.

Have you heard of C.P. Ellis? Mr. Ellis was a Ku Klux Klan leader. He was the Exalted Cyclops of the Durham, NC chapter of the KKK and led raids on black communities. Through his "leadership" the Klan terrorized African Americans in the late 1960s. But God had other plans for Claiborne Paul Ellis. Through the guidance and caring of Ann Atwater, a black civil rights activist and committed Christian, God used her genuine love and the gift of gospel music to change Ellis' heart. Ms. Atwater followed God's commands by loving her enemy. She reached out to Ellis and a friendship developed between these two mortal enemies. Through the love of Ms. Atwater, spurred by the grace of God, Ellis renounced his Klan membership and, under death threats from the KKK, became an activist for desegregation in the South. He turned his life over to Jesus and sought forgiveness of his sins.

Jesus transforms lives and takes hearts of stone and breaks them.

B. What About Good Works?

As we have established, you can't do anything to earn God's love, it is freely given. However, you better do something with that love when you get it! By placing your trust in Jesus and claiming the mantle of salvation, your sins are wiped clean. But what do you do with a God who loves you so much that He will allow his Son to die a cruel and painful death for the sake of your sins? If works do not save you why do good works? Good works are described by Jesus as the fruit of the spirit. He likened it to a tree that grows and bears good fruit.

"Every tree that does not bear good fruit is cut down and thrown into the fire," Jesus said. The person who believes and puts their faith in Jesus will bear good fruit - or do good works. "Thus, by their fruit you will recognize them." (Matt. 7:17-20). If you claim to have faith but do not act accordingly, you are like an apple tree that does not bear apples. The barrenness of this sort of faith demonstrates its real character – the faith that says but does not do is really unbelief. Jesus was not suggesting that works are meritorious, but that true faith will not fail to produce the fruit of good works. This is precisely the point of James 1:22–25; 2:26."[126]

Once you receive the guarantee, you have experienced the ultimate love of God. So how do you show love in return? If you believe that Jesus died for you it stands for reason that you love Him with all your heart. For those of you who are or were married you understand this love and the ultimate desire to return love to your spouse. If you are a parent you experience this immersive love for your children. This depth of love is a form of surrender to a feeling that overwhelms you. This form of love manifests itself in your desire to do anything within your power to please your better half and/or your children. This love shows as a focused desire to make them happy. My good friend Joe said that he did not truly understand the love his father had for him until he had children himself. Becoming a father provided him with an overwhelming sense of desire to give all of his love to his children. He finally understood the caring, loving protection and affection his dad had for him and his siblings. A parent's love for his children and a spouse for her betrothed is a small glimpse into how much our heavenly Father loves us.

So, how do we express, in return, our love for God? Jesus gave us a very straightforward, but challenging answer. "If you love me," He said, "you will obey what I command." He was asked this same question again and again. Each time He gave basically the same answer. "Whoever has my commands and obeys them, he is the one who loves me" (John 14:15, 21, NIV). Therefore, you ask, what did Jesus command us to do? The answer was illustrated quite clearly by a series of events that occurred just before Jesus was executed on the cross and just after His resurrection.

---

[126]John MacArthur, *One Perfect Life*, Part V notes

During the trial of Jesus, His disciples stayed their distance from Him, afraid that they too would be tried and convicted. In a prior chapter I recounted the story of how Peter acted when he was recognized outside the courtroom where Jesus was on trial. A woman recognized Peter as a follower of Christ. When exposed, he denied ever having even known Christ. Not once but three times – just as Jesus told Peter he would. After the cock crowed and Peter realized what he'd done (disown the man he pledged his life to follow) he was beside himself with grief. The self-loathing Peter experienced lingered until after Christ's resurrection.

When Jesus appeared to Peter following His resurrection Jesus asked Peter, "Do you love me?" In fact, Christ asked Peter this question three times, mirroring the three denials by Peter during Jesus's trial. With each question from Jesus came the same answer from Peter, "Yes Lord, you know that I do." Jesus followed up Peter's response with three different (but similar) commands. First, Jesus said if you love me "Feed my lambs." After the second reply from Peter Jesus said, "if you love me then take care of my sheep." After the third question was asked and after Peter gave the same response, Jesus concluded, "Peter, if you love me feed my sheep."

Jesus was answering the responses of Peter with a litmus test of faith, not only for Peter, but for each of us. Jesus, who placed the foundation of His Church on Peter, illuminated the fruit that he (and we) should bear if we love Jesus. If you love Jesus for giving his life for you, will you return His love by feeding and taking care of His lambs and sheep? John 21:15-17, NIV.

The words Jesus used to tell Peter how he can express his love for Jesus, in turn, show us that there is a connection between the love we have for Jesus and the love we should have for each other. Matthew 25:40 says that whatever we do for the least of our brothers, we do for God. This command was contained within the parable Jesus told of the sheep and the goats. The thing that separates the forgiven children of God (sheep) from those who reject God (goats) is the love we have for each other – both friends and enemies. This form of love is a common theme that we find woven throughout the Bible.

This desire of God for us to love and care for each other was also echoed by Jesus in the parable of the good Samaritan that was referenced earlier. As you will remember, a lawyer sought to trap Jesus by asking him which of God's commands was the most important. Jesus, without equivocating, responded by saying that all of the commands are based on the first two: loving God and loving your neighbor as yourself. Jesus shamed the lawyer by encapsulating the entire Old and New Testaments and boiling them down to the first two commandments. By doing so, you can get a good picture of the love that Jesus asks us to display – the fruit that belief produces. If we truly believe in Jesus as the resurrected Savior who died so that we can claim the guarantee of salvation then we should bear the fruit of that love by loving God with all our heart, mind, and soul, and loving all others as we do ourselves. We bear such fruit by taking care of His flock – whoever they are and wherever they may be. Those who love Jesus will bear good fruit by feeding, sheltering, and clothing His children and doing those things that God would do for the least of our brothers. "Thus, by their fruit you will recognize them" (Matt. 7:20). Philip Yancey and Brenda Quinn remind us that

> [There is a] direct correlation between loving [God] and loving others in need. Love for Jesus is not simply an inward feeling that issues from us to his Spirit. If true love, it will manifest itself in caring for people toward whom Christ feels compassion. That same love he showed for every kind of

person while here on earth will become a living love that flows from him through us and touches others. Jesus does not imply that a list of good deeds will save us in the end. The Bible is clear - we are saved by grace through our faith in him. But [in Matthew 25:31-46] Jesus tells us that the proof of our love is how we care for others. Our faith saves us, and our faith also compels us to help people in need. Each person we help, Jesus explains, carries a part of him. In loving them, we are directly loving him.[127]

As Paul explains in Ephesians, "For we are God's handiwork, created in Christ Jesus to do good works, which God prepared in advance for us to do" (Eph. 2:10). Note the placement of these words directly after Paul says that works do not guarantee our salvation. What he is echoing is Jesus's command to all who love him to take care of your neighbor as you would yourself. These two concepts (grace and good works) therefore are not mutually exclusive, they are two sides of the same coin!

C. Seeing is Believing

Contracts, as we have explored, are usually written or recorded in some form. People must see the written warrantee that manufacturers provide before they take the leap and pay thousands of dollars for a new car. Most people will not rely simply on the slick words of a salesperson. "Only physical or concrete evidence is convincing, as in 'She wrote us that she's lost twenty pounds, but *seeing is believing.*'

---

[127] Philip Yancey & Brenda Quinn. "Meet the Bible." P. 1530-31. Zondervan. iBooks.

This idiom was first recorded in this form in 1639."[128] So, does God provide us proof that the guarantee is real and reliable?

"I will believe it when I see it" is the phrase that was attributed to the disciple Thomas after he was told that Jesus was alive following His crucifixion. Thomas heard the accounts of the women who went to the tomb on the Sunday after Jesus's death and saw Him in his resurrected body. After this interaction with Jesus, the women immediately reported to the assembled, yet terrified, disciples exactly what they saw and heard. Thomas was there to hear the report. Despite the report of the women, Thomas still insisted on concrete proof. A few days later Jesus appeared to the disciples when Thomas was absent. Thomas was not there in the locked room where the other disciples were holed up in fear for their lives. Thomas, despite these two sets of eyewitness accounts still demanded proof. Each of the disciples told Thomas in great detail how Jesus came into their midst and spoke with them. But Thomas said he would not believe until he could see Jesus with his own eyes. He would not believe unless he could feel the wounds that Jesus experienced during His crucifixion.

Let us remember that Jesus told all the disciples on numerous occasions before his crucifixion that He was going to be put to death and then rise from the grave. Thomas was present during those predictions but still doubted Jesus was alive. After all, Thomas saw *with his own eyes* that Jesus died a horrible death on the cross. He witnessed the Roman guard thrusting his spear into Jesus's side. He knew that Jesus was entombed, a stone was rolled across the grave and guards were standing watch over the cave where Jesus was laid to rest.

Some people want to apply that same standard or test when determining if they have the guarantee of salvation. However, just

---

[128] dictionary.com

like Thomas, they fail to heed Jesus's words and become blind to the mountains of proof that were displayed for all to see while Jesus walked the earth[129]. The gospels record in excess of thirty-five miracles that Jesus performed while He was on earth. Dead people were brought back to life. The deaf and blind had their senses restored. People with incurable diseases were cured. Time and time again these acts were done in full view of the disciples and the people who crowded around this charismatic man. In fact, some of the recorded accounts of these miracles attest that *Jesus healed many.* Jesus told those who were present that He was performing these miraculous things because only God could do such things. Thomas was an eyewitness to most of these miracles, yet Thomas doubted.

Jesus then appeared to the disciples for the second time and fixed his gaze on Thomas. Jesus showed disappointment but also compassion. Without shaming him, Jesus asked Thomas to probe the nail marks in His hands and feet and put his hand into the wound in His side. Thomas was broken. *How could he have doubted,* he asked himself. *After everything Jesus said. After all his teachings and all those miracles, how could he have doubted?*

But Jesus said, "Thomas because you have seen Me, you have believed. Blessed are those who have not seen and yet have believed." Thomas was humbled by Jesus allowing his unbelief to be transformed into belief by *seeing* the resurrected Savior once again. But John, in his gospel, was quick to remind us that "Jesus did many other miraculous signs in the presence of His disciples" which were not recorded in his gospel. Miracles that were well known to the people Jesus met and touched. "But these are written that you may believe that Jesus is the Christ, the Son of God, and that believing you may have life in His name." John 20:24-31.

---

[129] this proof will be detailed in later chapters

Despite not being in the presence of Jesus while He walked the earth, we nevertheless have many advantages that Thomas lacked. We have the ability to read the whole story set forth in the pages of the Bible. It is all here in black and white! We also have the benefit of knowing how the story of Jesus's time on earth ends. And how ours will end if we accept the guarantee.

It's like reading the last chapter of a murder mystery, understanding the plot twist, then going back and reading the whole novel. It spoils the ending but, in our case, it removes the doubt that Thomas labored under. As I will discuss and analyze in the next chapter we also have the perspective of history. As I discovered when I was researching this book, recorded history (apart from the Bible) confirms and underpins the message portrayed in the pages of the Old and New Testaments. I found out that history proves that the Bible is true and that Jesus is who He said He was. The Bible is a reliable and accurate account of Jesus's teachings, trial, death, and resurrection. As I hope you will "see", archaeology has also provided another layer of proof to the life and times of Jesus and His disciples.

D. Self-Righteousness Blinds Us to the Guarantee

Seeing is difficult if you are blind to the truth. We are blind to the truth when we presuppose we know it all. Many people have a self-sufficient and self-righteous point of view. They feel as if they are good enough already. They believe that Jesus may have existed but that he was only a man who died and was never seen again. These people only rely on what they were taught in school about science and history. They believe that these teachings prove that the story of the Bible is not worthy of belief. They, like Thomas, must see the evidence in order to believe. They say that the Bible is an ancient document that was written centuries ago and the words are clouded by the faith and commitment of the authors. I will directly address this in the next chapter. However, this attitude of self-righteousness is the tool of those who want to blind you to the truth.

As I have noted in the previous chapters, C.S. Lewis used *The Screwtape Letters* as a way for us to gain the perspective of the devil in his dealings with humans. One of the themes addressed was just this sort of self-righteousness – an attitude that turns us away from our Creator. Some may view Christians as self-righteous but they miss the point completely. Someone who is self-righteous is convinced that he or she is righteous based on his own actions or demeanor. Christians owe their righteousness to the atoning death of Jesus, not to any act of their own or self-determination.

C.S. Lewis describes it this way in his sequel to *The Screwtape Letters, Screwtape Offers a Toast* (1959). Screwtape, a fictional demon, appears to understand the nature of human minds and weaknesses. And, in this segment of the toast, Screwtape is addressing the darker side of self-righteousness:

> I'm as good as you is a useful means for the destruction of democratic societies. But it has a far deeper value as an end in itself, as a state of mind which, necessarily excluding humility, charity, contentment, and all the pleasures of gratitude or admiration, turns a human being away from almost every road which might finally lead him to Heaven.
>
> Different types of Pharisee[130] have been harvested, trodden, and fermented together to produce its subtle flavor. Types that were most antagonistic

---

[130]I believe that Lewis is analogizing a "Pharisee" to grapes used for wine

to one another on Earth. Some were all rules and relics and rosaries; others were all drab clothes, long faces, and petty traditional abstinences from wine or cards or the theatre. *Both had in common their self-righteousness* and the almost infinite distance between their actual outlook and anything the Enemy really is or commands[131]. The wickedness of other religions was the really live doctrine in the religion of each; slander was its gospel and denigration its litany. How they hated each other up there where the sun shone! How much more they hate each other now that they are forever conjoined but not reconciled.

All said and done, my friends, it will be an ill day for us if what most humans mean by "religion" ever vanishes from the Earth. It can still send us the truly delicious sins. The fine flower of unholiness can grow only in the close neighbourhood of the Holy. Nowhere do we tempt so successfully as on the very steps of the altar. [132]

This toast gives us a picture of someone that "leans on their own understanding" and does not "trust in the Lord with all [their] heart" (Prov. 3:5, NIV). John MacArthur, in his commentary *One Perfect Life*, says that "[t]he Pharisees thought they were well - religiously pure and whole. The outcasts knew they were not. Salvation can't

---

[131] Here again the "Enemy" is God. Lewis is discussing the disconnect between who God is and what the self-righteous "think" or "believe" God is. Emphasis added

[132] The Screwtape Letters: Annotated Edition, notes 39-42

come to the **self-righteous** (i.e., those who think they are whole and therefore fail to seek healing)...The Pharisees tended to focus on the outward, ritual, and ceremonial aspects of God's law to the neglect of its inward, eternal, and moral precepts. In doing so, they became harsh, judgmental, and **self-righteously scornful** of others. Jesus repeated this same criticism in Matt. 12:7.[133]"

It is a comfort to me to understand that I cannot be righteous on my own. It is consoling to know that I cannot do this – I cannot be good – and what I have attempted to substitute for good does not make me right. It takes a commitment on my part to repent of my transgressions and depend on God to make me righteous. I must surrender to God's will and subvert my own.

I like the way Eugene Peterson describes this surrender. "It is deciding that you have been wrong in supposing that you could manage your own life and be your own god; it is deciding that you were wrong in thinking that you had, or could get, the strength, education, and training to make it on your own; it is deciding that you have been told a pack of lies about yourself and your neighbors and your world. And it is deciding that God in Jesus Christ is telling you the truth."[134] This truth is the key to finding the freedom that only Jesus can provide. The righteousness that only God can give.

Jesus was constantly being challenged by the self-righteous. These so-called learned men of those days, the Pharisees, knew that Jesus claimed to be God's Son and they tried to show that He was a fraud. In chapter eight of John's gospel one of those attempts led to *testimony by Jesus* of His divinity. At one point the Pharisees asked Jesus, point-blank, who He was.

---

[133] Part V, notes. Emphasis added. Also see: Luke 5:27–32, NIV

[134] Eugene H. Peterson. "A Long Obedience in the Same Direction." Chapter 2, Repentance. InterVarsity Press, 2012-04-25. iBooks.

In reply, He said, "Just what I have been claiming all along"[135] (John 8:25, NIV). Jesus then summed it all up by saying that if the people who hear His words listen and understand, then they would "know the truth, and the truth will set [them] free" (John 8:32). This is the opposite of self-sufficiency. Self-sufficiency and self-righteousness lead you away from God and the truth. Your truth becomes what you tell yourself. This self-sufficient truth tells you that your life on earth is your own and that you will do things for the benefit of your family and you. Your education is sufficient because it tells you that there is nothing more important than your gods of success, status, money, and pleasure. This type of self-gratification puts you directly at the center of your own world. This self-centered lifestyle is one that you believe is the source of your happiness. And God has no room in your life because you totally fill up the center of your own universe.

Be wary of the traps of the world. If you have success, power, and accomplishments they can fill your mind with thoughts of what you have done to bring you these forms of *happiness*. Rich and powerful politicians and leaders often find themselves ensnared in such traps. They listen to people telling them how great, intelligent, skilled, and successful they are – and they begin to believe that they are the product of their own making. In doing so they become convinced that they are the center of their own universe. People (entourages) start circling them like moons circumnavigating a planet. They begin to believe their own press clippings. They become completely self-righteous to such an extent that they feel, as country music singer Travis Tritt described, "ten feet tall and bulletproof."

---

[135]Let's remember the credibility of a witness when their past words conform with their present testimony

175

And then comes the fall from grace. This commonly used phrase has its origins in Paul's letter to the Galatians. This letter was written as a defense of the central core of the guarantee: that we are justified by faith in Jesus, nothing more and nothing less. We cannot justify ourselves. We cannot gain the kingdom of heaven through our own acts, successes, accomplishments, or achievements. Galatians 5:4, NIV. We may feel self-justified in our own universe but sin invades us every day. We fall from grace. We may feel ten feet tall and bulletproof but we are just setting ourselves up for the fall. As Tritt says in his song, they feel as if they are a super hero who is invincible ... until they find out that their nemesis is holding kryptonite! Indeed, just as you get to the point where you feel like Superman – at the center of your own world where no one can vanquish you – your self-righteous persona suffers a fall from grace.

"A person who is filled with himself has no room for God in his life. Self-sufficiency can ruin one's appetite for the things of Christ." These words, from Billy Graham, say it better than I possibly could.[136] Jesus said that if you believe in Him, He will indeed set you free from the sin that inhabits (and enslaves) each of us. John 8:36, NIV. If you are set free, you have the guarantee that you will be reunited with your Creator. Self-righteousness and self-sufficiency divorce and exile us from God. "Talent, a pleasing physical appearance, and the adulation of crowds tend to shove aside the qualities of humility and selflessness and love that Christ demands of those who would bear his image." [137] This is the trap of success.

Jesus told many parables/stories warning of the poison of success that leads to self-righteousness. The stories told by Jesus also tell of how wealth leads to feelings of self-worth. And you can see these

---

[136] The Secret of Happiness, Chapter 5, iBooks.

[137] Philip Yancey & Paul Brand. "In His Image." Chapter 3. Zondervan. iBooks

themes repeating themselves in all aspects of life. The workaholic rises in his company to become president, only to fall prey to corruption and eventually, prison. The world-class athlete climbs to the top of his sport only to succumb to illegal performance-enhancing substances that result in his banishment from the sport he loves. The politician with the charismatic personality ascends to national prominence only to lose her husband and children when her many extramarital affairs finally come to light. It is an ever-repeating circle of the upward rise and downfall with a self-centered person at the middle of it all. Fortune and all its trappings make it difficult for a life of humility and dependence on God.

As mentioned previously in chapter four, the parable of the Rich Young Man (Ruler), told in the Gospels of Matthew (Chapter 19) and Mark (Chapter 10) highlights Jesus's teaching on the self-centered and self-righteous life.

As the story goes, Jesus encounters a wealthy man who asked what he needed to do to enter the kingdom of heaven. By the tenor of the question, I could imagine that this successful man was confident that he had already done what he needed to do to secure salvation. Confidence is often associated with successful people. This is so because their financial accumulation allows them to believe they are truly self-sufficient. Jesus sternly warned that wealth can keep people from the kingdom of God by tempting them to depend on themselves rather than on God.[138]

In answering the question of the rich young ruler, Jesus first told him that he should demonstrate that he loves God by following His commandments. These include not committing murder, having an extramarital affair, lying, or stealing. Jesus also said that he should honor his mother and father and love his neighbor. You could tell

---

[138]Philip Yancey & Brenda Quinn. "Meet the Bible." P. 1502. Zondervan. iBooks

that this self-assured successful young man thought that following these commands of God would assure him of salvation because, after all, they are all included in the Ten Commandments.

The young man said with pride that he has done all of this. Then Jesus told him the ultimate requirement – that he must also sell everything he has accumulated, give the money to the poor and follow Him. This way, Jesus explained, his true treasure will be in heaven and not in the self-centered life the young man had created for himself on earth. The man was broken-hearted. Why, if he followed the commandments, would he need to surrender his wealth and power? He was rich, young, and successful. He had achieved much and enjoyed a high standing in society.

He was unwilling to surrender everything he had accomplished and accumulated. He was unable to put God in the middle of his self-centered, self-righteous life. He had achieved a life that he believed followed all God's commands. Why wasn't that enough? Because he refused to put his Creator before the god of money and power. He had been worshiping that false god and it had brought him fame and fortune. He was not willing to give in to his need for God's forgiveness, because he was satisfied with his successful life of riches, prestige, security, and money. A life that allowed *him* to satisfy all of *his* physical needs. "As [Jesus] explains it, money operates much like idolatry. It can catch hold and dominate a person's life, diverting attention away from God. Jesus challenges people to break free of money's power - even if it means giving it all away."[139]

Jesus was telling this rich man that he had to choose who he was going to serve. His god of money and power over his Creator. "No servant can serve two masters. Either he will hate the one and love the other, or he will be devoted to the one and despise the other. You

---

[139]Supra. P. 1493

cannot serve both God and Money." The Pharisees, even though they were upright people who followed all the rules, were also like this young man. They looked down on Jesus and, as we know, challenged him on every occasion they could. As Luke records in his gospel, Jesus said to these self-described men of faith "[y]ou are the ones who justify yourselves in the eyes of men, but God knows your hearts. What is highly valued among men is detestable in God's sight." This successful rich young ruler "had it all" and was highly esteemed "among men". Jesus saw right through him (and us) and got to his heart. Luke 16:1–31.

Do not lose the point that Jesus is making. This parable does not tell us that if we want salvation, that we are to sell everything, give it to the poor and follow Jesus in the literal sense. It tells us that we must rid our lives of the gods of wealth, power, infidelity, drug addiction, or anything that dominates our hearts. We must surrender our very will to God's offer of true joy and happiness. We must turn to our Creator and put him at the center of our lives. We must not love money, we must love God with every fiber of our being.

After Jesus told this parable there was also a disappointing response from Jesus's own followers. When the disciples heard what Jesus said – that following the Commandments was not enough – they were unable to admit this simple truth to themselves. They thought that following the law (like the Pharisees) was all they needed to do. But, if they had taken a moment to think of what Jesus was saying and the context within which the statement was made, they would have known what Jesus meant. After all, they had witnessed the law-abiding Pharisees challenge Jesus. But Jesus used this as a teachable moment. Jesus lamented how hard it was for those who trust in riches to enter the kingdom of God. The key phrase is to "trust in riches." Many successful people, who have become rich, trust in their money because they believe money can buy them freedom. When they store up their treasures in banks and investments, they become like Ebenezer Scrooge. Money becomes firmly placed at the center of their world. Rich people, who have become rich by virtue of their hard work and determination and who allow themselves to become self-centered, replace their relationship with God with their earnings. When they do so, they leave no room for their Creator.

My favorite verse in the Bible is, "What good is it for someone to gain the whole world, yet forfeit their soul?" (Mark 8:36, NIV). I have tried to remind myself of this powerful admonition. This speaks to me and is a warning to the success-driven person. It is a verse that I need to read – and heed -- often. I lose sight of this verse when money or success cloud my vision. I start thinking that I have achieved all I intended and have accomplished what I have set my sights on. When we gain a large bank account and acclaim we often go off course. We lose the compass that guides us because worldly values pull us away from God. Success, acclaim, wealth, status, and possessions are not inherently bad, but they can be the siren songs that cause us to veer off course and lead us to wreckage on the rocks. When my children went off to college filled with hope, big dreams, and limitless horizons, I wanted to remind them of this verse. I wish I had received this warning myself because there were many times that I strayed from the course God wanted me to follow – all because of the lure of success and achievement.

Luckily for me, God was always by my side, whispering in my ear and helping me get back on course. God's desire for me has been, and will always be, that I do His will. And my desire is that I show my love for God by surrendering all to Him, no matter the cost, because He has guaranteed my salvation. God does not want to deprive us of achievements, money, acclaim, or success, He just wants us to put them in their proper place - or rather He wants to be in His rightful place. At the center of our lives.

Money is not the root of all evil, the *love* of money is at the root of evil. "For the love of money is a root of all kinds of evil" (1 Tim. 6:10, NIV). Money and riches do not set you free. When you place them at the center of your life they enslave you to an endless cycle of wanting more. The truth sets us free. And Jesus is the way, the truth, and life – not money, success, power, and prestige. Therefore, you can be *assured* that you have the guarantee if you give up your self-centered life and put God at the center. You can do so by claiming the guarantee that was offered by Jesus to all people – no matter how long you have kept God out of the center of your life. No matter how full your life is with false gods. All you have to do is surrender your attitude of self-righteousness and rely on the truth that Jesus speaks to you.

E. Conclusion

I hope that I have shown how you can claim the guarantee of salvation. I have illustrated how God laid out the promise through a series of contracts that have been recorded in the pages of the Bible. God has made this agreement with His creation and has fulfilled his end of the bargain. Through the terms of His covenant, you determine that the guarantee given by God applies to you. He has spelled out why you need the guarantee and how you can claim the promise of eternal life. The covenant promise has been fulfilled. God sent His Son to earth to put in place the final condition of the agreement. Jesus taught us how to claim the promise and then paid the premium needed for you to gain this assurance.

I have explained, using God's own words, how you can get the guarantee and how your own actions will evidence the proof that the guarantee has been claimed by you. I have shown that *good works* are the byproduct of a life that has been committed to Christ. You can't do anything to earn the reward of eternal salvation because you can't be good enough to earn the guarantee. You will never be able to actually see the proof that will enable you to take hold of the guarantee because seeing is not always believing. But it is set forth in black and white for you to see and read within the pages of the Word of God – the Bible.

And finally, I have warned you about the blindness the world will cause – it will blind you to the will of God. How the self-righteous and self-sufficient think that they have it all and need nothing. How the trap of success will snare the unwary so that they will refuse to even look for something they feel they do not need. These people have a god at the center of their lives but refuse to see the urgent need to have their Creator at the core of their being.

CHAPTER EIGHT

HOW HISTORY & SCIENCE PROVE THE GUARANTEE

L adies and gentlemen of the jury, I would now like to provide you with proof that the primary book I have been quoting throughout this trial (the Bible) is a reliable source – something that you can count on as truthful and accurate. I do not expect you to take for granted that the Bible is a dependable source. I will not presume that you will consider it authentic and worthy of belief. I will not dare to think that you will believe in God's promise of salvation based on faith alone. However, I will attempt to show you how the Bible is a genuine source of proof by providing what I believe is cogent evidence of the reliability and trustworthiness of this book, written by a succession of authors. These writers begin with Moses, who wrote the book of Genesis in approximately 1446 BC, and end with John, who penned Revelation about 95 AD.

Genesis begins with the statement explaining how God created the universe and human beings. The first four books of the New Testament conclude with Jesus proclaiming that He is God, that He will be crucified, buried, and will rise from the dead. These fundamental truths set forth in the Bible will be examined through the microscope of history, archeology, science, and mathematics to determine the reliability of the claims made in this book called the Bible.

Authenticating a book that took 1540 years to complete may seem daunting, but I believe that when we are finished with this chapter you will have a level of confidence that will allow you to be convinced that the contractual guarantee of salvation recorded within the pages of the Holy Bible is true, accurate and reliable.

Philip Yancey tells us that

> [It cannot be a coincidence that] this diverse collection of manuscripts written over a period of a millennium by several dozen authors possesses as much unity as it does. To appreciate this feat, imagine a book begun five hundred years before Columbus and just now completed. The Bible's striking unity is one strong sign that God directed its composition. By using a variety of authors and cultural situations, God developed a complete record of what he wants us to know; amazingly, the parts fit together in such a way that a single story does emerge.[140]

There are many treatises and hundreds of volumes of books that tackle this subject. If I were to devote the remainder of this book to offering proof that the Bible is historically accurate, I would not even scratch the surface of the mountains of evidence by hundreds of scholars on this subject. Since I do not have the time nor the inclination to do so (after all I am retired and enjoying my leisure time) I will try to provide you with a bullet-point summary of facts that I feel are convincing. If you want to conduct further inquiry

---

[140]Yancey, Philip. "The Bible Jesus Read." Zondervan, 2017-03-01. iBooks. P. 23

on your own, please delve into the books and articles I cite in this book – and particularly in this chapter.

Most of the relevant parts of the Bible that deal with the guarantee of salvation are contained in the New Testament. These books of the Bible contain the stories of Jesus's birth, teachings, trial, death, and resurrection. If these portions of the Bible are true and accurate then you can be confident in the words uttered by Jesus and recorded during and soon after He walked the earth. Also, if the accuracy of the New Testament can be proven, then, by direct correlation, the Old Testament's truthfulness can also be shown.

This is so, as will be revealed in this chapter, because Jesus himself quoted the Old Testament. If what Jesus said can be believed as true, His quoting of portions of the Old Testament has similar accuracy. I will also prove, through legal evidentiary maxims, that statements made, long before the birth of Jesus, are recorded in the Old Testament. These messages foretold aspects of Jesus's life that could not have been known when these portions of the Old Testament were written, hundreds of years before the birth of Jesus. I will attempt to provide this proof, primarily by showing that the New Testament is an accurate account of Jesus's life on earth and that Jesus is who he said He was.

A. Historical Proof

The impact of Jesus's life on earth is so far-reaching that the very way we count and keep track of time starts and ends with His life. The period of time before His birth is designated as B.C. and the period since his birth is designated as A.D. "The idea of counting years has been around for as long as we have written records, but the idea of syncing up where everyone starts counting is relatively new. Today the international standard is to designate years based on a traditional reckoning of the year Jesus was born – the "A.D." and "B.C." system."[141] The fact that the international system of counting years was based on the time Christ walked the earth shows, in and of itself, the validity of the nature of Jesus in history.

Throughout this book, I try to use the Socratic method of teaching and analysis of issues (referenced earlier). This allows you to look at both sides of an argument instead of being fed one-sided information. Therefore, I want to tackle an issue frequently brought up by those persons who question the authenticity of the Bible. These persons would assert that the bedrock story of the New Testament – that Christ died and rose from the dead to save mankind from sin – is just a story that has been told and re-told in ancient cultures. The argument goes that this *story* is just a myth that was in circulation long before the New Testament was written and adopted as fact by authors of the New Testament.

Therefore, they will argue, it is neither unique or distinctive. "As applied in the scholarly literature, 'dying and rising gods' is a generic appellation for a group of male deities found in agrarian Mediterranean societies who serve as the focus of myths and rituals that allegedly narrate and annually represent their death and resurrection."[142] If the story of a god dying and then raising from the dead existed before the New Testament, how can you have confidence that the "story" of Jesus is historically correct? That it really happened? Why is Jesus's death and resurrection any different than these myths? In fact, the stories from ancient cultures had other striking similarities.

---

[141] Live Science. www.livesicence.com

[142] https://www.encyclopedia.com/environment/encyclopedias-almanacs-transcripts-and-maps/dying-and-rising-gods

Beyond this sufficient criterion, dying and rising deities were often held by scholars to have a number of cultic associations, sometimes thought to form a 'pattern.' They were young male figures of fertility; the drama of their lives was often associated with mother or virgin goddesses; in some areas, they were related to the institution of sacred kingship, often expressed through rituals of sacred marriage; there were dramatic reenactments of their life, death, and putative resurrection, often accompanied by a ritual identification of either the society or given individuals with their fate.[143]

Why is the biblical account any different? Jesus was born of a virgin, He was hailed by the angels and wise men as a King. He died and came back from the dead.

A closer look at these stories by scholars reveals, however, a different perspective. "[T]he category of dying and rising deities is exceedingly dubious. It has been based largely on Christian interest and tenuous evidence. As such, the category is of more interest to the history of scholarship than to the history of religions. Therefore, these ancient stories, once dissected reveal that '[t]he category of dying and rising gods, once a major topic of scholarly investigation, must now be understood to have been largely a misnomer based on imaginative reconstructions and exceedingly late or highly ambiguous texts.' "[144] The one thing the scholars can agree on is that there are vague stories of a deity who dies and rises from the dead, only

---

[143]Supra.

[144]Supra.

to die again for good. What then do we make of the story of Jesus of Nazareth?

I have tried to use logic for my explanation. How do I explain these vague stories that allegedly existed before the New Testament was written and why didn't the gospel writers just pick up on those stories when they wrote the account of Jesus's life?

In addition, how do I explain how the Old Testament's description of how the universe and mankind were created in light of modern scientific discoveries? In doing so I have tried to put the Old Testament to rigorous examination in trying to understand how God, our Creator, endeavored to teach us how the universe that He created worked. I thought about how I could logically explain such things to my children and specifically how I could explain to them the story of the birth, death, and resurrection of Jesus.

As a parent and teacher, I taught my children through the use of stories and rhymes. I used nursery rhymes and stories from Hans Christian Anderson. I read them classic children's stories such as *Where the Red Fern Grows*. Together, we watched *Old Yeller*. Through these auditory and visual means, I was able to teach them moral lessons of right and wrong. These stories of courage, faith, perseverance, and loss taught them the value of morality, kindness, friendship, and how to deal with death. I used these stories to help teach my children about life and love and loss. Stories gave my children perspective and reinforcement so that they would better understand concepts and principles that I thought were important. As they grew in wisdom and understanding they could fall back on the understanding they gained from these early stories. Nursery rhymes that were so primitive and basic allowed them to have a foundation for later understanding of more weighty subjects as they grew.

I believe that God tries to convey ideas in the same way. How do you describe the creation of the world to people in the year 1446

BC? Do you try to explain that God created matter that later led to the Big Bang, which eventually resulted in God's creation of the earth, its land, water, and atmosphere? Or do you explain it in the way that Moses did in Genesis? Moses wrote that, "God said, 'Let there be lights in the vault of the sky to separate the day from the night, and let them serve as signs to mark sacred times, and days and years, and let them be lights in the vault of the sky to give light on the earth.' And it was so. God made two great lights – the greater light to govern the day and the lesser light to govern the night. He also made the stars. God set them in the vault of the sky to give light on the earth, to govern the day and the night, and to separate light from darkness."[145] Humans were only *children* in our understanding of such things in 1446 B.C. and God explained Himself to us in the Bible as if we were children.

What does this have to do with the retelling of the birth, death, and resurrection of Jesus in the New Testament and that story being similar to the ancient stories? I cannot explain it better than C.S Lewis.

> And what did God do? First of all, He left us [a] conscience, the sense of right and wrong: and all through history there have been people trying (some of them very hard) to obey it. None of them ever quite succeeded. Secondly, He sent the human race what I call good dreams: I mean those queer stories scattered all through the heathen religions about a god who dies and comes to life again and, by his death, has somehow given new life to men. Thirdly, He selected one particular people and

---

[145]Genesis 1: 14-18, NIV

spent several centuries hammering into their heads the sort of God He was—that there was only one of Him and that He cared about right conduct. Those people were the Jews, and the Old Testament gives an account of the hammering process.

Then comes the real shock. Among these Jews there suddenly turns up a man who goes about talking as if He was God. He claims to forgive sins. He says He has always existed. He says He is coming to judge the world at the end of time. Now let us get this clear. Among Pantheists, like the Indians, anyone might say that he was a part of God, or one with God: there would be nothing very odd about it. But this man, since He was a Jew, could not mean that kind of God. God, in their language, meant the Being outside the world, who had made it and was infinitely different from anything else. And when you have grasped that, you will see that what this man said was, quite simply, the most shocking thing that has ever been uttered by human lips. — from Mere Christianity[146]

Basically, God was getting mankind ready for the story of Jesus. He was planting the seeds for the greatest story ever told. He planted these seeds in the ancient world and then planted them in the Old Testament (as will be explained below). God was teaching us like parents teach their children.

[146]C. S. Lewis. "A Year with C. S. Lewis." P. 45-46. HarperCollins. iBooks

We do not teach first graders algebra, we teach them that 1+1=2. We get them slowly ready by teaching basic arithmetic of addition and subtraction, then multiplication and division. Later comes algebra and then advanced calculus. We are taught by laying the groundwork with simple equations. Simple concepts develop later into complex understanding. We are taught this way because this is the way we learn.

1. Documentary Authentication:

The best way to authenticate a document (the Bible) is to use other reliable documents that were in existence when the New Testament was written. If these other documents, which are authenticated independently, are consistent with the story set forth in the New Testament, there is a separate source of reliability for the Bible. Lee Martin McDonald is a well-known scholar on the historical accuracy of the Bible[147]. He is a big proponent of determining the historical accuracy of the New Testament based on comparative publications, known to be accurate in and of themselves. In his textbook, *The Story of Jesus in History and Faith*, he references Greek and Roman writers of the first century as independent sources that cite

---

[147] President and Professor of New Testament Studies, Acadia Divinity College (1999-2007) and Dean of the Faculty of Theology, Acadia University, Wolfville, Nova Scotia (1999-2007); Past President, Institute for Biblical Research, (2006-2012); Visiting Professor, Princeton Theological Seminary (June 2007- June 2008) Adjunct Professor of Biblical Studies, Fuller Theological Seminary (1985-1999 and 2008-2010) Adjunct Professor of Biblical Studies, Arizona State University, Tempe, Arizona (2010 to present). His educational background includes: a B.A., Biola University, La Mirada, California, (Religion); a B.D., Talbot Theological Seminary, La Mirada, California (Magna Cum Laude) ; Th.M., Harvard University, Cambridge, Massachusetts, (Honors) and a Ph.D., University of Edinburgh, Scotland

the accuracy of biblical accounts. These writers were unbiased. They did not identify as Christians and did not profess a belief in Christ.

The publications McDonald used were independently documented to be written shortly after the death and resurrection of Jesus. These authenticated documents and books were written contemporaneously with the books in the New Testament. After reviewing these known-source writings, McDonald came to this conclusion:

> These passages [from 1st century Greek and Roman writers who were not Christians] show, among other things, that the early Christians were often persecuted for their faith, that by and large they did not draw on the wealthy and learned classes, that they worshiped Jesus as a divine being, and that they cared for those of their number who were imprisoned by reason of their witness. Further, there was a perception on the part of the non-Christian world that many of the Christians were not afraid to face the consequences for being Christians (confiscation of property, imprisonment, or death), and that their eschatological hope was a primary source of encouragement to them. This supports the New Testament witness in these matters.[148]

Logic and reason dictate that people would not be willing to forgo their life, family, and material possessions for a fictional character that taught the value of loving others as much as a person loves themselves. Rational people would not be willing to choose death

---

[148]The Story of Jesus in History and Faith, P. 382. iBooks.

over life unless they knew with certainty that Jesus died and was resurrected to fulfill His promise of redemption.

There is also proof that the physical Bible was in existence at the same time as these other non-Christian first-century publications. These books and documents reference many of the events from Jesus's life. McDonald examined the Gospel of John to determine if it was a reliable document. In doing so he said that

> [T]he consensus is that it was written sometime during the last decade of the first century. The evidence of its early use comes from Egypt, where a small fragment of the Gospel of John from around AD 125 has been found. The fragment offers evidence that John was written not much later than the early decades of the second century, but more likely it was written several years earlier. John's Gospel was known among Gnostic Christians no later than AD 130."[149]

This independent authentication of the Gospel of John lends credibility to the New Testament. Similarly, the Gospel of Matthew has also been documented as historically accurate. Professor McDonald has reviewed the work of noted historians and found that there is general agreement on the accuracy of Matthew's accounts of Jesus's ministry and the events surrounding His death and resurrection. "Matthew mingles what can reliably be argued as history by all fair-minded historians with remarkable theological statements about Jesus's identity that are beyond the historian's craft

---

[149]Supra. at P. 316

to investigate."[150] In fact, there is plenty of proof that the Gospel of Matthew was widely used by the early church of the first and second centuries. It was relied on by people who either knew eyewitnesses to the ministry of Jesus or were eyewitnesses themselves. If the Gospels of John and Matthew were not historically accurate, they would not have been relied upon as the factual telling of the story of Jesus. This adds great credibility to the accounts of Jesus's life, death, and resurrection as these same stories are echoed in the other gospels and the remaining books of the New Testament.

B. Historical Correctness of the Resurrection

The most important aspect of Jesus's life, in my opinion, is the claim that He rose from the dead. All of Jesus's teachings can be dismissed as a nice man giving good advice regarding how to live life in harmony with each other if the claim that He rose from the dead and appeared to many people can be shown to be a fantasy. Jesus's claim to be God incarnate is a lie if His claim that He rose from the dead is false. If, however, it can be proven by reliable sources that Jesus died and then rose from the grave all of His statements about who He was and why He came to earth are given credibility and are, therefore, foundational truth. Thus, I would like to spend some time examining this claim of resurrection to determine its historical correctness.

The most prolific New Testament author is Apostle Paul. As mentioned previously, this man began his adult life as "Saul of Tarsus." He was born approximately five years after Jesus's death. His parents maintained dual citizenship, both Hebrew and Roman. This gave Saul a great deal of privileges that solely Hebrew citizens

---

[150]Supra. chapter 2, the Gospels

did not enjoy. When Saul was between fifteen and twenty years old he began his studies of the Hebrew Scriptures. These included extensive studies of Jewish law. He became so proficient and knowledgeable that he moved up the ranks of the Jewish religious establishment.

In this position of power, he became an ardent "defender of the faith" and sought out Christians for arrest and imprisonment. He even participated in the deaths of many Christian believers. He was a true zealot for the Jewish faith. Everything about Saul indicated that he had no first-hand knowledge of the birth, life, or death of Jesus. The prime focus of his life was to track down Christians and stop (by whatever means) the spread of Christianity.

Saul instigated the capture and imprisonment of first-century Christians. Once captured, all a Christian had to do to escape imprisonment or death was to renounce their belief that Jesus died and rose from the dead for the remission of their sins. Keep in mind that Jesus's resurrection occurred some thirty to forty years before Saul persecuted believers of Christ. In this period of time, "there is no record of any followers of Jesus who denied his passion and resurrection prior to or during the ministry of Paul."[151] Let that *fact* sink in for a moment. In this almost forty-year period following the death of Christ, not one single Christian is recorded in any document to have renounced their belief that Jesus died and rose from the grave. No one renounced their faith to avoid imprisonment or death. And, these consequences were imposed by both the Roman authorities and Jewish religious leaders – foremost among them, Saul. How can it be that there are no records, from any recognized source, of a denial of the death and resurrection of Jesus?

---

[151] *The Story of Jesus in History and Faith*, p. 199

After Jesus's death, all of the remaining eleven disciples – who went far and wide to preach of the atoning death and resurrection of Jesus – died at the hands of their accusers instead of renouncing their faith. These eyewitnesses to the life, death, and resurrection chose death over the abdication of their eyewitness testimony. If Christ's resurrection from the dead was a false premise, made up by eleven co-conspirators who were telling people a made-up story, how did that false narrative hold up as they were systematically hunted down and put to death? Remember, the people in power (the Roman government and the Jewish religious leaders) had every motive to record any person renouncing this story of resurrection. Yet **no record** of such a renunciation has been found!

Put that choice in the perspective of today's justice system. How many co-conspirators turn state's evidence and testify against their fellow conspirators to save themselves from prison?

Chuck Colson served as Special Counsel to President Richard Nixon from 1969 to 1970. Once known as President Nixon's 'hatchet man,' Colson gained notoriety at the height of the Watergate scandal for being named as one of the Watergate Seven. After he was confronted with the evidence against him, he plead guilty to obstruction of justice for attempting to defame Pentagon Papers defendant Daniel Ellsberg. In 1974 he served seven months in the Federal Maxwell Prison in Alabama, as the first member of the Nixon administration to be incarcerated for Watergate-related charges.[152]

---

[152]https://en.wikipedia.org/wiki/Charles_Colson

Colson gave his life to Christ in prison and went on to found the Christian-based Prison Fellowship International. This ministry supports prisoners and helps them repent of their criminal ways. Since his incarceration, Colson has brought many prisoners to believe in Christ and has received accolades from international criminal rights organizations for his work in helping prisoners turn their lives around.

Before Colson became a Christian in prison, he spent a great deal of time examining the factual basis for the story of Christ. In doing so, he was struck by the fervent, unshakable belief of the disciples and the first century Christians. *Why,* he asked himself, *would they sooner face death or imprisonment* (like him) *over renouncing their belief in the atoning death and resurrection of Jesus?* Colson looked at this question because of his intimate first-hand knowledge of conspiracies and prosecution. He was part of the cover-up plan that was hatched once the burglars were caught in the Watergate offices of the Democratic party. As noted above, he was the first of the Watergate co-conspirators to be sent to prison. He experienced, firsthand, the unraveling of the coverup and how, when faced with the consequences of prison, conspirators would "sing like canaries." Seeing his fellow conspirators fall like dominos once confronted with the realities of jail time he began to see parallels to the supposed eyewitnesses to Christ's resurrection. After studying the claims of the Bible, he came to the conclusion that the story of the death and resurrection of Christ must be true. His experience with the Watergate conspiracy taught him that a lie cannot live long when the pressure of prison (and in the case of the disciples and first-century Christians, death) is applied.

"Here were the ten most powerful men in the United States," (referring to the Watergate cover-up attempt). "With all that power, and we couldn't contain a lie for two weeks." Under the threat of prison, the Watergate coverup (and the lies that were told pursuant thereto) folded like a cheap tent. Contrast this with the deaths and imprisonment of Jesus's followers. The disciples (who were so frightened that they locked themselves away after Jesus's death) were suddenly emboldened to venture far and wide to testify to the truth of the story of the death and resurrection. After witnessing Jesus walking and talking after His resurrection they surrendered to death rather than renounce the fact that Jesus claimed to be God. [Only God could be resurrected from such a horrible death as being crucified] "Take it from one who was involved in the conspiracy, who saw the frailty of man firsthand, there is no way the eleven apostles who were with Jesus at the time of the resurrection, could ever have gone around for forty years proclaiming Jesus's resurrection unless it were true."

Colson, a lawyer, investigated the accounts of the Bible and the facts of history that recorded the deaths of the disciples and the first-century Christians and came to the only logical conclusion. Had the New Testament account not been true, Colson continued, "Peter would have been exactly like John Dean." Dean, you may remember, was the first of the Watergate co-conspirators who talked to prosecutors to save his own skin. It would have taken just one of Jesus's inner circle to say that Jesus did not die and resurrect to unravel the story of the guarantee. If just one of the disciples said that Jesus did not rise from the dead, the Christian faith would have gone the way of the Watergate coverup. "They," Colson said, "would have sold out to save their skins." Christians, however, chose to be fed to lions at the Roman Coliseum rather than renounce their faith. This, to me, is clear and convincing proof of the factual reliability of the Gospel accounts of the death and resurrection of Christ from the dead.

1. Proof of the Resurrection

One argument that has been made against the resurrection is that the Hebrew religious authorities believed that the followers of Jesus stole his body and buried it in another (undisclosed) location so that the tomb was found empty on Easter Sunday. "Even the Jewish leaders did not deny the reality of the empty tomb, but concocted the story that the disciples had stolen Jesus's body" (Matt. 28:11-15). The idea that the fearful (John 19:19), doubting (Luke 24:10-11) disciples somehow overpowered the Roman guard detachment and stole Jesus's body is absurd. That they did it while the guards were asleep is even more preposterous. Surely, in moving the heavy stone from the mouth of the tomb, the disciples would have awakened at least one of the soldiers. And in any case, how could the guards have known what happened while they were asleep? Many other theories have been invented over the centuries to explain away the empty tomb, all of them equally futile."[153] Doug Becker posits it this way:

> The resurrection of Jesus is a true historical event. Our confidence in this does not come from our ability to refute mythicists, but from the testimony of the Scriptures and, to a lesser extent, from the historical evidence of the resurrection. Jesus's crucifixion under Pontius Pilate; his burial in the tomb owned by Joseph of Arimathea; the empty tomb; his post-mortem appearances to the women, the eleven disciples, and to other eyewitnesses; the rise of early Christianity in Jerusalem where many of these things had taken place; the lack of

---

[153]One Perfect Life, John F. MacArthur, Chapter X Notes, iBooks

embellishment and theologizing in the Gospels' crucifixion and resurrection accounts; the use of women as the primary witnesses[154] - all these factors and more should establish a very high degree of confidence in the resurrection of Jesus...[155]

John MacArthur has also weighed in on the issue of the reliability of the Bible as it relates to the death and resurrection of Jesus. He notes that the Old and New Testaments are consistent as they reference the facts surrounding the resurrection. As pointed out above there are hundreds of years that passed between the recorded statements of the Old and New Testaments. How could authors, writing hundreds of years before Jesus was born, know that the Savior would die and rise from the dead? "Neither Peter nor John understood that Old Testament Scripture said Jesus would rise (Ps. 16:10). This is evident in the reports of Luke (24:25–27, 32, 44–47). Jesus had foretold His resurrection (Matt. 16:21; Mark 8:31; 9:31; Luke 9:22; John 2:17), but they would not accept it (Matt.16:22; Luke 9:44–45). By the time John wrote his gospel, the church had developed an understanding of the Old Testament prediction of Messiah's resurrection (cf. "as yet").[156]

I will discuss these Old Testament statements about Jesus, his life, death, and resurrection in further detail later in this chapter.

2. Historical Reliability of the Death and Burial of Jesus

As referenced at the beginning of this chapter, the way we record time is based on the markers of Jesus's birth and death (BC and AD).

---

[154]In this time women were not allowed to testify in court, own property or vote.

[155]Was the Resurrection of Jesus a Repackaged Pagan Myth? Doug Becker, Pastor of Theology, Emergence Ministries. April 2, 2018

[156]One Perfect Life, John F. MacArthur, Chapter X Notes, iBooks

However, is there any reliable proof of the death and burial of Jesus? One way to judge the accounts of Jesus's death and burial that are set forth in all four gospels and the Book of Acts is to compare these accounts with how things were done in the Jewish culture during the time of Roman rule.

Professor McDonald in his book[157] devotes a significant amount of time to this question. He reviewed historical accounts of executions by the Romans and compared them to the biblical accounts of Jesus's death. He notes that the "Roman practice of execution by crucifixion may have been learned from the Carthaginians. Its practice dates from at least the sixth century BC and was banned in the Roman Empire by Constantine in AD 337 out of respect for Jesus." (P. 648). All the gospel accounts of Jesus's crucifixion are in agreement that his crucifixion occurred during the day. Historical accounts of the Roman Empire show that daylight executions were the norm because they were expected to attract public attention. This was something the Roman authorities wanted for the "deterrent effect" of such executions. This type of capital punishment was also staged in public places "to instill fear in all who observed the execution and to deter actions similar to those that led to the crucifixion. "Torture, humiliations, and beatings were common in both Carthaginian and Roman crucifixions which were considered more horrible than hangings. Hanging was quick but crucifixion took much longer and involved much torment and pain before death. Besides the usual beatings that preceded such executions, those crucified were often hung naked to add to their humiliation." (P. 649-50). The accounts in the gospels are, therefore, in conformance with the accepted methods employed by Roman authorities of the time.

---

[157] The Story of Jesus in History and Faith

McDonald also studied two prominent authors of the day, Philo and Josephus, to contrast their accounts with the books of Matthew, Mark, Luke, and John. He notes that:

> Philo and Josephus both claim that in general the Romans honored the Jewish customs (Philo, Embassy 300; Flaccus 83; Josephus, Ag. Ap. 2.73), and this is similar to the Roman law cited in the Digesta. The relevant text for exceptions to the usual practice reads as follows:
>
> > *The bodies of those who are condemned to death should not be refused [to] their relatives; and the Divine Augustus, in the Tenth Book of his Life, said that this rule has been observed. At present, the bodies of those who have been punished are only buried when this has been requested and permission granted; and sometimes it is not permitted, especially where persons have been convicted of high treason...The bodies of persons who have been punished should be given to whoever requests them for the purpose of burial. (Digesta 48.24.1–3)*
>
> From this, it is clear that the Roman practice of allowing the burial of the bodies of crucifixion victims was common if the body was requested. Joseph of Arimathea's request to bury the body of Jesus following the crucifixion (Mark 15:42-45) does have precedent in Roman law. (P. 652-53)

McDonald also noted the tie-in between the death of Jesus by crucifixion and how the Jewish religion viewed such a death. He says that this form of execution was despised[158] and because of this, the Jews had a very hard time accepting that *their* Messiah would meet His death in this manner. (P. 654-55.) The death of Jesus by crucifixion would cause even a *casual* Jew to reject the notion that Jesus was the redeemer of the Jewish people. Why would a new religious movement which sought to convert Jews and then Gentiles describe the death of Jesus this way? The only logical answer, to me, is that it would not – unless it were true.

3. What About the Different Accounts in the Gospels?

There are those who point out the slight differences between the gospel accounts of the death, burial, and resurrection as inherent untrustworthiness of the gospels. However, in my experience, this has proven to be a false narrative. In fact, these slight differences in descriptions by eyewitnesses have been shown to be the norm by those who study eyewitness accounts of accidents or crimes. In a March 2019 peer-reviewed article, a team of three respected scientists from the Department of Psychology at Stockholm University, in Sweden, concluded that:

> Evaluating eyewitness testimonies has proven a difficult task. Recent research, however, suggests that incorrect memories are more effortful to retrieve than correct memories, and confidence in a memory is based on retrieval effort. We aimed to replicate and extend these findings, adding

---

[158]Deuteronomy 21:23

retrieval latency as a predictor of memory accuracy. Participants watched a film sequence with a staged crime and were interviewed about its content. We then analyzed retrieval effort cues in witness responses. Results showed that incorrect memories included more "effort cues" than correct memories. While correct responses were produced faster than incorrect responses, delays in responses proved a better predictor of accuracy than response latency. Furthermore, participants were more confident in correct than incorrect responses, and the effort cues partially mediated this confidence-accuracy relation. In sum, the results support previous findings of a relationship between memory accuracy and objectively verifiable cues to retrieval effort.[159]

The authors found that eyewitnesses who viewed the exact same incident had slightly different accounts when asked to retell what they had seen. When I encountered the same thing in my trial practice I came to the same conclusion. People view the same tragic events with slightly different accounts. In fact, if I found two or more eyewitnesses giving the *exact* same account of an event, I would be skeptical of their testimony, believing that they rehearsed their versions of the accounts (most probably with the lawyers for the parties they testified for) before testifying.

Here is how McDonald evaluates the gospels:

---

[159]Gustafsson, Lindholm & Jonsson. Predicting Accuracy in Eyewitness Testimonies With Memory Retrieval Effort and Confidence. Front. Psychol., 29 March 2019. https://doi.org/10.3389/fpsyg.2019.00703

Despite the several variations in the Gospel accounts of the burial story, all agree, including Acts 13:29, that Jesus of Nazareth was buried. This is also supported by the earliest New Testament reference to Jesus's burial in 1 Corinthians 15:4, a tradition that precedes Paul and was handed down to him (1 Cor. 15:3). P.679

Although there are a number of variations in New Testament traditions, the writers of the New Testament are agreed that following his death, Jesus was buried (Mark 15:42–47; 16:1–3; Luke 23:50–56; 24:1–3; Acts 13:28–29; Matt. 27:57–66; 28:1; John 19:31, 39–42; 20:1; 1 Cor. 15:3–4). The canonical Gospels, the Gospel of Peter 2:3–4 and 6:23–24 (mid-second century AD?), and the Acts of Pilate[160] 15:5–6 (perhaps as early as the late second century or even as late as the fourth century AD) agree that Joseph of Arimathea buried the body of Jesus. (P.680)

...

It is possible that Joseph acted at the behest of the Sanhedrin to keep Jewish law and ensure that the body would not defile the land (Deut. 21:22–23; cf. Ezek. 39:14–16). This may be implied in John 19:31 and Acts 13:29—that is, the Jewish leaders were concerned about burial practices, and the law

---

[160]Another separate, independent and verifiably accurate historical source

led them to request the body of Jesus for burial—but if so, it is strange that John reports that Joseph went to Pilate secretly for fear of the Jews (John 19:38). If he went to Pilate as a member of the Sanhedrin (Mark 15:43; Luke 23:50) at the behest of the Jews (John 19:31), his discipleship did not have to be declared, and there would be no need for a private meeting with Pilate as well as no occasion for fear. On the other hand, if Joseph was a secret disciple of Jesus, or eventually became one, that could account for his name being included in the biblical narratives and in subsequent Christian sources (Gos. Pet. and Acts Pil.). (P. 680-81)

I contend that Mark 15:42–47 is the earliest story of the burial of Jesus and that all seven traditions (all four canonical Gospels, 1 Cor. 15:4; Acts 13:29; and Gos. Pet. 2:3 and 6:23–24) agree that Jesus was appropriately buried in accordance with Jewish custom. Attempts to deny the burial of Jesus, the empty tomb, and ultimately the resurrection of Jesus go against the multiple attestations of this tradition in antiquity. P. 684-85

Therefore, sight differences in the Gospel accounts are consistent with research about eyewitness accounts and with my experience of dealing with the testimony of eyewitnesses in the cases I handled.

4. Does Archeology Provide Proof of Reliability?

There is another way that history is recorded. Written documents are not the only things that attest to the history of a time and place. Archeological findings document what is occurring at a particular time and place, sometimes in a more concrete and convincing fashion than written records. This is especially true for the period of time before Jesus was on planet earth. There are many books in the Old Testament that deal with Israel being conquered by the Babylonian empire and the Jewish people being taken captive (see e.g. Daniel and Esther). The descriptions of this period of the Jewish nation are detailed in the pages of the Bible and archeology has proven the reliability of these accounts.

> Today, archeologists in Iraq must dig through layers of dirt to find any remnants of Babylonian culture. Nebuchadnezzar is a mere footnote of history. Yet the prophecies of Jeremiah and Daniel have been preserved and are still studied by millions around the world. And if the messages concerning Moab and Philistia and Assyria and Babylon proved true in precise detail, then what of their message about the end of all history?[161] P. 293

C. Testimonial Proof of Authenticity of the Gospels

In civil cases I handled, timelines were often important to show the reliability of testimony. For instance, I once handled a case for a manufacturer of fetal heart monitoring devices. The lawsuit alleged that the monitor malfunctioned and the low heartbeat warning alarm didn't sound. The alarm had a programmed notification

---

[161] Yancey, Philip. "The Bible Jesus Read." P. 293. Zondervan, 2017-03-01. iBooks.

function that would sound and alert hospital personnel if the fetus was going into cardiac distress. In my case, the timeline of events was critical. The lawyers handling this case for the mother, the hospital, nurses, and my client, the manufacturer, had to determine where the hospital personnel were at all times leading up to the fetus's heartbeat slowing down.

The timeline was crucial because we needed to understand whether the nurses were properly attending to the mother, who was hooked up to this monitor, on their scheduled intervals, and at what point the doctors were alerted to the problem. We then had to compare the testimony of all of the witnesses to see if caregivers were credible when their testimony was juxtaposed to computer-recorded low heartbeat rates and the timeline of events.

Was it possible that nurse "A" was meeting the required protocols for his rounds when he testified that he checked the mother five minutes before the fetus was recorded going into distress? Could he have been administering medication to patient "D" in the far wing of the maternity unit at 10 am and still been following doctor's orders by checking the heartbeat of the fetus five minutes before the slowing of the heartbeat? The established timeline was a test that I used to judge the reliability of the testimony of each witness.

I have used this same method to test the reliability of the *testimony* as set forth in the Bible. As noted above, the accounts of the trial, execution, burial, and resurrection of Jesus as set forth in the gospels have been tested on the timeline of history. I have already shown that the gospel accounts are consistent with the use, at the time of Jesus's death, of the methods of burial and crucifixion as practiced by the Romans and Jews of the time. I have also examined the timeline of history with the conversion of Saul of Tarsus and his remarkable change from a persecutor of Christians to Apostle Paul. "The conversion of Paul took place sometime around AD 33-35 at the latest (Gal. 1:11-17), and he claims that his gospel was acknowl-edged by the leadership (pillars) of the church in Jerusalem (Peter, James, and John) and that he and his gospel were accepted by them in Jerusalem (Gal. 2:2–10). Paul's gospel is compatible with the pas-sion and resurrection stories of the canonical gospels. The gospels were all written some thirty to seventy years – at most – following the death of Jesus, and they clearly reflect earlier traditions about Jesus."[162] In such a case, the timeline fits, and the testimony of Paul is consistent with the testimony of the eyewitnesses to the events in the life of Christ.

Historians have also studied the Gospel of John and have con-cluded that his account of the life, death, and resurrection of Jesus was historically accurate. McDonald observed that:

> John had no doubt that what he reported about Jesus actually happened, and that the conclusions he drew about Jesus's identity were true. While he packs his narratives full of symbolic and theolog-ical meaning (e.g., Jesus's words to the woman at the well in Samaria in 4:10–14), there is nothing to suggest that he had little or no interest in the truth-fulness of the stories he presented in his gospel.
>
> John's *chronology* of the story of Jesus, although often different from that of the Synoptic Gospels, is not necessarily wrong. Despite the traditional description of John as the "spiritual Gospel," one cannot conclude that John was uninterested in pre-senting a story about Jesus in history as well as in

---

[162]Lee Martin McDonald. The Story of Jesus in History and Faith. Chapter 2

faith. More scholars are now suggesting that behind John's interpretation of his stories about Jesus are credible historical events that cannot be ignored.[163] Emphasis added

John, described as the disciple "whom Jesus loved," accurately described Jewish customs and traditions in his gospel. His descriptions are consistent with eyewitness accounts. It is believed that he was greatly influenced not just by his ability to see, receive and write about what he saw, but was also very familiar with the Old Testament (see e.g. John 1:1-5). It is believed that John wrote his gospel about 80-85 AD.

The trial and death of Jesus have been discussed herein. However, the reliability of the assurance of salvation is tied to the resurrection. Jesus said that His resurrection was the final piece of the puzzle that solved the problem of sin. Jesus also said that His resurrection from the dead was the key that unlocked the chains of sin that prevented us from entering into fellowship with God. Therefore, proof of Jesus's resurrection is foundational. It forms the "quid pro quo[164]" for the guarantee.

We have discussed the historical accuracy of the Gospels and how each disciple wrote a firsthand eyewitness account of seeing Jesus after the resurrection. We have also discussed how the Bible says that the first people to see Jesus after the resurrection were

---

[163] Supra. P. 322-23

[164] The failed attempted impeachment of President Trump in early 2020 is occurring during the time that I am writing this section of this book so perhaps I do not need to explain what this latin phrase means. However, we all have short memories so here goes: **Quid pro quo** ("something for something" in Latin) is a Latin phrase used in English to mean an exchange of services, in which one transfer is contingent upon the other. The granting of salvation was contingent on the resurrection of Jesus from the dead.

women. At the time of Jesus's death, women were not allowed to give testimony in court. If a Jew of that time were to accredit witnesses to the fact of an event, they would not be women. This, in my opinion, lends credibility to their firsthand account because if one were going to make up the story of the resurrection at that period of history you would not say that women were first eyewitnesses to this significant event.

There were also secondary sources who can attest to the eyewitness accounts of the disciples.

> [T]hree leaders of the early church named Clement of Rome, Polycarp, and Ignatius, mention Jesus's resurrection. Two of them, Clement and Polycarp, probably knew the apostles Peter and John. Clement of Rome and Polycarp are probably repeating some of the information they had heard from Peter and John. Though Ignatius is fairly early and was a friend of Polycarp, there is no evidence suggesting he had met one of the apostles. Although it is possible he did, historians must primarily concern themselves with matters that are probable. Since it is probable that Clement and Polycarp heard about Jesus's resurrection from Peter and John, they are primary sources related to that event.[165]

Licona concludes that:

---

[165] What are the Primary Sources for Jesus' Resurrection? Michael R. Licona. Houston Baptist University, Spring 2016

We have surveyed a number of sources that mention Jesus's resurrection and are able to summarize our findings. Our primary sources include some of Paul's letters, Matthew, Mark, Luke, John, and Acts, Hebrews, 1 Peter, Clement of Rome, and Polycarp. Of these Hebrews, 1 Peter, Clement of Rome, and Polycarp inform us that Jesus's resurrection was being proclaimed. However, they do not provide any details about the event itself or the nature of Jesus's resurrection. Paul's letters, the Gospels and Acts inform us that Jesus's resurrection involved his corpse, and that he had appeared to others. From Paul, we have rock-solid evidence that this is also what the Jerusalem apostles were proclaiming.

Paul writes in 1 Corinthians 15:3-8 that the resurrected Christ was seen by over 500 people. As mentioned above, there are no records of any of the 500-plus people ever retracting their testimony that they witnessed the resurrected Christ. As a trial lawyer, this is an amazing fact. I agree with Chuck Colson that this lack of retraction in the face of imprisonment or death belies human understanding. This was not a conspiracy devised by the apostles. 2 Peter 1:16. Put another way, consider how strong the account of Christ's resurrection would be in a court of law. "If each of these 500 people were to testify in a courtroom for only six minutes each, including cross-examination, you would have an amazing fifty hours of first-hand eyewitness testimony. Add to this the testimony of the many other eyewitnesses and you could well have the largest and most lopsided trial in history."[166] The number of eyewitnesses is over-whelmingly convincing.[167]

Two of the eyewitnesses to the resurrected Christ were Peter and John. In the book of Acts (3:1-26) they describe what they saw to the Jewish leaders – the very people who could have them executed or imprisoned. They did so knowing that they could be imprisoned or killed for their statements. They also performed the types of miracles Jesus did – all the while pointing to Jesus as the source of their power. "The God of Abraham, Isaac and Jacob, the God of our fathers has gloried his servant, Jesus. You handed him over to be killed, and you disowned him before Pilate, though he had decided to let him go. You disowned the Holy and Righteous One and asked that a murderer be released to you. You killed the author of life, but God raised him from the dead. *We are witnesses of this*. By faith in the name of Jesus, this man whom you see and know was made strong. It is Jesus's name and the faith that comes through him that has given this complete healing to him, as you can all see."[168]

In chapter ten of Acts, Peter again testifies to seeing and encountering[169] the resurrected Christ. He says that he and the other disciples "...are **witnesses** of everything [Jesus] did in the country of the Jews and in Jerusalem. They killed him by hanging him on a tree, but God raised him from the dead on the third day and caused him to be seen. He was not seen by all the people, but by **witnesses** whom God had already chosen – by us who ate and drank with him after

---

[166]Josh and Sean McDowell, Evidence for the Resurrection, Regal (Ventura, CA: 2009), p. 196

[167]Eye-witness Evidence of Christ Resurrection. Heath Henning. May 11, 2019

[168]Philip Yancey & Brenda Quinn. "Meet the Bible." P. 1781-82. Emphasis added. Zondervan. iBooks.

[169]Eyewitness testimony

He rose from the dead. He commanded us to preach to the people and to **testify** that he is the one whom God appointed as judge of the living and the dead. All the prophets testify about him that everyone who believes in Him receives forgiveness of sins through his name." (Emphasis added) Peter is boldly proclaiming the death and resurrection of Jesus and further, that these things transpired so that Jesus's death would act as payment for the sins of all that believe in him. See Acts 10:1-48, NIV.

Further verifying the reliability of eyewitness testimony is the date when these eyewitness accounts were recorded. If the statements of the eyewitnesses were recorded while they were still alive it would lend reliability to the accounts. This is important because if the recorded testimony of the eyewitnesses was wrong or erroneously recorded, the eyewitnesses could recant or correct the recorded testimony. The testimony of the eyewitnesses set forth in the Bible was recorded within twenty years of Jesus's death and resurrection. "First Thessalonians, dating probably from A.D. 50 or 51, is our earliest record of the life of a Christian community. As such, it provides a firsthand account of Paul's relationship with a missionary church barely twenty years after Jesus's departure."[170]

The importance of eyewitness testimony is not lost on C.S. Lewis. "I have to believe that Jesus was (and is) God. And it seems plain as a matter of history that He taught His followers that the new life was communicated in this way. In other words, I believe in His authority. Do not be scared by the word *authority*. Believing things on authority only means believing them because you have been told them by someone you think trustworthy. Ninety-nine percent of the things you believe are believed on authority." [171]

---

[170]Philip Yancey & Brenda Quinn. P. 1890. "Meet the Bible." Zondervan.

[171]C. S. Lewis. "A Year with C. S. Lewis." P. 47. HarperCollins. iBooks.

D. Prior Consistent Testimony

I have mentioned the power of testimony in court by an expert or an eyewitness. That testimony is especially persuasive when it is consistent with earlier statements that were made by that witness. The theory is that if the prior statements are consistent with their in-court testimony, their testimony under oath is more credible. In examining the truth of the New Testament accounts of the life of Jesus I looked at *predictions*, made hundreds of years before Jesus's birth. If those prior statements were consistent with the historical accounts of Jesus's life and the statements made by Jesus; they can be used to attest to the truth of the accounts of Jesus's life as set forth in the New Testament.

When I confronted a witness in a trial, using the art of cross-examination, I would challenge the witness's veracity by reviewing prior statements made by that witness that dealt with the same subjects the witness was testifying to in court. In the case of the truth of the gospels, I examined Old Testament transcripts to determine if they were consistent with the key aspects of who Jesus was, what He said, and what happened to Him. Using this method of "truth-seeking," I could see if the stories of Jesus's birth, life, death, and resurrection had been recently fabricated or were based on predictions made long before the great, great, great... grandfathers of the New Testament authors were born.

> ...one passage alone, Isaiah 53:2–12, foretells twelve aspects of Christ's passion, all of which were fulfilled - he would be rejected, be a man of sorrow, live a life of suffering, be despised by others, carry our sorrow, be smitten and afflicted by God, be pierced for our transgressions, be wounded for our

sins, would suffer like a lamb, would die with the wicked, would be sinless, and would pray for others.

> Some of the other major predictions about the Messiah, all of which were fulfilled in Jesus, was that he would be born of a woman (Genesis 3:15) who would be a virgin (Isaiah 7:14), of the seed of Abraham (Genesis 12:1–3; 22:18), of the tribe of Judah (Genesis 49:10), of the house of David (2 Samuel 7:12–16), in Bethlehem (Micah 5:2); he would be heralded by the Lord's messenger (Isaiah 40:3); he would cleanse the temple (Malachi 3:1); he would be "cut off" 483 years after the declaration to reconstruct Jerusalem in 444 B.C. (Daniel 9:24–27); he would be rejected (Psalm 118:22); he would have his hands and feet pierced (Psalm 22:16); he would be pierced in his side (Zechariah 12:10); he would rise from the dead (Psalm 16:10); he would ascend into heaven (Psalm 68:18), and he would sit down at the right hand of God (Psalm 110:1). [Geisler and Brooks, When Skeptics. Ask, 114–15.][172]

This is very compelling evidence that the birth, life, death, and resurrection of Jesus was not a recent fabrication concocted by his closest associates and written down in the pages of the New Testament. Just these few passages from the Old Testament (recorded hundreds of years before a word of the New Testament was written) verify every aspect of the guarantee of salvation.

---

[172]Ravi Zacharias, Who Made God? Emphasis added. iBooks

If an expert in the field of mathematics and statistics was called to examine whether there was any proof of Christ's claim of divinity, that expert could be cross-examined to determine if his or her claims were reliable. If that expert opined on the validity of the claims of the New Testament writers, just on the subject of Christ's claim of divinity, I could find proof to determine if this claim was valid or lacked credibility. What if the expert concluded that Jesus's statements about his own death, burial, and resurrection were backed by that expert's analysis of the chances that the Old Testament predictions came to pass? Could a skilled cross-examiner question the expert in such a way as to shake his or her testimony? Could that lawyer find any area of weakness in the expert's testimony that statistically speaking, Jesus was who He said he was: the Son of God?

This question was, in fact, studied by experts. The question was posed as follows: what are the odds that the prophecies of the Old Testament about the coming Savior would be fulfilled? In reaching their conclusions, they said that "[t]he odds against Jesus fulfilling the prophecies by accident would be staggering. In fact, Professor Peter Stoner, who was chairman of Westmont College's science division in the mid-1950s, worked with six hundred students to come up with their best estimate of the mathematical probability of just eight New Testament prophecies being fulfilled in any one person living down to the present time. Taking all eight prophecies together, Stoner then calculated the odds at *one chance in a hundred million billion*. [See Peter W. Stoner, Science Speaks (Chicago: Moody Press, 1969).] This is equivalent to the number of one-and-a-half-inch squares it would take to tile every bit of dry land on the planet."[173] Therefore, it is statistically impossible that Jesus was not who the Old Testament said He wouldbe. Jesus was exactly who

---

[173] Supra.

he said he was. The chances that any one man would fulfill all these eight prophecies is almost too much to comprehend. This leads to just one conclusion – Jesus was who he said he was. No further questions of the witness, your honor!

One of the eight such prophetic statements dealt with a significant event in Jesus's life. The beginning of the end of Jesus's life started in triumph on Palm Sunday. The Gospels of Matthew, Mark, Luke, and John all record the scene. "...They brought the donkey and the colt to Jesus, laid their clothes on them, and they set Jesus on the colt."[174] The gospel writers all recorded this amazing scene. However, it was actually predicted by the prophet Zechariah. (Zech. 9:9, cf. Isa. 62:11). "The precise fulfillment of this messianic prophecy would not have escaped the Jewish multitudes, who responded with titles and accolades fit only for the Messiah (cf. Rev. 7:9)."

And as He went, many spread their clothes on the road, and others cut down leafy branches from the trees and spread them on the road. Spreading one's garments on the street was an ancient act of homage reserved for high royalty (cf. 2 Kings 9:13), suggesting that they recognized His claim to be King of the Jews.[175]

---

[174]Matt. 21:1b–11, 14–17; Mark 11:1b–11; Luke 19:29b–44; John 12:12–19

[175]John F. MacArthur, One Perfect Life, Part VIII Notes

The prophecy of Zechariah, written sometime before 480 B.C., about Jesus's entry into Jerusalem is just another example of the testimony set forth in the Old Testament that occurred exactly as it was foretold. What do you think the odds are that the twelve disciples conspired with Jesus to assemble a crowd of adoring fans along a dusty road in Jerusalem, gave them palm branches and cloaks to spread out before Him, and incited them to play it all out exactly as it was described some 500 years before it actually happened? Add these astronomical odds to the calculated chances of the above mathematicians and you get a number that takes many pages just to write out. Convinced yet?

As the commercials say, "Wait, there's more!" In court there are a few levels of proof that must be established to prove your case. In criminal court, the proof of guilt required is "beyond a reasonable doubt." The standard of proof in a civil case, however, is "the greater weight of the evidence." This proof is often described as the 51% test. The plaintiff in a civil case must "tip the scales" of justice in their favor to win.

There is a higher level of proof in some civil cases, however, called "clear and convincing." Clear and convincing proof is evidence that is "highly and substantially more probable to be true rather than untrue." I believe the remarkable link between the Old Testament predictions of the Messiah and the actual proof of Jesus meets both the criminal standard of "beyond a reasonable doubt" and the higher civil court standard of "clear and convincing" evidence. "[T]hese detailed prophecies, recorded many centuries before Jesus's birth, offer *convincing proof* that God is revealing his plan for the ages through the ancient prophets. He has not permanently severed his covenant with the Jews. Rather, out of Jewish roots – King David's own stock – he will bring forth a new king, a king like no other, to reclaim all the earth."[176]

Jesus, through his teachings and the very way He lived, connected the dots between the long-sought Messiah of the Jewish people and the salvation promised by God. "[I]n a dramatic scene early in his ministry, Jesus quoted from one of Isaiah's servant passages. After reading aloud in the synagogue, Jesus rolled up the scroll, gave it back to the attendant and sat down. The eyes of everyone in the synagogue were fastened on him, and he began by saying to them, 'Today this scripture is fulfilled in your hearing' (Luke 4:20-21). At last, a link snapped into place for some, but not all, of Jesus's listeners. The Messiah had come at last – not as a conquering general but as a carpenter's son from Nazareth."[177]

In order for Jesus to truthfully say such a thing, He had to be God's Son. Otherwise, as I have said before, He was a liar or a madman. "The Gospels record some three dozen miracles performed by Jesus, and he states plainly why he does them: 'Believe me when I say that I am in the Father and the Father is in me; or at least believe on the evidence of the miracles themselves' (John 14:11). They serve as convincing proofs that he is the Messiah, the Son of God."[178]

I have heard some say that this type of proof is using a forbidden legal device known as *pulling oneself up by one's own bootstraps*. I have mentioned this before when talking of the testimony of experts. Bootstrapping is a suspicious form of reasoning that verifies a source's reliability by checking the source against itself. Theories

---

[176]Philip Yancey & Brenda Quinn. "Meet the Bible." P. 1284, emphasis added. Zondervan. iBooks.

[177]Supra., P. 1278

[178]Supra., P. 1404

that endorse such reasoning face the bootstrapping problem. Critics, therefore, say that using the Old Testament prophesies to prove the reliability of the New Testament accounts of the life, death, and resurrection of Jesus face the bootstrapping problem. However, you can defeat this type of attack when you verify the reliability of the source. We have already examined this on many occasions in this chapter and this book. By showing that what the Old Testament predicts about Jesus came true and that this truth is backed up by eyewitness testimony we have built a clear and convincing case that Jesus was the Son of God. This is not a bootstrapping attempt to provide validity of testimony.

The gospels record many instances of Jesus talking in parables. In fact, even writers who do not believe Jesus was raised from the dead marvel at the wisdom Jesus conveyed in the many parables He used to teach people of God's plan for them. Psalm 78:2 talks of such a person speaking in such a way. "I will open my mouth in parables, I will utter hidden things from of old...". Yancey and Quinn say that by "[u]sing simple, homespun images, Jesus expresses profound truths in a way that holds his audience captive. His parables, or concise short stories, have won high praise even from literary experts who do not accept their message."[179] These parables are just the type of *utterance of things of God* that the Psalmist speaks of in Psalm 78.

There are many other instances of statements that are contained in the Old Testament that have proven to be remarkably accurate. There is but one explanation: Jesus is the Son of God foretold by the prophets of the Old Testament as the coming Messiah. As I have done previously, I will "string cite" some of them for those of you who are still unconvinced. These include:

---

[179] Supra., at P. 2541

1. Predictions of the birth of Jesus[180]
2. Predictions that John the Baptist would prepare the way for Jesus[181]
3. Predictions about how Jesus would appear to the Jews[182]
4. Examples of how God would allow His Son to be sacrificed[183]

---

[180]God puts his reputation on the line. He will answer the Hebrews' bitter complaint with an act of boldness, imagination, and courage that none of them could have dreamed of, an event that will test the limits of human credibility and divine humiliation. God agrees to join them on planet Earth, "to write himself on the pages of history," in Jacques Ellul's words. The mysterious Servant Songs of Isaiah plainly foretell the Incarnation (as the New Testament points out at least ten times). Philip Yancey & Brenda Quinn. "Meet the Bible." P. 311 Zondervan. iBooks.

Yet, as Isaiah makes clear, the God who visits Earth comes not in a raging whirlwind, nor in a devouring fire. "Behold, a virgin shall conceive and bear a Son, and shall call his name Emmanuel, 'God with us.'" He arrives instead in the tiniest, least threatening form imaginable: as an ovum, and then fetus, growing cell by cell inside a peasant virgin. That egg divides and redivides until a fetus takes shape, and finally a single baby bursts forth from Mary's loins to join the puny human beings on their speck of a planet. P. 312. Supra.

[181]Malachi 3:1-18

[182]According to Isaiah, what happened to Judah was not God's defeat. God has in mind a new thing, a plan far more wonderful than anything seen before. The book of Isaiah explains why the future holds hope—not just for the Jews but for the whole world. A mysterious figure called "the servant" will, through his suffering, provide a means of rescue. Philip Yancey & Brenda Quinn. "Meet the Bible." P. 1272. Zondervan. iBooks.

[183]Now it came to pass after these things that God tested Abraham, and said to him, "Abraham!" And he said, "Here I am." Then He said, "Take now your son, your only son Isaac, whom you love, and go to the land of Moriah, and offer him there as a burnt offering on one of the mountains of which I shall tell you." Genesis 22:2. Also: Remember what God said about Jesus after he was baptized? Here is my Son whom I love.

5. Statements relating to Jesus carrying a wooden cross[184]
6. Examples of the method of death employed by the Romans[185]
7. A prediction that Jesus would be betrayed for thirty pieces of silver[186]
8. Predictions of how Jesus would send the disciples out to preach the good news[187]

E. Pascal's Wager: The Logic of it All

In chapter two I made mention of Pascal's Wager and how it relates to using logic to explain the guarantee. It is also helpful, I believe, to show how math and science underscore the validity of the biblical story of salvation. Blaise Pascal was a seventeenth-century

---

[184]Abraham took the wood for the burnt offering and placed it on his son Isaac,... "Later, this same mountain will become home to Jerusalem, the place where God will provide his only Son as the final sacrifice for all people." Philip Yancey & Brenda Quinn. "Meet the Bible." P. 149. Zondervan. iBooks., P. 149

[185]...SO MUST THE SON OF MAN BE LIFTED UP. Cf. John 8:28; 12:32, 34; 18:31–32. This is a veiled prediction of Jesus' death on the cross. Jesus referred to the story of Num. 21:5–9, where the Israelite people who looked at the serpent lifted up by Moses were healed. The point of this illustration or analogy is in the "lifted up." Just as Moses lifted up the snake on the pole so that all who looked upon it might live physically, those who look to Christ, who was "lifted up" on the cross, will live spiritually and eternally. John F. MacArthur, One Perfect Life, Part IV Notes, iBooks.

[186]Zechariah 11:10-13

[187]The last part of Isaiah, addressed to a people facing deep despair, opens the door for the Jews to become a gift to all people. According to Isaiah, word about God will go out to nations nearby and faraway and to distant islands that have never heard of him (66:18-21). This prophecy sees fulfillment in Jesus, who recruits disciples to carry his message worldwide. Through his life and death, the suffering servant indeed introduces the gospel to the entire world. In this and other soaring chapters, Isaiah describes the future with such eloquence that New Testament books like Revelation cannot improve on the language; they merely quote Isaiah. Meet the Bible, P.1289

mathematician who was one of the most celebrated scientists of his time. Along with scientists Descartes and Bacon, he was involved in not only an examination of the way the world works through science and math, but how scientific thought should be developed. They literally changed the way people constructed knowledge. They were pioneers, I believe, in the use of science to determine the truth set forth in the Bible. These men challenged the church's belief at that time which insisted one must believe the Bible *solely* on the basis of faith. They used scientific and analytic methods to examine the claims made in the Bible. These scientists viewed the faith-based method of belief through the lens of mathematical skepticism. Pascal thought that the foundational truths set forth in the Bible must be put to and withstand rational examination. These biblical truths, they contended, must make sense when scrutinized by prudent scientific methods. In contrast to the blind faith required by the church, Pascal started from the premise that nothing can be taken as a "given."[188] This, he theorized, when taken to its logical extreme, would mean that not even God can be viewed as *a given*. Belief in God, he thought, must have a rational basis.

His analysis of belief in God was published, posthumously, in his book, "Pensees" (or Thoughts) in the 1600s. One of the premises that Pascal examined was the scientific and mathematical acknowledgment of the notion of infinity. Both scientists and mathematicians agreed that infinity is a discernable "thing." While it is not subject to calculation, they know it exists. Pascal acknowledged that scientists know infinity exists even though they could not see or calculate infinity. As such, he thought, why do people claim that God cannot exist because He cannot be seen or calculated?

---

[188] Descartes professed this premise in a three word latin phrase: Cogito, Cogito, Ergo. He believed that he couldn't even take his own existence as a given

Mathematicians have never observed infinity, yet they know it exists. Pascal wanted to calculate "the odds" of belief vs non-belief to determine if belief in God was "worth the gamble."

One of the philosophical and scientific methods used for the analysis of a complex question or theory such as this is a Cartesian Plane. This tool, developed by Descartes, was used by Pascal to analyze the question of God's existence. To explain Pascal's wager or theory, I have borrowed this method of investigation and put it into a decision matrix (shown below). This matrix has two essential parts: **Existence** (the top row) & **Belief** (the left column). These two essential parts are then broken down into a four-quadrant matrix. These four quadrants are: **Upper right** (God does not exist but I believe); **Upper left** (God exists and I believe); **Lower right** (God does not exist and I do not believe); **Lower left** (God exists but I don't believe).

	God exists (G)	God does not exist (¬G)
Belief (B)	$+\infty$ (infinite gain)	$-c$ (finite loss)
Disbelief (¬B)	$-\infty$ (infinite loss)	$+c$ (finite gain)

When quantifying his wager Pascal determined four possible outcomes. The **upper left** quadrant results in an *infinite* gain because, as Jesus testified, if God exists and we believe, we are going to heaven. In heaven, we have fellowship with God and we will have no pain, suffering, or sorrow *forever*. The **upper right** quadrant results in a *finite loss*. Our *loss* is that through our belief we have given up some things during our life on earth. Our belief has caused us to go to church and we have forgone some earthly pleasures because of that belief in God. But this quadrant results in no infinite gain.[189] The **lower right** quadrant results in a *finite* gain because those who do not believe in God are living life on their own terms and are not "confined" by the things a person would do if they live a life of faith. But, again, there is no infinite gain. The **lower left** quadrant results in an infinite loss. This is so because if God exists and a person does not believe, they will be excluded from heaven and will suffer eternal separation from God. Jesus said that they will never be happy, will always experience pain, and will forever feel stress.

Pascal's philosophical and mathematical conclusion, based on this analysis, is that **belief in God** (i.e., God exists) results in a finite loss vs. infinite gain. However, **non-belief** (God does not exist) presents us with a finite gain vs. an infinite loss. Pascal, therefore, looked at the loss vs. gain in the form of a wager. Would you rather wager your money on the chance of a finite gain or put your money on a payout of infinite rewards? Mathematically, Pascal therefore determined that the risk/reward calculation of outcome clearly pointed to belief in God as the best choice because of the infinite reward that this belief brings. For non-believers, this decision matrix clearly pointed to the best result: the gain that resulted from belief in God and the guarantee of eternal life (*infinite* reward). This is a much better wager than the *finite* reward that the denial of the existence of God brings. Jesus and his promises of salvation are well worth the wager.[190]

Put another way, Pascal's argument is rooted in game theory. Using this analysis one must conclude that the best course of action is to believe in God regardless of any lack of evidence because that

---

[189]However, this is also weighed against the gain of living a "good" life as a Christian.

[190]I acknowledge the assistance of an explanatory video provided by Tom Ritchey which really helped me understand this analysis (Tomritchey.net)

option gives the biggest potential gains. Ravi Zacharias in his book, *The End of Reason*, says it this way "...the fact that the universe cannot explain itself, added to the obvious intelligence behind the universe, linked to the historical and experiential verification of what Jesus taught and did, make belief in him a very rational and existentially fulfilling reality."[191]

F. Truth?

Ladies and gentlemen of the jury, I do not have all the answers. However, as promised, I have tried to explain, in the time allotted to me by this court, why I believe the promises of salvation are true and are based on historically verifiable sources. As you have heard from my esteemed opponents, there are many historians and mathematicians that dispute the evidence set forth in this argument. However, I believe that the greater weight of the evidence – in fact the clear and convincing evidence – shows that Jesus was a man who walked the earth and who taught many truths by which to live your life. I think that I have shown that this clear and convincing evidence also demonstrates that Jesus was much more than a mere man. His words were much more than wisdom from a virtuous person. History proves that the guarantee that He promised was based on foundational proofs that have been proven to have happened. These include that Jesus was convicted of blasphemy by a Jewish tribunal (the Sanhedrin) because He professed to be God. That He was sentenced to death by crucifixion at the hands of the Roman authorities. He was tortured and died on a cross. He was buried according to Jewish traditions. And, most importantly, that history and the

---

[191]Zondervan, 2008. iBooks

eyewitness testimony of over 500 people attested to the fact that, just as He said, Jesus overcame the grave and rose from the dead.

The passages of the Bible that detail God's plan of salvation are true, historical records. These records are as verifiable as any history book written in ancient times. In fact, the Bible has been verified as reliable by contemporaneous writers. Lee Martin MacDonald says that

> The credibility of the Gospels is that they were written when some of the eyewitnesses of events described in them were still alive. Had the evangelists reported something far afield from what had been circulating orally about Jesus in the churches, the churches would surely have rejected it as they did other unreliable portraits of Jesus... The Gospels themselves also display evidence of dependence on earlier sources about Jesus, some of which may well have been produced before the death of Jesus and were included in the post-Easter stories about Jesus that were taught in the churches and informed the evangelists in writing their Gospels. The canonical Gospels contain no major departures from the received traditions about Jesus that were circulating in the churches in the first century; at least, scholars have not been able to show that.

> ...[T]here is no evidence that the evangelists invented stories about Jesus's life and teachings to satisfy the needs of a later generation of his followers. If a story is repeated in other traditions and if it coheres with other facts that we have been able

to establish about Jesus, then from a historical perspective we can make a case for its authenticity as a genuine part of the earliest traditions about Jesus. We can say further that, in the case of Christianity's most important events—the death and resurrection of Jesus—though many of the details surrounding them in the Gospels differ, their essential message is the same; namely, that Jesus of Nazareth, who died, is now alive and worthy of our faith, and that this has great significance for all who will receive it.[192]

In fact, the word Apostle was understood to the first century Christians to mean "eyewitness." C.S. Lewis discusses this in his book *Miracles*. He explains that only eyewitnesses were allowed to teach the early Christians about Jesus and his lifesaving message of redemption.

> In the earliest days of Christianity, an 'apostle' was first and foremost a man who claimed to be an eyewitness of the Resurrection. Only a few days after the Crucifixion when two candidates were nominated for the vacancy created by the treachery of Judas, their qualification was that they had known Jesus personally both before and after His death and could offer first-hand evidence of the Resurrection in addressing the outer world (Acts 1:22). A few days later St Peter, preaching the first Christian sermon, makes the same claim—'God raised Jesus,

---

[192]Lee Martin MacDonald. The Story of Jesus in History and Faith. P. 331-36. iBooks

of which we all (we Christians) are witnesses'
(Acts 2:32). In the first Letter to the Corinthians,
St Paul bases his claim to apostleship on the same
ground—'Am I not an apostle? Have I not seen the
Lord Jesus?' (1:9)[193].

Pascal's philosophical and mathematical analysis of the existence
of God and the price of not wagering on belief in Jesus and his guarantee of salvation can only convince you so much. "...Christianity is
not a statistical view of life. Indeed it is not. Not when a shepherd
barely shuts the gate on his ninety-nine before rushing out, heart-
broken and short of breath, to find the one that's missing. Not when
a laborer hired for only one hour receives the same wage as an all-day
worker. Matthew 20:1–16. Not when one rascally sinner decides to
repent and ninety-nine upstanding citizens are ignored as all heaven
erupts in a great party. Luke 14:4-7."[194]

Logic dictates, ladies and gentleman, that these types of things
are not the type of behavior that human beings would invent to
entice their fellow citizens to believe in a "religion" meant to inspire
people to blindly follow. In fact, this is further proof of the reliability of the Bible. What religion would be formed this way if man
had created it? Would it not be formed to appeal to the majority?

G. God and Creation

What are we to make of the universe? Does everything that
science tells us about the creation of the cosmos point to a mathematical and scientific explanation that everything was created

---

[193] C. S. Lewis. "A Year with C. S. Lewis." P. 288. HarperCollins. iBooks.

[194] Philip Yancey and Dr. Paul Brand. Fearfully and Wonderfully Made. iBooks

out of nothing? Or does the scientific explanation of the universe merge with a creator-God? Do modern scientific discoveries of the building blocks of the creation of the universe point toward a Creator or does the explanation that order was created out of chaos hold the key to how the universe came about?

Time magazine, in an April 27, 2014 article by Amir D. Aczel, looked at this question and started from this hypothesis advanced by scientists: "We know so much about how the universe works, their authors claim, that God is simply unnecessary: we can explain all the workings of the universe without the need for a Creator." Mr. Aczel went on to examine how far scientific knowledge has advanced.

> The sum total of human knowledge doubles roughly every couple of years or less. In physics and cosmology, we can now claim to know what happened to our universe as early as a tiny fraction of a second after the Big Bang, something that may seem astounding. In chemistry, we understand the most complicated reactions among atoms and molecules, and in biology we know how the living cell works and have mapped out our entire genome. But does this vast knowledge base disprove the existence of some kind of pre-existent outside force that may have launched our universe on its way?

After acknowledging all that science has discovered and determined, Aczel had to admit, however, that scientific knowledge cannot explain how and in what way the initial particles of energy and matter came into existence. In addition, even though science can advance the theory of evolution, it cannot explain such basic things as "how the first living organisms emerged from inanimate matter on this planet and how the advanced eukaryotic cells—the highly structured building blocks of advanced life forms—ever emerged from simpler organisms." While psychologists and neurologists have mapped and explained some of the most complicated functions of the human brain, no scientific theorem can tell us how consciousness arose in living beings. As will be shown below, scientists, mathematicians, philosophers and academics. are at a total loss to explain how all of the elements of matter and energy came together at just the right time and in just the right order to create human beings on this planet called earth.

Aczel frankly acknowledges that all the scientific research and study over recorded time cannot answer this question:

> Why is our universe so precisely tailor-made for the emergence of life? This question has never been answered satisfactorily, and I believe that it will never find a scientific solution. For the deeper we delve into the mysteries of physics and cosmology, the more the universe appears to be intricate and incredibly complex. To explain the quantum-mechanical behavior of even one tiny particle requires pages and pages of extremely advanced mathematics. Why are even the tiniest particles of matter so unbelievably complicated? It appears that there is a vast, hidden 'wisdom', or structure, or knotty blueprint for even the most simple-looking element of nature. And the situation becomes much more daunting as we expand our view to the entire cosmos.

That entire cosmos started (as explained above) in the Big Bang some 13.7 billion years ago. It initiated from a burst of energy "whose nature and source are completely unknown to us and not in the least understood by science." Mr. Aczel then went on to explain that "as if by magic, the 'God particle'—the Higgs boson discovered two years ago inside CERN's powerful particle accelerator, the Large Hadron Collider—came into being and miraculously gave the universe its mass." While the scientists can explain the likely structure and composition of this aptly named "God particle" they cannot tell us how or why it came about. Without the God particle, nothing could exist. The sheer immensity and complexity of events and circumstances that had to go right for the universe to come into existence in the way it has begs the question of how this occurred. Aczel explains it this way:

> Why did everything we need in order to exist come into being? How was all of this possible *without some latent outside power to orchestrate the precise dance* of elementary particles required for the creation of all the essentials of life? The great British mathematician Roger Penrose has calculated—*based on only <u>one</u> of the hundreds of parameters of the physical universe*—that the probability of the emergence of a life-giving cosmos was 1 divided by 10, raised to the power 10, and again raised to the power of 123. This is a number as close to zero as anyone has ever imagined. (The probability is much, much smaller than that of winning the Mega Millions jackpot for more days than the universe has been in existence).

Emphasis added

The only explanation for this, the only answer to the question posed by Aczel is that God created the universe. God created the God particle. God, as the creator, gave the universe order. God caused the Big Bang and then "orchestrated the precise dance" that led to the orderly formation of the universe. God caused the particles and energy to align to allow human beings to emerge and for the world to be balanced in such a way as to sustain life. Mr. Aczel concludes by saying that the "incredible fine-tuning of the universe presents the most powerful argument for the existence of an imminent creative entity we may well call God. Lacking convincing scientific evidence to the contrary, such a power may be necessary to force all the parameters we need for our existence—cosmological, physical, chemical, biological and cognitive—to be what they are." Put another way:

> ...As we go back in time, everything was closer and closer together. Ultimately, at some point in the finite past, the entire known universe was contracted down to a mathematical point, which scientists call the "singularity," from which it has been expanding ever since. The farther back one goes in the past, the denser the universe becomes, so that one finally reaches a point of infinite density from which the universe began to expand. This initial event has come to be known as the "Big Bang." Nothing existed prior to the singularity, for it is the edge of physical space and time. It therefore represents the origin, not only of all matter and energy, but also of physical space and time themselves. Physicists John Barrow and Frank Tipler observe, 'At this singularity, space and time came

into existence; literally nothing existed before the singularity, so, if the Universe originated at such a singularity, we would truly have a creation out of nothing.' Why does the universe exist rather than nothing? There can be no natural, physical cause of the Big Bang event, since, in philosopher Quentin Smith's words, 'It belongs analytically to the concept of the cosmological singularity that it is not the effect of prior physical events. The definition of a singularity...entails that it is impossible to extend the spacetime manifold beyond the singularity.... ***This rules out the idea that the singularity is an effect of some prior natural process.***' Sir Arthur Eddington, contemplating the beginning of the universe, opined that the expansion of the universe was so preposterous and incredible that 'I feel almost an indignation that anyone should believe in it—except myself.' He finally felt forced to conclude, 'The beginning seems to present insuperable difficulties unless we agree to look on it as frankly supernatural.' Emphasis added.[195]

As can be seen, scientists agree that the Big Bang theory explains the creation of the whole known universe out of...nothing. Scientists however cannot explain how "nothing" caused the existence of everything. These same scientists cannot agree that God created the universe. Why? Because God cannot be measured and known. Just like the beginning of everything. I will let Mr. Zacharias answer that question. He said:

---

[195]Ravi Zacharias, Who Made God, iBooks

It is not just the probability of one universe or another existing, but the probability of a life-permitting universe existing. Thus, the correct analogy would be a lottery in which a billion, billion, billion black balls were mixed together with one white ball, and you were invited to reach in blindfolded and pick out a ball. While every ball has an equal improbability of being picked, nevertheless, it is overwhelmingly more probable that whichever ball you pick, it will be black rather than white. To complete the analogy, imagine now that your life depended on the ball's being white; pick out a white ball, or you'll be killed! If you reached, blindfolded, into those jillions of black balls and discovered that you had pulled out the one and only white ball, you would rightly suspect that the whole thing was rigged. If you are still skeptical, imagine that in order to stave off execution you had to succeed in doing this three times in a row. The probabilities involved would not be significantly different, but you would be nuts if you thought you had accomplished this by chance.

This example shows the way science explains how the universe (including the existence of all life on earth) came into existence. The chances that elements and pressure and energy all came together to create the cosmos as we know it, and earth as we experience it, is akin to the examples given above. This "chance" is quantified as the ability of a human pulling out the one white ball out of billions of black balls three times in a row! Or, just as impossible: the chance of winning the Mega Millions lottery every day from the time of the Big Bang until the present day. Now, as rational humans, what is easier to believe? Is it just as logical, scientifically, that God created the universe in the way the scientists say - through the Big Bang? And is it also as logically reasonable to believe that God created people in his image in a way that humans have existed over the history of people on this earth[196]? Or, keeping in mind the unthinkable odds described above, do you think it is logically reasonable that everything occurred out of nothing? And that we exist today because nothing caused a chain reaction of events in the precise way that our complex bodies function on planet earth? In your opinion, based on the evidence presented by the expert scientists and mathematicians, do you believe that God exists and that Jesus came to earth to save you from your sins or is it more likely that the universe was created out of nothing, by chance?

H. The Reliability of the Bible.

Ladies and gentlemen of the jury, as I admitted at the start of this closing argument, I do not have all the answers to the possible

---

[196]For the technology of life, the functional parts are generally proteins made up of linked chains of 20 different types of amino acids. The odds of getting a comparatively short chain of 150 amino acids to fold into any sort of useful protein, any sort of remotely possible useable part in the machinery of life, is about one in a number with 74 zeros. In the real world, those are impossible odds to overcome. It's not clear there have been that many mutations in the entire history of all life on Earth, even if you assume that life has existed for billions of years. And that's just one protein. To get any sort of new technology you need dozens or hundreds of new proteins coordinated to fit together and work together just right. The odds of doing that are less than one in a number with a thousand or so zeros, like the odds of winning a powerball lottery more than a hundred times in a row. And life has millions of different systems, technology that supposedly was created by accident, by the Darwinian process of keeping the best mistakes. Counting To God: A Personal Journey Through Science to Belief. Douglass Ell, Chapter 12

questions relating to the claims made in the Bible that God created the universe and human beings. I was not present when Jesus walked the earth proclaiming that he was God. I told you that I was unable to provide my testimony that I heard Jesus's promises of salvation.

However, I promised that I would not ask you to accept, by blind faith, the claims made by Jesus of his divinity. I said that I would not ask you to believe, by faith *alone*, in Jesus's predictions that he would be betrayed, tried, sentenced to death by crucifixion, killed, buried, and would rise from the grave. I promised you proof by documents, eyewitness testimony and expert analysis.

I have attempted to show you how the Bible is a genuine source of reliable proof of these things by providing what I believe is cogent evidence of the trustworthiness of this book, written by a succession of authors. I have provided evidence, based on trustworthy outside sources, that verifies the claims made in the Bible relating to the creation of the universe. I have shown how the life of Jesus has been documented by accepted historical texts written by non-Christians at the same time the gospels were written. These fundamental truths set forth in the Bible have been investigated by me through the microscope of history, archeology, science, and mathematics. While the claims made in these pages are subject to honest debate, I hope I have provided clear and convincing proof that the contractual guarantee of salvation recorded within the pages of the Holy Bible is true, accurate, and reliable.

If, as shown, God is the Creator of the universe and of all that exists on the earth and if, as shown, the Bible is a historically reliable source of truth; then the guarantee set forth in the pages of the Bible is a guarantee worthy of steadfast trust. There is a general trend in modern physics that indicates that the more the universe is examined, the more complex it appears to be. Scientists and mathematicians have determined that the closer they look at the universe and the deeper they penetrate the cells in our bodies, the greater the level of sophistication they find. The more deeply science probes the structure of matter, the greater mathematical order is found. The order we see in nature does not come from chaos – it is distilled out of more fundamental order.

The deeper one looks [into the universe], the more remarkable the mathematical structure one sees.

Four hundred years ago, for example, Johannes Kepler discovered three marvelous geometrical laws that describe planetary motion. So impressed was he by the beauty of these laws that he wrote this prayer in his treatise Harmonices Mundi (The harmonies of the world): 'I thank thee, Lord God our Creator, that thou hast allowed me to see the beauty in thy work of creation.' Decades later, Newton succeeded in explaining Kepler's laws but he did not explain them 'down,' if by down we mean reducing what we observe and experience to something more trivial or brutish. On the contrary, he explained them by deriving meaning from an underlying order that is more general and impressive, which we now call Newton's laws of mechanics and gravity. Newton's law of gravity was later explained, in turn, by Einstein, who showed that it followed from a more profound theory of gravity called general relativity. And it is now generally believed that Einstein's theory is but the manifestation of a yet more fundamental theory, which many suspect to be superstring theory.

Physicists have found beauty in the mathematical principles animating the physical world, from Kepler, who praised God for the elegant geometry of the planets' orbits, to Hermann Weyl, for whom mathematical physics revealed a 'flawless harmony that is in conformity with sublime Reason.' Some might suspect that this beauty is in the eye of the beholder, or that scientists think their own theories beautiful simply out of vanity. But there is a remarkable fact that suggests otherwise. Again and again throughout history, what started as pure mathematics—ideas developed solely for the sake of their intrinsic interest and elegance—turned out later to be needed to express fundamental laws of physics.[197]

The precision of the universe points to a Creator rather than to a random series of events culminating in the creation of the universe. The historical accuracy of the Bible and the testimony of eyewitnesses all point to the truth that Jesus was (and is) who He said He is – God. And God is Creator of everything!

Scientists themselves who calculate the odds of the universe coming into existence by accident suggest such boggling figures as one in 10 to the 60th. Physicist Paul Davies explains, 'To give some meaning to those numbers, suppose you wanted to fire a bullet at a one-inch target on the other side of

---

[197] Fearful Symmetries – From First Things by: Stephen M. Barr. Philip Zaleski & Philip Yancey. The Best Spiritual Writing 2012. iBooks

the observable universe, twenty billion light years away. Your aim would have to be accurate to that same part in 1060.' Stephen Hawking admits that if the rate of expansion one second after the big bang had varied by even one part in a hundred thousand million million, the universe would have recollapsed. That's only the beginning: if the nuclear force in certain atoms varied by only a few percentage points then the sun and other stars would not exist. Life on earth depends on similarly delicate fine-tuning; a tiny change in gravity, a slight tilting of earth's axis, or a small thickening in its crust would make conditions for life impossible.[198]

Impossible! The evidence that has been presented confirms the historical accuracy of the Bible. I have shown that independent historical texts confirm that the gospel accounts of the life, death, and resurrection of Jesus are accurate. As has been argued, there is no getting away from the over 500 eyewitnesses who saw Jesus before his crucifixion and then later saw the resurrected Christ. The fact that none of these eyewitnesses ever retracted their testimonies to this effect speaks volumes. The remaining eleven disciples of Jesus (a rather large conspiratorial group) never recanted their testimony. Despite the threats of imprisonment and death, not one of those who were present in the Upper Room at the Last Supper and who witnessed the death of Jesus denied the resurrection of Jesus from the dead. After Jesus appeared to his disciples and the women who were with them in His resurrected form, not one of the eleven disciples nor any of the women in the locked room (who were terrified

---

[198]Philip Yancey. Vanishing Grace. P. 178. iBooks

of persecution after the death and burial of Jesus) were afraid to go far and wide to preach the gospel of redemption by belief in Jesus.

> "...[E]ach one of the Twelve—including the three eyewitnesses of the Transfiguration—abandon Jesus in his hour of deepest need. Somehow the import of who Jesus is, God in flesh, never really sinks in until after he has left and then comes back. ... Actually, the fact of the disciples' abrupt change makes compelling evidence for Jesus's resurrection. The cowering disciples portrayed in [the Gospel of] Mark hardly resemble the bold, confident figures in the book of Acts. Something incredible had to happen to turn this bunch of bumblers into heroes of the faith." Mark 9; 1–41[199]

Therefore, ladies and gentlemen of the jury, the greater weight of all the evidence proclaims the truth of God our Creator and the biblical accounts of the life, death, and resurrection of Jesus, just as the Old Testament prophets said would happen. Science and math do not belie this truth. In fact, these branches of intellectual realism proclaim the truth contained in the biblical stories of creation and the wondrous life and time of Jesus. If these truths are valid, then the promises made by Jesus can be taken to the bank. The guarantee of salvation is real, reliable, unreproachable, and resilient.

---

[199]Philip Yancey & Brenda Quinn. Meet the Bible. P. 1604. Zondervan. iBooks.

CHAPTER NINE

WHAT DOES THE GUARANTEE PROVIDE?

Every guarantee comes with benefits. If it's the warranty you get when you buy a new car, the agreement spells out the benefits that come with the assurance that the car will work as intended for a specific time or number of miles after you get the keys. The transmission will shift the car smoothly and will work as it was designed for three years or 30,000 miles, whichever comes first. The on-board navigation screen will display the route you have selected, the air conditioner and heating will operate at the proper temperature, the engine will fire on all cylinders... you get the picture. You purchased this new car with the assurance that it will perform as advertised for a certain period of time or the dealer will fix it for free. This warranty gives you the peace of mind that you need in order to make what is often described as the second most expensive thing Americans will buy – only exceeded by the cost of a house.

When choosing to buy a car you may want to consider using the Pascal cost/benefit analysis in selecting the automobile that best fits your needs. In your evaluation you determine, for example, that a Mazda 626 provides a longer power train warranty than a Hyundai Elantra but the cost of the 626 may be 10% more than the Elantra.

When weighing the benefits of the longer power train warranty you may consider the higher purchase price of the Mazda versus the shorter warranty provided by the Hyundai[200]. This type of cost/benefit analysis gives you a better understanding of the issues involved in the decision when making this all-important purchase.

As a trial lawyer, I often would assist my clients by providing advice to enable them to determine the best type of protection needed for their business. I endeavored to help them make informed decisions by explaining the type of insurance policies on the market for the risks they may potentially have in the distribution of a particular product. In doing so, I tried to assist my clients in the selection of policies that provide protection for expected risks weighed against the costs of obtaining the indemnity that the policies cover. The clients could then rationally evaluate those risks to make an informed decision as to how much, if any, guaranteed protection they wanted to purchase.

Logically you may also want to understand God's guarantee of salvation based on the blessings that this guarantee provides. Perhaps, like Pascal, you may want to examine the cost/benefit relationship between what you are "giving up" during your lifetime if you believe in the guarantee versus what benefits you can expect. Or, like me, you may want to dream of what life on earth may hold and what eternity in heaven may be like with God's assurance firmly in hand. You may want to envision what your future may entail as you navigate life's good and bad times. Perhaps you wonder what tomorrow holds as you experience the joys and heartaches of living in an unpredictable and broken world.

---

[200]These are merely hypotheticals and do not represent the true nature of costs or warranties. How is that for lawyerly double-speak and hedging?!

To understand the benefits provided by God's guarantee of salvation we have only to look at the contract God has established for all and spelled out in the Bible. It is all there in black and white. To realize the bounty of God's blessings we will investigate God's covenant. Sometimes the terms of the contract are evident to anyone by simply finding and reading the words in the Bible. But some guarantees are more complex and contain words or phrases that are difficult to understand. In such cases perhaps you want to seek the counsel of someone who has investigated the words and studied these promises to make sense of them. Therefore, let's see what the Bible says and what some of the best scholars have opined on the subject of the benefits of the guarantee.

A. Two Guarantees

Pascal's wager considered the costs and benefits of belief in God's grant of salvation. The costs associated with the belief in Jesus and his promise of forgiveness, according to Pascal, included giving up some things and following certain commands once a person has committed his life to Christ. These things you will relinquish are: not committing adultery, loving your enemies, and treating others as you would yourself. As discussed, if a person commits to belief in Jesus and entrusts her life to Him she *surrenders* herself to love the Savior. Believers love Jesus by doing as He asked. Believers are known by the fruit of the spirit. The one who loves God will care for others as themselves. They give their time and money, they worship and pray. These are all of the things that Pascal hypothesized a believer would expend in costs. Pascal did, however, mention that these costs could also be viewed as benefits because they actually resulted in living a better life. Pascal noted that by not committing adultery, not lying, and by giving oneself to others,[201] believers were actually receiving the benefits of living a good life. It should also be mentioned that these hallmarks of living a Christian life are not exclusive to believers. Non-believers often follow biblical principles without committing themselves to a life of following Christ.

When examining the benefits of the guarantee we must consider two essential hallmarks of the guarantee. The first, as I have discussed, is the guarantee of salvation (John 3:16). This guarantee comes to fruition upon our death. However, God also so loved the world that He provided us with a *helper* during our lifetime. "The giving of the Spirit suggests the realization of the future divine blessings in one's present experience"[202] (John 7:38-39; 16:7; 20:22-23). Jesus assured us that while his work on the earth would end in his death and resurrection, He was going to give us the indwelling presence of God in the form of the Holy Spirit. Jesus describes this as the "Counselor," a Spirit to guide us during our life.

As you know, lawyers and psychologists are also described as counselors. In this role, they give guidance on legal or psychological problems. Jesus was quoted as saying in John chapter 16 that the Counselor will "convict the world of guilt in regard to sin and righteousness and judgment..." What this means is that the Holy Spirit will open our eyes to what is right and wrong and, in doing

---

[201]Studies have shown that people who give to charitable organizations and give of their time to others in need actually live a happier, healthier and longer life. "Many studies point to the possible positive consequences of generosity for the giver. Giving social support—time, effort, or goods—is associated with better overall health in older adults, and volunteering is associated with delayed mortality. Generosity appears to have especially strong associations with psychological health and well-being." According to a white paper prepared for the John Templeton Foundation by the Greater Good Science Center at UC Berkeley. May 2018

[202]Lee Martin MacDonald, The Story of Jesus in History and Faith, iBooks

so, guide us on the path that God wants us to follow. Jesus describes this guide as someone to be with us at all times, helping us in our journey of faith. David S. Dockery defines it this way:

> The Counselor, the Spirit of truth, teaches and reminds believers regarding the things of Jesus Christ. This teaching and this reminding are done in close connection with Jesus, just as Jesus had carried out his mission in conjunction with the Father. The [Counselor] leads believers into all truth and presents this truth in light of the resurrection. The Spirit, who defended the disciples in the Synoptics (see Mark 13:11), is the defender of the truth about Jesus in John.[203]

Jesus inspired the disciples to follow Him by direct examples and by modeling behavior. Jesus, during His ministry on earth, expressly taught the disciples by living a holy life and by giving them instructions and lessons in the form of parables. These educational examples, often crafted through parables, also included direct teachable moments.

At the end of Jesus's ministry, he conferred the Holy Spirit, the Counselor, on the disciples. After His resurrection from the dead Jesus appeared to the disciples "on the evening of the first day of the week." As we know, Jesus had already appeared to the women who came on Sunday to attend to his entombed body. They related the story of Jesus's appearance, in bodily form, to the disciples who immediately rejected the notion of Jesus's resurrection. That next day, Jesus came to the disciples who were locked away in a hidden

---

[203]https://www.biblestudytools.com/dictionary/counselor/

room, frightened that they would be sought out and arrested. The disciples were astonished when He appeared to them, despite the locked doors. However, upon recognizing Jesus, they were overjoyed. They marveled at the resurrected Jesus when he exhibited the punctures in His hands and feet and the cavity that was left when His side was pierced by the soldier's lance. After Jesus wished them, "Peace," He reminded them that he was entrusting His ministry to them. They were to carry His message to all the world.

However, Jesus knew that such a mission was fraught with uncertainty on the part of the disciples and anxiety over this very important task to which they were assigned. Therefore, He left them with the Holy Spirit, who would fill them with hope and a feeling of confidence and support. After exhibiting His scars to the disciples-in-hiding, His very next words were, "receive the Holy Spirit" (John 20:19-21). Jesus was giving his disciples (and by inheritance to all believers) the Holy Spirit, the Counselor, to guide them (and us) in their walk of faith.

Jesus must have realized that since we are constantly in a state of sin and temptation, we need the power of the Holy Spirit to dwell within us to give us strength to overcome the things that pull us away from God. The apostle Paul addressed this very problem in chapter eight of the book of Romans. In this chapter, he tried to explain the purpose and power of the Holy Spirit. In his letters to the church in Rome, he gave those new Christians hope that their sins would be forgiven and that the presence of the Spirit in a person's soul can fortify him against the wages of sin.

> First, Paul sets to rest the nagging problem of sin he has just raised so forcefully [in the preceding chapters of the Book of Romans]. "There is now no condemnation...," he announces. Jesus Christ, through

his life and death, took care of "the sin problem" for all time. Elsewhere (ch. 4), Paul borrows a word from banking to explain the process. God "credits" Jesus's own perfection to our accounts, so that we are judged not by our behavior but by his. Similarly, God has transferred all the punishment we deserve onto Jesus, through his death on the cross. In this transaction, human beings come out the clear winners, set free at last from the curse of sin.[204]

As Paul explains, the indwelling of the Holy Spirit does not prevent all sin from entering our lives and does not prevent the temptation of sin from luring us away from the narrow path (through belief in Jesus) that leads to salvation. This Counselor, however, can act like a trusted attorney to warn you of the dangers of breaking the law (of God) and the consequences of doing so. "The God within" can do for us what we could never do for ourselves. The Spirit works alongside us as we relate to God, helping us in our weakness, even praying for us when we don't know what to ask.

It is written, "I believed; therefore I have spoken." With that same spirit of faith we also believe and therefore speak, because we know that the one who raised the Lord Jesus from the dead will also raise us with Jesus and present us with you in his presence...we groan and are burdened, because we do not wish to be unclothed but to be clothed with our heavenly dwelling, so that what is mortal may be swallowed up by life. Now it is God who has

---

[204]Philip Yancey & Brenda Quinn. "Meet the Bible." P. 1972. Zondervan. iBooks.

made us for this very purpose and has given us the Spirit as a deposit, **guaranteeing what is to come.** 2 Corinthians 4:1–5:10, NIV, emphasis added.

This indwelling guarantee of the Holy Counselor is one of the primary benefits of the guarantee of salvation. The Holy Spirit is like an insurance policy we need to be Christ's representatives on earth and to enable us to love God with confidence. To love Him with all our mind, body, and spirit. [205]

> [On] Pentecost, the disciples get what they have been waiting for. The Holy Spirit, the presence of God himself, takes up residence inside ordinary bodies—their bodies. The disciples hit the streets with a bold new style that the world has never recovered from. Soon everyone in Jerusalem is talking about the Jesus followers. Clearly, something is afoot. To their amazement, pilgrims from all over the world hear the Galileans' message in their own native languages. Peter, coward apostle who denied Christ three times to save his own neck, brazenly takes on both Jewish and Roman authorities. Quoting from King David and the prophet Joel, he proclaims that his audience has just lived through the most important event of all history. "God has raised this Jesus to life, and we are all witnesses of the fact[206]," he says and goes on to declare Jesus as the very Messiah, the fulfillment of the

---

[205]Supra.

[206]Again, referring to the Apostles and the people in the audience as eye-witnesses

Jews' long-awaited dream. Three thousand people respond to Peter's powerful message on that first day. And thus the Christian church is born.[207]

The first prong of the guarantee, as I have discussed thus far, is the guarantee of salvation. This guarantee provides a "get-out-of-hell-free card." As a civil trial lawyer representing a client accused of wrongdoing, my job was to obtain a "defense verdict" in a trial. If I did my job, the jury would find that the plaintiff (who is accusing my client of negligence and resulting damages) is not entitled to a judgment. This is the equivalent of a judgment of acquittal in a criminal trial. If the jury finds the defendant in a criminal case *not guilty* of the crime, he is acquitted of the charges and released from jail. The guarantee of salvation works this way. The benefit conferred on a believer is akin to being acquitted of the sin that convicts our soul.

B. Forgiveness of Debts

How wonderful would it be if you received an unexpected certified letter in the mail one day? "I am the attorney for the estate of your great-Aunt Millie" the letter begins, "and I am pleased to inform you that Ms. Millie has been watching your life from afar." The attorney explains that she "has recently died of natural causes at the age of ninety-five and has specified in her will that your mortgage, car loan, your children's educational loans, and your credit card debt are to be paid in full." The lawyer goes on to say that "Ms. Millie wanted you to be freed from the burden of your debts and wishes you and your family a happy and healthy life." The attorney

---

[207]Philip Yancey & Brenda Quinn. "Meet the Bible." P. 1777-78. Zondervan. iBooks.

The Guarantee

encloses a satisfaction of debt receipt showing that all your outstanding debts have been canceled. Wouldn't that be a nice surprise? As mentioned earlier, the penalty of sin is death. (Romans 6:23.) The judgment that would be rendered for our sin, therefore, would be the finding of guilt and would warrant the imposition of the death penalty. This means that sin separates us from God and bars us from eternal life. The need to be found innocent is therefore conditioned on either not ever committing a sin (which is impossible) or being forgiven of the sin by God (our judge). These are the only two ways to be granted an acquittal. I like the way John F. MacArthur described this process.

> Forgiveness...a permanent and complete acquittal from the guilt and ultimate penalty of sin - belongs to all who are in Christ (cf. John 5:24; Rom. 8:1; Eph. 1:7). Yet Scripture also teaches that God chastens His children who disobey (Heb. 12:5–7). Believers are to confess their sins in order to obtain a day-to-day cleansing (1 John 1:9). This sort of forgiveness is a simple washing from the worldly defilements of sin, not a repeat of the wholesale cleansing from sin's corruption that comes with justification. It is like a washing of the feet rather than a bath (cf. John 13:10).[208]

The center point of the guarantee of eternal rewards, therefore, is forgiveness. Forgiveness is a primary benefit that is conferred by the guarantee. Since we can never be sin-free, we must be able to be acquitted of the sin that infects us. Without the promise that all

---

[208]One Perfect Life, Part V, notes. iBooks

our sins will be forgiven, we will forever be prevented from reunification with God, our Creator. The written covenant that God has given provides the peace of mind that we will not only be forgiven, but that God will not hold the sins we have committed over our heads as a looming sentence. We are assured of this because God not only forgives...but forgets. As King David said in Psalm 103, God removes our sin from our ledger "as far as the east is from the west, so far has he removed our transgressions from us." "But now He has appeared ***once for all*** at the end of the ages to do away with sin by the sacrifice of Himself" (Hebrews 9:26, NIV), emphasis added. Philip Yancey phrases this hallmark of the guarantee as follows:

> "Shusaku Endo, the Christian novelist from Japan, centered many of his novels on the theme of betrayal. To Endo, the most powerful message of Jesus was his unquenchable love, even for - especially for - people who betrayed Him. When Judas led a lynch mob into the garden, Jesus (seeing his betrayer with the mob close behind) addressed him as 'friend'. During the ordeal of a trial, the mocking heaped upon Jesus by the soldiers and the awful death on a cross, the remaining disciples deserted Jesus despite their constant assurances that this would never happen. And what was Jesus's response? He still loved them. His own nation (Israel) had him executed. Yet, while stretched out naked on the cross in posture of ultimate disgrace, Jesus roused himself for the cry, 'Father, forgive them.'[209]

---

[209]Philip Yancey. The Jesus I Never Knew. P. 193-94. iBooks

Isn't that remarkable? One of the very last things Jesus said before He died was a request that God forgive the very people who were executing him. This request was something Jesus absolutely was sure would be granted. We know this from everything Jesus said during His ministry. The greatest example of this was the statement Jesus made when He performed perhaps His greatest miracle – the raising of Lazarus from the grave four days after he died. Jesus, in affirming the power God gave Him to raise people from the dead, said, "Father, I thank you that you ***have heard*** me. I knew that you **always** hear me, but I said this for the benefit of the people standing here, that they may believe that you sent me" (John 11:41-42, NIV), emphasis added. Jesus uses the past-tense "have heard" and the definitive "always" in describing the power of prayer and the guarantee of forgiveness. We should, therefore, be confident in all the power that Jesus possessed.

God has a great capacity for forgiveness, in fact, an unlimited capacity. The Bible is filled with instance after repeated instance of God forgiving the sins of mankind. "The book of Jonah powerfully expresses God's yearning to forgive, and these two brief chapters fill in the lesser-known details of Jonah's mission. To the prophet's disgust, a simple announcement of doom sparks a spiritual revival in pagan Nineveh. And Jonah, sulking under a shriveled vine, admits he has suspected God's soft heart all along. He could not trust God; could not, that is, trust him to be harsh and unrelenting toward Nineveh. As Robert Frost so eloquently says in his poetic drama, *A Masque of Mercy*, "After Jonah, you could never trust God not to be merciful again." What a great way of putting it! We can never fail to trust God's capacity for forgiveness.

How comforting is the guarantee of forgiveness to a sinner like me! Someone who sins every day, asks for forgiveness every night, and then commits the same sins again the next day! Jesus was God's ultimate answer for repeat offenders. C.S. Lewis put it this way: "What God does for us, He does in us. The process of doing it will appear to me (and not falsely) to be the daily or hourly repeated exercises of my own will in renouncing this attitude, especially each morning, for it grows all over me like a new shell each night. Failures will be forgiven; it is acquiescence that is fatal, the permitted, regularized presence of an area in ourselves which we still claim for our own. We may never, this side of death, drive the invader out of our territory, but we must be in the Resistance, not in the Vichy government."[210]

God has fashioned a way to eternally forgive our sins. He paid a hefty penalty for our sins. He allowed his one and only Son to suffer the humiliation of taking on a human form. Jesus gave up his position at the right hand of God to become human and to suffer human frailties. God permitted mankind to heap all of its sin on the back of His Son, like a scapegoat. Jesus gave license to the Roman and Jewish authorities to convene a Kangaroo Court of "justice" to convict an innocent man and impose a death sentence so cruel that it is hard to even imagine. God let His Son die a horrible death. He decreed these things because he has an unlimited capacity for forgiveness. How else can this be explained?

Another way to view the benefits of the guarantee is to think of sin as a debt that we owe God. When I was a kid my mom would use a device for paying off debt known as a "layaway plan." If my mom wanted, for instance, to buy train set for me for Christmas she would go to the five-and-dime store three months before Christmas and put some money down to hold the trains. She would pay some money each week to the store until the price of the train set was paid in full. Once that happened, my mom would pick up this cherished

---

[210]"A Slip of the Tongue (The Weight of Glory)"

toy that I wanted for Christmas, wrap it and place this present under the tree for an excited son to open on Christmas Day.

Jesus is the answer to our layaway plan of sin-debt. He paid the ultimate price for our sins on Good Friday. Once that was accomplished, God marked our debt "paid in full" and gave us the gift of salvation.

Sin is a debt that only Jesus can pay and only God can forgive. Billy Graham tells a story that illustrates, for me, a person who knows he has the guarantee and therefore has no fear of death. It goes like this:

> Some time ago a Christian workman was fatally injured when he fell from a high scaffolding on a construction job. A minister was called, and when he saw the serious condition of the man, he said, "My dear man, I'm afraid you're dying. I exhort you, make your peace with God!" "Make my peace with God, sir!" said the man. "Why, that was made nineteen hundred years ago when my Savior paid all my debt upon the cross. Christ is my peace, and I do know God—I do know God!"[211]

What a great example of a man who positively understands that he has been freed from the debt of sin. This was a person who knows he is dying but also knows that he is forgiven because his sin-debt has already been paid in full.

A number of years ago I had the opportunity to travel with three of my dear friends on a fly-fishing trip to Goose Bay, Canada. We had been planning this trip for years. Goose Bay was one of the

---

[211]Billy Graham, *The Secret of Happiness.* Chapter 8, iBooks

Holy Grails for fly fishermen. It took us a full day to fly from our home cities in the United States to Nova Scotia. We all arrived by supper and spent the night at a hotel, before flying to Goose Bay the next morning. This very remote area of the world, however, was only our launching point for the final destination. In Goose Bay, we boarded a 1953 Otter seaplane for a noisy two-hour flight further into the wilderness of northeastern Canada. We eventually landed on a lake with one small building - the first structure we had seen in over an hour. After the water landing, we taxied to a dock and were greeted by a man and woman who would be our caretakers for the next five days. The remote wilderness was a fitting environment for four good buddies to sit on the deck overlooking the lake after dinner and philosophize about the meaning of life. We were all trial lawyers from the four corners of America and we came together with our thoughts.

After a number of glasses of red wine and cigars, numerous tall tales of adventure and interesting jury trials spilled out. We enjoyed each story with nods of our heads and smiles of delight. Before long, however, the laughter subsided and our discussion turned serious. We were all very like-minded. Each man was committed to doing good in the world. Each one of us loved our wives, our children, and our jobs. Each was involved in his community and profession. We led good lives and had achieved a modicum of success.

However, when the subject of death reared its head we realized that we were not all the same. My friend from Texas and I professed an unwavering belief that death was nothing to be feared. Death did not scare us. It was just a gateway to eternal life. It was the path to being reunited with our Creator. Death was the beginning of an existence where all fear, anxiety, pain, and sorrow were banished forever. My wonderful friends from Michigan and California expressed just the opposite view. They confessed that death was the thing they feared most. They both firmly believed that death was the end. Two of us were committed Christians and the other two described themselves as an atheist and an agnostic. Even though my buddy from Texas and I were sinners – the same as our good friends from California and Michigan – we had the "peace that surpasses all understanding"[212]. We *knew* that our debts had already been paid. We *had* the guarantee firmly in hand.

Nothing, not even death, was frightening to us because we knew that eternity awaited. Why should we be afraid of a point in time (our deaths) when we were certain that there was no end? Why should we be afraid of transitioning from a place where sin, anxiety, and pain were part of our lives to a place where there is no more suffering, pain, anxiety, envy, conflict, or strife? Why be fearful? C.S. Lewis, in the book, *Miracles*, described the lack of hold death has over us as follows:

> On the one hand Death is the triumph of Satan, the punishment of the Fall, and the last enemy. Christ shed tears at the grave of Lazarus and sweated blood in Gethsemane: the Life of Lives that was in Him detested this penal obscenity not less than we do, but more. On the other hand, only he who loses his life will save it. We are baptized into the death of Christ, and it is the remedy for the Fall. Death is, in fact, what some modern people call 'ambivalent'. It is Satan's great weapon and also God's great weapon: it is holy and unholy; our supreme disgrace and our

---

[212]Philippians 4:7

only hope; the thing Christ came to conquer and the means by which He conquered. [213]

Philip Yancey echoes this way of looking at sin and death when he says,

> Jesus was God's way of paying sin's debt once and for all, and his death on the cross gives us the greatest picture of God's grace and his love for us. God has every reason to walk away from us because of our failures at loving him well. Instead, through Jesus, he walks toward us and forever silences our pleas for mercy. Jesus is our picture of a holy, loving God who draws believers near once and forever.[214]

When you realize that your debt to God, which was caused by your sin, has been paid, you have no fear of death. *Death, where is thy sting?* 1 Corinthians 15:55 KJV. "Somehow, in Gethsemane Jesus worked through a crisis by transferring the burden to the Father. It was God's will he had come to do, after all, and his prayer resolved into the words, 'Yet not as I will, but as you will' (Matt. 26:39)."[215]

I long for the internal fortitude to have that type of trust, that type of faith. So did Yancey. He said that he prayed for "that sense of detachment, of trust. I pray that I could see my work, my life, as an offering to God each day. God alone is qualified to help me negotiate the slippery path between love for others and love for myself." Through Jesus, God transferred the burden of the debt of sin from

---

[213]C. S. Lewis. "A Year with C. S. Lewis." P. 234. HarperCollins. iBooks.

[214]Philip Yancey & Brenda Quinn. "Meet the Bible." P. 1333. Zondervan. iBooks.

[215]Philip Yancey. Church: Why Bother? P. 98. iBooks

us to His Son. No longer will sin be an anchor around our necks. No longer will our transgressions be held against us. No longer will we fear death.

Max Lucado, in his book about the fears we have, came to this conclusion about the fear of death. "Someday we will all stand before God. All of us will be present. All of us will have to give an account for our lives. Every thought, every deed, every action. Were it not for the grace of Christ, I would find this to be a terrifying thought. Yet, according to Scripture, Jesus came to 'take away the sins of the world' (John 1:29). On the day when I appear before the judgment seat of God, I will point to Christ. When my list of sins is produced, I will gesture toward him and say, 'He took it.'"[216] Jesus took the fall for our sins. He paid the price and bore the burden for us.

That prepaid forgiveness is the greatest benefit conferred by the guarantee of salvation. It qualifies us for an eternal reward because it pays, in full, our heavy debt of sin.

C. Healing and Cleansing

Sin takes a toll on our lives. It causes heartache, headache, and bellyaches. It breaks hearts and results in broken marriages. It leads to stress and anxiety. And, foremost, it causes a chasm to form between God and His creation. In order for all of these things to heal, we need three things. First and foremost, we need God to forgive us. And, just as importantly, we need to forgive others. Lastly, we need to forgive ourselves! The guarantee allows us to do all these things because it cleanses our bodies of the stain of sin.

The apostle Paul reminds us that God wants us to "[g]et rid of all bitterness, rage, and anger, brawling and slander, along with every

---

[216]*Anxious for Nothing.* P. 45. iBooks

form of malice" (Eph. 4:31, NIV). This is the type of forgiveness that cleans and heals in order for us to offer forgiveness to others. This type of forgiveness heals our neighbors, our loved ones, and our enemies. This, Paul said, will make us like Christ. "Be kind and compassionate to one another, forgiving each other just as in Christ God forgave you" (Eph. 4:32, NIV). Now that is a tall order.

From the book of Matthew, a parable was told by Jesus about forgiving others in the same manner as God has done for us. It is called the *parable of the servant*. Jesus is triggered to use this parable to teach when Peter asked him, How many times must I forgive another... "up to seven times?" Jesus, responding to this question, gives him an answer that floored both Peter and the rest of the disciples. Matthew 18:21-22, NIV tells us, "Peter was a devout Jew, and as such, he knew all about the rabbinical teaching on forgiveness. It was a settled rule that forgiveness should not be extended more than three times. Therefore, if a good Jew extended forgiveness three times, he was fulfilling the rabbinical teaching. For the religious Jew in Jesus's day forgiveness had become like everything else in religious life, a rule, an act, a performance. Forgiveness was never an expression of the heart, or of reconciliation or love – it was just a rule."[217] Jesus, who came to break the stereotypes associated with a rules-based faith, answered Peter's question directly. "I tell you, not seven times, but seventy times seven." That radical forgiveness is the type of forgiveness (and more) that God gives us. And just the type of forgiveness that I need for my constant cycle of sin!

But Jesus did not stop there. He told Peter and the disciples the story of the unmerciful servant. This servant owed a large sum of money. Unable to pay, he went to the person he was indebted to

---

[217]Alan Wilson, Hamilton Road Baptist Church, Bangor, Maine. http://www.contemporarychristianity.net/econiroot/LionLamb/027/forgive.html

and asked for forgiveness of the debt that he had accrued. In Jesus's time, if the debtor couldn't pay his debt, he would have been thrown in a debtor's prison. In fact, this servant's debt was so high that he, his wife, and children could be sold to pay for the debt. Knowing this, the servant threw himself "upon the mercy of the court" (in this case the holder of the debt – the creditor). He begged for the forgiveness of his debt.

The creditor heard his plea and was moved. Instead of prison, the creditor showed the servant grace and forgave the entirety of his debt. The servant was jubilant and went away toward home counting his blessing of forgiveness. On his way home to tell the good news to his family, this debtor came upon a person who owed him money. This person owed the unmerciful servant far less than he had owed his creditor. Upon hearing that the debtor could not repay the meager sum owed, the unmerciful servant "grabbed him and began to choke him." The debtor who owed this small sum broke the chokehold, fell to his knees, and begged for mercy and forgiveness. And how did the unmerciful servant respond? He refused and had the debtor thrown in prison. Later, upon hearing of the servant's refusal to show mercy on his debtor, the man who forgave the unmerciful servant's debt called the servant to appear before him and explain. "Shouldn't you have had mercy on your fellow servant just as I had on you?" he exclaimed. Having no answer to give, the unmerciful servant was punished and turned over to the jailers.

Jesus then turned to Peter and his fellow disciples and said "[t] his is how my heavenly father will treat each of you unless you forgive your brother from your heart." Matthew 18:35. Jesus is telling each of us that we are not fully cleansed and healed of our own sins unless we show our neighbors and debtors the same forgiveness and mercy that God gives us.

Each of us can recite the Lord's prayer, "Our Father, who art in heaven" from memory. It is drilled into us as kids and we recite it on cue. But, how many of us stop and listen to each word? How many of us blindly recite this most common (yet wonderful) prayer that Jesus taught us? It is the only prayer Jesus asked us to pray, yet we treat it in a cavalier manner. In this prayer, we ask God to forgive our sins. But the prayer doesn't stop there. We also ask God to forgive us "*as we forgive others.*" Do we really mean that? What if we treated others like the unmerciful servant treated the person who owed him money? Is that the type of forgiveness we are asking God to give us? I certainly hope not. The parallel passage in Luke 11:4 uses a word that means "sins." Therefore, in this context "debts" actually mean spiritual debts. "Sinners are debtors to God for their violations of His laws (cf. Matt. 18:23–27). This request is the heart of the prayer..."[218]

There are certain things we do each day to cleanse ourselves. We wash our face, brush our teeth and take a shower or bath. No matter how we spend our day, working outside at a construction job or inside in an office, we need to clean ourselves regularly. Cleaning in these ways not only provides the benefit of good hygiene but also makes us feel good and refreshed.

Our daily sins must be attended to in the same way. We need to cleanse sin's stain on our souls each day. When we do this, our spiritual hygiene is served and we feel refreshed. The mark of sin is removed from our hearts. Jesus provided a way for the grime of sin to be washed from our souls. His atoning death on the cross washed away the scourge of sin through the mechanism of substitutional sacrifice. His death allowed us to purge sin from our lives by a simple, but important, process. Once we have accepted Jesus as *the* way for

---

[218]John F. MacArthur. One Perfect Life. Part V, Notes. iBooks

forgiveness to cleanse us of sin, all we have to do is sincerely place our sins before God and ask that He remove them from our soul. Once this has been done, God not only forgives but forgets our transgressions. Hebrews 8:12, Isaiah 43:25, NIV.

At the last supper, Jesus humbled himself by washing the feet of his disciples. In doing so he impressed upon them not only a servant's heart but the power of forgiveness. When it was Peter's turn to have his feet washed, he asked Jesus why a lowly sinner such as himself should have his feet washed by his Lord. In response, Jesus said, "Unless I wash you, you have no part with Me." If we do not accept the cleansing forgiveness of Jesus's death for us we can have no part of eternal life with Him. "The cleansing that Christ does at salvation never needs to be repeated – atonement is complete at that point. But all who have been cleansed by God's gracious justification need constant washing in the experiential sense as they battle sin in the flesh. Believers are justified and granted imputed righteousness (Phil. 3:8-9) but still need sanctification and personal righteousness (Phil. 3:12-14)."[219] In other words, the guarantee of salvation provides an unconditional grant of forgiveness made possible by the payment Jesus made on the cross. This provision of the covenant (contract) is a benefit that is provided by the guarantee. There are no conditions, exceptions, or limitations on forgiveness. All one must do to utilize this conferred benefit of cleansing is to continually ask for forgiveness, knowing that all those heartfelt requests will be granted.

The author of the book of Hebrews reminds us that we must be cleansed of our sins to enter the kingdom of heaven. We "have been made holy through the sacrifice of the body of Jesus Christ once for all ...Therefore, brothers, since we have *confidence* to enter the Most

---

[219]Supra., Part IX Notes.

Holy Place by the blood of Jesus, by a new and living way opened for us through the curtain, that is, his body, and since we have a great priest over the house of God, let us draw near to God with a sincere heart in *full assurance* of faith, having our hearts sprinkled to cleanse us from a guilty conscience and having our bodies washed with pure water" (Heb. 10:19–23). [220] Cleansing of sin's stain on our soul is, therefore, a primary benefit of the guarantee.

D. Mercy

As the parable of the unmerciful servant so forcefully illustrates, mercy and forgiveness go hand in hand. God shows, throughout the Old and New Testaments, the power of mercy to people who do not *deserve* or *earn* the right to receive this most precious gift. The story of Joseph and his coat of many colors (referenced also in chapter six) is just one of those examples. One of Billy Graham's secrets of happiness is the gift of mercy. Reverend Graham talks of this gift as God's way of showing a sinful world that He loves us and wants to be close to us.

> Perhaps no more beautiful illustration of it exists in the Bible (apart from God's mercy to us in Christ) than that of Joseph and his undeserving brothers.
>
> ...
>
> Where vengeance and just retribution were certainly justified, Joseph showed only mercy and

---

[220]Philip Yancey & Brenda Quinn. "Meet the Bible." P.2133. Zondervan. iBooks. Emphasis added.

loving kindness. In fact, he says to his apprehensive brothers (in Genesis 50), "...ye thought evil against me; but God meant it unto good...Now therefore fear ye not: I will nourish you, and your little ones. And he comforted them, and spake kindly unto them" (vv. 20–21). What mercy!

...

If we have no mercy toward others, that is one proof that we have never experienced God's mercy. Mercy Is Not Self-Centered to paraphrase this Beatitude we might say, "They which have obtained mercy from God are so happy that they are merciful to others."

...

Jesus is emphasizing the fact that we are to be unchoked channels through which His love and mercy flow out to other people. You become an instrument of mercy, compassion, and love through which He manifests Himself to the world

...

If we embrace a spiritual, aesthetic gospel only and disregard our obligation to our fellowmen, we annul it all. The gospel of the New Testament can come into full blossom only when the seed of the Spirit is buried in the rich soil of human mercy. [221]

The guarantee of salvation is therefore inextricably tied to mercy. God grants us salvation because He is merciful. Because He is merciful He forgave our sins. He forgave our sins through the atoning death of His Son on the cross. God had every right to condemn us for our sins. God is totally and completely righteous and therefore our sin sentences us to death. However, He is also merciful and therefore grants us His grace. This grace is the vehicle through which we are forgiven through belief in Jesus. Once forgiven, death no longer has a hold on us. The apostle Paul writing to the church in Rome starts his letter by saying that "there is now no condemnation for those" who believe in Christ. Romans 8:11.

Remember that the former Saul of Tarsus actually met the resurrected Christ and was converted into an evangelist. "In Romans 8, Paul sets to rest the nagging problem of sin he just raised so forcefully...Jesus Christ, through His life and death, took care of 'the sin problem' for all time."[222] Yancey goes on to explain how that occurred. "God 'credits' Jesus's own perfection to our accounts, so that we are judged not by our behavior but by his. Similarly, God transferred all the punishment we deserve onto Jesus, through his death on the cross. Romans chapter 8 ends with a ringing declaration that nothing – absolutely nothing – can ever separate us from God's love."[223]

When we are forgiven, we are freed of sin's hold over us and thus we are reunited with God. The guarantee provides us the blessed

---

[221]Billy Graham, The Secret of Happiness. Chapter Six. iBooks

[222]Philip Yancey. Meet the Bible. P. 596. iBooks

[223]Supra.

assurance that we will never be separated from God's loving arms again. That is the purest definition of mercy that has ever existed! The mercy that comes with the guarantee is a precious gift of immeasurable value.

E. Redemption

Growing up in Florida in the early 1960's involved going to the grocery store with my grandmother and mom. They went to Winn Dixie food stores because of the S&H Green Stamps that were provided at checkout. As a perk of shopping there, Winn Dixie would give Green Stamps to shoppers based on how much they spent. After coming home and putting away the groceries, I was assigned the wonderful "chore" of putting these stamps in a coupon book that the store also provided. I would lick the back of the stamps and place them in the book, page by page, until the Quick Saver Book was filled. The larger the denomination of stamps, the quicker it would fill up the pages of the book. Mom and Grandma also had catalogs that Winn Dixie would supply that would exhibit, within their pages, various items that could be exchanged for the filled stamp books. The books were the currency that we used to get electric coffee pots, waffle irons, and various household items. We would go to the local Redemption Center to exchange the completed books for our treasures. What fun my mother and grandmother would have filling the books and deciding on the items we could get in exchange.

Christ is known by many names, but one of the most important was the "Redeemer."[224] He was the Green Stamp payment for the

---

[224] See e.g. Isaiah 47:4, Psalm 19:14, Psalm 78:35, Deuteronomy 24:18, Romans 3:23-24, Galatians 4:4-5, Ephesians 1:13-14

redemption of the world. The redemptive death and resurrection of Christ is yet another benefit conferred by the guarantee. Like all sinners, we need to be redeemed from our wayward paths and placed on the road to heaven. Christ's death and resurrection redeemed us from sin's hold over us. We did not have to pay for our freedom.

F. Grace

The most extravagant benefit conferred by the guarantee is God's amazing grace. Grace is perhaps best described as the other side of the coin that holds mercy. Grace and mercy are the two sides of the same coin. The best part of grace is that it is something that cannot be bought, earned, or obtained by status in life. You can do nothing to "merit" grace. You can't redeem grace at the Green Stamps catalog store because you can never collect enough stamps for the price of grace. It is priceless.

"While everyone desperately needs it, grace is not about us. Grace is fundamentally a word about God: his un-coerced initiative and pervasive, extravagant demonstrations of care and favor. Michael Horton writes, "In grace, God gives nothing less than Himself. Grace, then, is not a third thing or substance mediating between God and sinners, but is Jesus Christ in redeeming action."[225]

The most poignant example of grace, in my opinion, is Jesus's parable of the Prodigal Son. In this story, Jesus focuses on the younger of two sons of a wealthy landowner. When I first read this story, I was confused. I identified with the eldest son and not the prodigal son. This is not only because I am the oldest of three children in my family but because, by my nature, I am a rule follower. I saw a bit of myself in the firstborn son, who stayed on the family

---

[225]Justin Holcomb, "What is Grace?". *Christianity Today*, January 23, 2013

land, worked hard, obeyed his father, and respected his father's authority. The oldest boy was the one who did as he was asked and took care of his chores. The younger brother was the free spirit, a renegade. He decided to "sow his wild oats" by asking his father for his inheritance early. He then took his newfound riches, left home, and kicked up his heels. He visited a far-off country and spent his money on wine, women and song. He never looked back. In doing so, he went through all of his inheritance and wound up penniless. The very definition of "prodigal" is one who spends money freely and recklessly. Someone who is "wastefully extravagant."

He sunk so low that he was forced into indentured servitude – subjected to feeding the pigs. "He longed to fill his stomach with the pods that the pigs were eating, but no one gave him anything" (Luke 15: 11-31, NIV). He finally hit rock bottom. His heart was broken and regret was now in his belly. He realized that he must now humble himself and repent. He decided to "go back to [his] father". And so, his long journey back to his family began. He was ashamed and emotionally damaged, afraid of what most assuredly would await him when he returned home. All these years away from his father and brother and he never sent so much as a card or letter. *How would he be treated upon his return?* he worried. He would most assuredly get the treatment he deserved, he thought, and be shunned, ridiculed, and punished. He would reap what he had sowed.

"But while he was still a long way off, his father saw him and was filled with compassion for him; he ran to his son, threw his arms around him and kissed him." (v. 20) The son knew he did not merit this reception. In fact, he deserved just the opposite. *How can this be?* the boy asked himself. He collapsed in his father's arms and pled for mercy. "Father I have sinned against heaven and against you." With all sincerity, he admitted, "I am no longer worthy to be called your son". (v. 21) His father would have none of this. Instead, much to the prodigal son's surprise, the father ordered that his youngest son be clothed in the "best robe" and as an outward symbol of his son's identity, he had a signet ring placed on his finger. What's more, his father ordered that a great feast would be given in honor of the prodigal son's return. A celebration was planned, "[f]or this son of mine was dead and is alive again; he was lost and now is found." What this prodigal son had done to his father was detestable. He squandered the family fortune. He consorted with prostitutes. He turned his back on the man who brought him into the world and raised him. This son disrespected the family name, spent his money on booze and women of the night, and ended up in the gutter.

On the other side of the farm, the eldest son was toiling away, doing his father's work. He was probably mending fences, tending to the flocks and crops. He was following his father's directions. This "good" son had done nothing to disobey or disrespect his dad. He had never taken a penny of his inheritance. He had done just the opposite – he worked hard on the family farm. From the other side of the farm, he heard all the commotion and went to see what was going on. He smelled the delicious scent of meat roasting on an open spit and heard the joyous sounds of music floating across the fields. "So he called to one of the servants and asked what was going on" (v. 26). The servant told him that his deadbeat brother had slunk back home. But the next words hit the eldest brother like a ton of bricks. "[Y]our father has killed the fatted calf because he has him back safe and sound." He thought to himself, *what? That derelict? He didn't even let us know where he was and what he was up to. We had to hear the stories of his drunken carousing from strangers. He was an embarrassment to our family. And now this? A celebration?* The good son was furious!

He stomped his feet and refused to join in the banquet. He went to his father and demanded an answer. All the time the youngest son was gone, he, the firstborn, did everything the father had asked. "I have been slaving for you and never disobeyed your orders," he screamed. And what did I get in return? "You never even gave me a young goat so I could celebrate with my friends" (v. 29). But the eldest son did not stop there. He reminded his father that the younger brother blew through his father's money and spent it on prostitutes and liquor. After listening to all of this the father, in response, modeled the type of grace that only the one wronged can provide. "My son," the loving father said, "you are always with me and everything I have is yours." But when one who is lost has returned and repented it is time to welcome him home and celebrate.

This is the great unmerited gift of grace!

Philip Yancey wrote an entire book on the subject called *What's So Amazing About Grace*. This title, playing off one of the most famous of all Christian hymns, provides an in-depth look at God's over-arching grace. To paraphrase his explanation of the lack of proportionality of grace versus our transgressions, he tries to compare what we deserve as opposed to what God grants. Just like the prodigal son, we do not deserve to be welcomed back into a loving Father's arms when we have sinned. "Yet if [we] care to listen, [we] hear a loud whisper from the gospel that [we] did not get what [we] deserved. [We] deserved punishment and God [gave] forgiveness. [We] deserved wrath and got love. We deserved debtors' prison and got a clean credit history. [We] deserved stern lectures and crawl-on-your-knees repentance; we got a banquet spread for [us]."[226]

The world teaches us just the opposite. It whispers in our ear that we only get what we fight for and what we earn. The world tells us

---

[226]P. 63-64. iBooks

that we only succeed when we exceed. No pain, no gain. In fact, the Darwinian model is the survival of the fittest. The world teaches us that the person who works hardest gets rewarded. But when we attempt to apply this way of thinking to God and his vision of salvation, the world's model fails miserably. As a matter of fact, if we get what we truly deserve from God we should get punishment and death. If the world's model of success and accomplishment was used by the father of the prodigal son, the boy would have received what his brother thought he should: ridicule, banishment, and punishment. But a loving God modeled grace. The prodigal son deserved to be penalized and the father showed compassion. He deserved to be derided but he received praise. The prodigal son should have paid his father back for the money he frittered away before he would even be allowed into the presence of his dad. That is the type of "justice" the world demands. Instead, he received a lavish celebratory banquet, a royal robe, and a signet ring.

No matter how hard we try to be good, we end up sinners. Like Martin Luther, when we try to purge our soul of sin we fail miserably. We cannot be good enough for God, but we cannot be "prodigal enough" for the denial of grace. Because of the death and resurrection of Jesus, we have been given the unmerited gift of God's forgiveness – His unending grace! "The author of Hebrews reminds believers that because of what Jesus has done for us, we can approach God with confidence. We do not need to feel afraid, unworthy, or unloved. We can come to God freely, without a guilty conscience, because of the forgiveness we've accepted."[227] "God gave his entire self, through Jesus, for all people. If some do not accept his gift, they are choosing to remain separate from God. If they do not respond to the Spirit of grace, they thus cut themselves off from God. Those

---

[227]Philip Yancey & Brenda Quinn. "Meet the Bible." P. 2136. Zondervan. iBooks.

following Jesus, however, have every reason for confidence. God is faithful, and no matter how things look in difficult times, his promises will come true."[228]

There is another parable told by Jesus that brings this concept into sharp focus for me. This story has sparked many hours of discussion in my Tuesday morning men's Bible study. The parable that has ignited this firestorm of debate is the parable of the laborers in the vineyard (See Matthew 20:1-16). Much like my Bible study, this parable has triggered debate and study in Christian circles. Saint Thomas Aquinas researched this story. He studied this powerful parable to try to understand the relationship between God's grace and human merit in light of the history of salvation. Aquinas concluded that this parable is evidence of how justice and mercy are present in everything God does.

The parable describes a landowner who owns a vineyard and was in need of day labor. In seeking workers, the owner goes to a location where persons congregate hoping to find work. Early in the morning, the owner picks out a crew of workers that he thinks can get the day's labor completed. He promises this crew that if they work a full day, they will receive one denarius[229] for a day's work. That crew begins work immediately, just as the sun is rising. As the morning progresses, the owner realizes he needs more workers. He goes back into the city and hires another crew and promises them that if they work the remainder of the day they will be paid "whatever is right." This crew begins work mid-morning. But the second crew is still not adequate to harvest all the grapes. The owner returns twice more in the afternoon for two more crews, one starts after

---

[228]Philip Yancey & Brenda Quinn. "Meet the Bible." P. 2136-37. Zondervan. iBooks.

[229]The equivalent of approximately $20 dollars today.

lunch and another begins work toward the end of the day. These last two crews were found in the marketplace "just standing around" because no one had hired them yet that day. They were delighted with the chance to make money for working, even if it was only for the three hours or, in the case of the fourth crew, the single hour that was left in the day. The last two crews were not promised a specific wage either.

That evening the owner called all of the workers together. He then asked the foreman of his vineyard to first call up to the office the last crew hired. Upon arriving at the office this last crew was paid one denarius each. The owner then called up to the payment desk the first crew he had hired – those workers who began at sunrise and worked all day. Each of these first crew members was also paid one denarius. Since they had witnessed the payment made to the last crew hired, they were shocked that they received the same payment. And they were angry. "These men who were hired last worked only one hour!" they shouted, "yet you have made them equal to us who have borne the burden of the work and the heat of the day." *This,* they cried, *was very unfair.* "Equal pay for an equal day," they chanted with their fists raised high in the air.

But the owner calmly responded with a question. To the leader of the first crew who shouted the loudest, he asked, "Didn't you agree to work the whole day for one denarius?" The man bowed his head and nodded "Yes." Then, the owner retorted, "Take your pay and go." The angry worker had no answer because he had been treated just as promised. The owner continued, "If I want to be gracious with my money and to give the last man hired the same as you, isn't that my right? It is my money, after all."

I can just hear my friend Doug say, "That is not fair." Then Joe would chime in, "This story shows that people who work hard at being good are treated just the same as those who are not as focused on doing God's will. And if that is true, why should we try as hard when everyone will receive the same reward?" Chuck would also add his words of wisdom and wonder whether justice is served by this parable? They have all made valid points. Using the world's standards, Doug, Joe, and Chuck are absolutely right.

But, I remind them (and myself) that we should thank God that we are not rewarded based on what we do or what we successfully refrain from doing. For we are all sinners, no matter how much we merit praise or deserve punishment. Thank God for undeserved grace! This lesson applies to our personal experiences. It's entirely possible to make sacrifices and difficult choices to serve God faithfully and watch others slip into the kingdom during deathbed conversions. Like the thief on the cross, they get to enter paradise by professing their faith in Jesus and confessing their sins in their last moments.

> This scandal of grace is a sign of the unbelievable goodness of God. It's possible that someone could look at a lifetime of service and feel, like the early laborers, that they were cheated. But this is the wrong way to look at faithfulness. When we truly recognize the lavish generosity of God's mercy, it's a game-changer. We stop focusing on what's "fair," and begin to humbly appreciate God's unbelievable benevolence. Hopefully, we recognize what the early laborers missed: It's a privilege to serve a God who is so kind and unselfish.[230]

---

[230]What Is the Parable of the Vineyard Workers About? Jesus Film Project. August 12, 2019

Instead of thinking about God's grace in terms of what is fair or unfair as defined by the world's standards, we should view grace in light of our own unworthiness as daily sinners. Without the guarantee of God's grace, and the payment made by Jesus for us, we would be hopelessly lost in our quest for eternity. We should not think like the older brother who pridefully believes that his father is unfair. His viewpoint is that of one who believes he has done everything right yet receives the same treatment as the unworthy prodigal son. Rather, we should rejoice that we are given the guarantee of salvation and that others are also forgiven when they repent and return to the Father.

We should look at that last crew of laborers and rejoice in their good fortune as they received the same unmerited grace as we have – for we are all laborers in God's vineyard. God's unmerited and overwhelming grace is a gift available to all sinners, no matter what sins they have committed and no matter when they seek the guarantee of redemption. We all were lost but now are found and were blind and now we see. How precious is that grace God gives, despite the lateness of the hour we first believe!

G. Justice

As a lawyer, justice was the focal point of everything I did, everything I worked for, and everything I hoped to accomplish in my professional career. The symbol of justice was an elegant and proud lady holding a scale while blindfolded. This statue was an emblem of how justice would be served. All people would be equal in the eyes of the law and their case or cause would be adjudged without regard to color, creed, or national origin (as symbolized by Lady Justice being blindfolded).

The justice each person seeks should be granted as if the jury was blindfolded and could not discern anything about a person or litigant except the content of their character. *Justice*, I believed, was not just a catchphrase. It was the pivot point upon which fairness would be perched. Lady Justice "is an allegorical personification of the moral force in judicial systems. Her attributes are a blindfold, a beam balance, and a sword."[231] The sword is a symbol of the power of the judicial system to provide justice swiftly and finally. While some would say that the American justice system has fallen short of this goal, it is nevertheless the greatest and most fair form of justice known to humankind, in my opinion.

My experience in a fallen world (where trials are conducted) shows me that even with the best justice system ever devised, truth, fairness, and righteousness are not always the result that juries and a fallible justice system deliver. *Life is not always fair*. Justice, in its purest form, is sometimes denied. There are many occasions when the person with the most money or influence will get the upper hand. There were also occasions where, I believe, the aggrieved person was given a judgment regardless of their fault because the jury favored that person over, say, a corporation. As it happened, the trier of fact or judge felt empathy or pity for the injured party. This world is filled with occasions where bad people gain the upper hand and innocent people go to jail. God, however, has promised to balance the books one day. "Justice will reign absolutely someday, and accomplishing that will require a time of cataclysmic violence against evil." [232] The only "pure" righteousness comes from God, and only He can deliver true justice.

---

[231]https://en.wikipedia.org/wiki/Lady_Justice

[232]Yancey, Philip. "The Bible Jesus Read." P. 216. Zondervan, 2017-03-01. iBooks

God provides the guarantee of everlasting life and the assurance that life everlasting will be just, righteous and fair. The justice that the guarantee provides is different from the civil and criminal justice systems devised by the world. God provides a system of judgment that guarantees that we will not be judged by the way we accord our lives in order to please Him but by the work of Christ on our behalf. If we were judged by God based on our own merit in securing our place in heaven (or by having the most power or money to buy the greatest lawyers to represent us) there is no way we could measure up to God's standard.

I envision God asking me, "Lewis, are you without sin? If so, you may enter my kingdom and commune with Me for eternity." My only answer to this question is "No." God would ask, "Then why should you be allowed to enter into eternity with me?" Without the guarantee, I would have no answer. However, with the blessed assurance I have in Christ, I can respond, with all certainty, "I have placed all my faith in your Son and He has forgiven my sins." God has thus guaranteed that He will say, in return, "Welcome into my eternal realm."

I am grateful that my sins are not placed on the scales of justice such as in a court of law. If they were, I would not measure up. Instead, God has accreted to my account the sacrifice of Jesus. My belief in His Son and my admission that I am a sinner in need of saving is all I need. No large sums of money, no powerful connections, and no Harvard-educated lawyer[233] needed. No lifetime of service such as Mother Teresa. "A simple fisherman, a scar-faced pilot, a paraplegic, a crone can take their rightful places there with joy. It is Christ's glory we take on, not our own. The cost may increase for those with wealth, physical attraction, and security. But for all of

---

[233] a tongue-in-cheek nod to my friend Charlie

us, the reward is the same: a chance to be judged not for what we are but for what Christ is. God looks upon us and sees His beloved Son."[234] That, in its purest form, is justice.

H. Contentment

More than thirty-five years ago I read something in my church's bulletin that really struck a chord with me. I saved that bulletin and, as soon as I got home, cut out this little quote. This clipping has been tacked to my home bulletin board in every house that we have lived in since. It is now a ragged, yellowed piece of paper but the words are as clear as the day I first read them. I also copied it and used this quote as a bookmark in my Bible. I keep it in these two locations so it can serve as a constant reminder of the importance of these simple words. I did this to under-score a critical gift given by God to me as part of the guar-antee. On this paper are simple words: "Contentment is not the fulfillment of what you want, but the realization of how 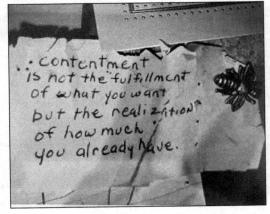 much you already have." I have attached a photo of this beautifully powerful principal as it appears on my family bulletin board.

Yes, the guarantee provides contentment. When you under-stand the guarantee, you realize how much God has provided you

---

[234]Philip Yancey & Paul Brand. "In His Image." Chapter 3. Zondervan. iBooks.

280

through the sacrifice of His son. We already have the gift of salvation – what more do we need to be fulfilled? I need the constant reminder of this fact, because the world keeps telling me the opposite.

When you have doubts (and we all do) do not think you are alone. Remember how the disciples reacted when they were first confronted by the risen Christ. In Luke, chapter 24, Jesus appeared to the disciples (minus Thomas) the day after he was seen by the women at the tomb. When this happened, Jesus reminded them of what He said so many times before His death. He told them that He would die and rise from the grave. And, to make matters worse, the last time He told them this astonishing fact was during the Last Supper, just hours before he was handed over to be crucified. It wasn't as if He only revealed this to them years before it happened. Nevertheless, look at their reaction when He appeared to them. "They were startled and frightened, thinking they saw a ghost." (v. 37). Really? Did they all have short-term memory problems? Jesus, seeing their response, asked "[w]hy are you troubled, and why do doubts arise in your minds?" Jesus then proceeded to provide proof positive that He was, in fact, the risen Savior. He showed them His hands and feet and invited them to touch Him. He was providing evidence that His promises were true. "This is what I told you when I was still with you" (v. 44).

Jesus reminded them that He had paid the price for forgiveness with his life so that whoever believed in him and repented of their sins would be absolved of those sins. He also said that they were "witnesses" to these events and were recipients of His atoning sacrifice. The scared and disbelieving disciples finally realized *how much they already had*. These true witnesses were then convicted of the guarantee of salvation and began to spread the word to a disbelieving world. These eleven, in the course of 2,000-plus years, brought forth the largest religious group on the planet, making up nearly one-third of the world's population. About 7.3 billion people.[235]

Therefore, the guarantee provides no doubt that if you believe in Jesus and you simply and humbly ask, you will receive forgiveness of your sins. As Max Lucado said in his book, *Anxious for Nothing,* "Christ-based *contentment* turns us into strong people. Since no one can take our Christ, no one can take our joy [because we have a guaranteed salvation]. ... He can give you a happiness that can **never** be taken, a grace that will **never** expire, and a wisdom that will ever increase. He is a fountain of living hope that will **never** be exhausted" (P. 98-99, emphasis added). Lucado reminded us that the Apostle Paul knew that his faith provided the guarantee of..."eternal life. He had the love of God. He had forgiveness of sins. He had the **surety** of salvation. He had Christ and Christ was enough. What he *had in Christ* was far greater than what he *didn't have* in life" (P. 98, emphasis added). That is the very definition of contentment.

> Focus more on what you do have and less on what you don't. The apostle Paul modeled this outlook. I have learned to be *content* whatever the circumstances. I know what it is to be in need, and I know what it is to have plenty. I have learned the secret of being *content* in any and every situation, whether well fed or hungry, whether living in plenty or in want. I can do all this through him who gives me strength. Philippians 4:11–13 NIV.[236]

---

[235]Pew Research Center, April 5, 2017

[236]Anxious for Nothing, P. 95, emphasis added.

True contentment, therefore is not the fulfillment of what you want. It's not getting the business partnership you worked so hard to achieve. Neither is it the house in the tony neighborhood you coveted, or the sports car you have wanted since you were a teenager. No. Contentment, in its purest form, is the realization of how much you already have. And you have the guarantee of everlasting life. The gift of immeasurable value is already yours.

I. Happiness

The United States Constitution provides many guarantees to citizens of the US. It was written by its framers to ensure that the tyranny of a monarch would not be allowed to impinge on our God-given rights. It was set on a foundational truth that the people of America had the ultimate power and would grant some of that power to its elected rulers – not the other way around. Some believe that the Constitution guarantees the right to life, liberty, and happiness. However, that is not the case. The authors of the Constitution knew that such a statement of principle would be impossible to insure. Instead, they said that the government would guarantee life and liberty, but only the "*pursuit* of happiness." "... '[T]he pursuit of happiness' means something like occupying one's life with the activities that provide for overall well-being. This certainly includes a right to material things, but it goes beyond that to include humanity's spiritual and moral condition.[237]" This fundamental right, written into the constitution by Thomas Jefferson was based on the philosophy of John Locke. He was an English philosopher and physician, widely regarded as one of the most influential thinkers of the Enlightenment Movement of his day. Thomas Jefferson was a big

---

[237]James R. Rogers. First Things, June 19, 2012. www.firstthings.com

fan of Locke. The US Constitution does not, and cannot guarantee "happiness" – only your ability to pursue something or someone that brings you this elusive state of wellbeing. As an American, you are guaranteed the right to seek any job you want and to spend your hard-earned dollars as you wish. None of these things, however, can or will bring you the guarantee of happiness.

King George V wrote on the flyleaf of the Bible of a friend, "The secret of happiness is not to do what you like to do, but to learn to like what you have to do." No document or Constitution can give you such a guarantee. Learning to like what you have to do can only be achieved by you. Learning to like what you have to do is one form of happiness.

There is another form of happiness that you seemingly have control over. It's the type of "happy" you get when your team gets to the Super Bowl.[238] It's akin to the feeling you experience when you head out in your first car after turning sixteen. It's the utter joy you feel as you cradle your newborn child. While these experiences bring happiness to your life, they do not guarantee happiness. These experiences, while joyful, do not bring lasting and eternal happiness. You get a ticket for speeding in your new car, your child stays out past curfew and you frantically wait on their arrival home. The joy suddenly fades.

The type of happiness that is guaranteed by faith in Christ is much different. That type of happiness is like the lack of fear you experience when you realize that cancer has no hold on you. Billy Graham in chapter one of his aptly titled book, *The Secret of Happiness*, says this:

---

[238]I am editing this passage ten days before 43-year-old Tom Brady is leading my hometown Buccaneers to the Super Bowl in our own stadium - a first in the history of the NFL. He eventually went on to beat the odds and win his 7th Super Bowl and the Buccaneers' 2nd Lombardi Trophy

The happiness which brings enduring worth to life is not the superficial happiness that is dependent on circumstances. It is the happiness and contentment that fills the soul even in the midst of the most distressing of circumstances and the most adverse environment. It is the kind of happiness that survives when things go wrong and smiles through the tears. The happiness for which our souls ache is one undisturbed by success or failure, one which dwells deep within us and gives inward relaxation, peace, and contentment, no matter what the surface problems may be. That kind of happiness stands in need of no outward stimulus.

That is the type of happiness my friend from Texas and I felt when discussing the issue of our own demise on the deck overlooking the lake in a remote region of Canada. This type of happiness can only be experienced through understanding the priceless gift of God's guarantee of salvation.

Eugene Peterson expressed this happiness, this utter joy, that I tried to communicate to my good friends on the first night of our fishing trip to Goose Bay.

Joy is characteristic of Christian pilgrimage. It is the second in Paul's list of the fruits of the Spirit (Gal 5:22-23). It is the first of Jesus's signs in the Gospel of John (turning water into wine)...Joy is not a requirement of Christian discipleship, it is a consequence. It is not what we have to acquire in order to experience life in Christ; it is what comes to us when we are walking in the way of faith and

> obedience...We cannot make ourselves joyful. Joy cannot be commanded, purchased or arranged. But there is something we can do. We can decide to live in response to the abundance of God and not under the dictatorship of our own poor needs.[239]

True, everlasting happiness and joy are what we experience when we realize that our sins have been forgiven and that the barrier between ourselves and our heavenly Father has been removed. We understand that no matter what we have done or how many times we have transgressed, we are forgiven. Because of the overwhelming love of God, he has allowed His Son to take on the burden of our sins so that we may be guaranteed everlasting life. Now that is happiness!

Peterson goes further to explain how happiness/joy is a guarantee from God. "The joy comes because God knows how to wipe away tears, and in His resurrection work, create the smile of new life. Joy is what God gives, not what we work up. Laughter is the delight that things are working together for good to those who love God, not the giggles that betray the nervousness of a precarious defense system. The joy that develops in the Christian way of discipleship is an overflow of spirit that comes from feeling good – not about yourself but about God. We find that **His ways are dependable, His promises sure.**" P. 146-47. Emphasis added.

True happiness is knowing that whatever happens – good or bad – it will not come close to knocking us down or counting us out. Happiness is knowing that all my transgressions have been wiped away and all of my faults have been overlooked. This type

---

[239]Eugene H. Peterson. "A Long Obedience in the Same Direction." P. 138-40. InterVarsity Press, 2012-04-25. iBooks.

of happiness is beyond the highest high I have experienced ever in my life.

J. Wisdom

King Solomon, as previously discussed in chapter four, was the wealthiest, most powerful person of his day. He had more possessions than anyone else. He ruled the largest number of people, over the greatest geographical region of the known world. He had multiple estates and more servants than he could possibly need. He simply had everything. Yet, during the last years of his life, he was depressed beyond consolation. If you want to read a real downer of a work by an unhappy author, read the first five chapters of the book of Ecclesiastes. Solomon starts out the book with these words: "'Meaningless! Meaningless!' Says the teacher. 'Utterly meaningless! Everything is meaningless'" (Eccles. 1:2, NIV). After all that he'd accomplished, built, conquered, controlled, and possessed, he felt that everything lacked meaning or purpose. He was not happy. He wondered aloud, *what was it all for? What did I really accomplish? Why did I strive for this?* He exclaimed, "Is there anything new under the sun?" (Eccles. 1:9).

In addition to his vast wealth and power, Solomon was viewed by many as the wisest man in the world. He had read all of the great works and was taught by the best teachers of his day. This education brought him great fame but this knowledge and discernment failed to fill his happiness bucket. He reviewed the education he'd received, all the books he'd read, the great advice he'd garnered from the best minds of his time and all he experienced in his conquests and travels and, in reflection, he concluded that it was nothing more than "chasing after the wind" (Eccles. 1:17). "Yet when I surveyed all that my hands had done and what I toiled to achieve, everything was meaningless...nothing was gained under the sun" (Eccles. 2:10). Even the pleasures of life brought him no joy, no happiness. All of the delights of his heart were fulfilled – he had it all. Everything he could imagine was in his possession. Listen to his words, "I denied myself nothing my eyes desired; I refused my heart no pleasure." Can you imagine? It's like the genie in the bottle granting you three wishes...and your third wish was for more wishes. Anything you wanted was given or taken or acquired by you. No pleasure you desired was denied! And after doing, getting, and experiencing everything, how did Solomon feel? Empty.

How would it feel if you had the most impressive house in your town? How would you look at your life if you could command a small army of workers to clean your mansion and cook your favorite meals? What if you were able to throw opulent parties and invite celebrities to your estate for drinks and dinner? How about if you had a fleet of cars, a bookcase filled with first editions, and photos lined up on your walls showing you with powerful politicians and sports stars? How would you react if you had more clothes in your closet than you could count? What if you vacationed in the most exclusive places on earth? If you had all this and more – you would have the life of Solomon.

Yet like Solomon, many people who are high achievers become disillusioned, depressed, and sad. Even the power of the world's greatest ruler could not serve Solomon's purposes. Despite having the wealthiest kingdom with the largest army and the wisest advisors, Solomon was powerless to solve the world's problems. "I saw the tears of the oppressed – and they have no comforter; power was on the side of the oppressors..." And after trying to right the wrongs of society through money, edicts, education, and force he realized that he failed miserably. "I declared that the dead, who have already died, are happier than the living, who are still alive" (Eccles. 4:2).

"Better the poor but wise youth than the old but foolish King..." he exclaimed. (Eccles. 4:13).

There is, however, a happy ending to Solomon's life as told in the Book of Ecclesiastes. King Solomon finally came to the realization in chapter five that life without God at the center of everything is unhappy and meaningless. The lack of God at the center of everything in his life is what makes it so. Solomon also realized that all the possessions, power, and authority do not make you wise or happy – and you can't take it with you! "Naked a man comes from his mother's womb, and as he comes, so he departs" (Eccles. 5:15).

Solomon, at the end of his life, finally came to the realization that despite conquering most of the world, **he** had not succeeded in vanquishing evil. Despite the best education that **his** money could buy, he felt lacking in true knowledge and understanding. He was not able to feel satisfied despite everything **he** had accumulated. All of his possessions were meaningless to him. **He** was not able to find peace inside his elaborate estates, temples, and fortresses. He finally realized that everything **he** accomplished was meaningless if God was not at the center of his life. Solomon finally attained true wisdom when he realized that everything was a gift from God (Eccles. 5:18-20). Things would fade away, but placing himself in a subservient position to God was the only path to true wisdom and happiness. Once he firmly placed God at the center of everything his depression faded and his gratitude shone through. "A good name is better than fine perfume and the day of death is better than the day of birth," he concluded. He realized that "wisdom, like an inheritance, is a good thing and benefits those who see the sun" (Eccles. 7:11). True wisdom, he concluded, comes from the reverence of God. "For this I have found: God made mankind upright..." Solomon finally got it: wisdom is better than possessions, pearls, or gold. Revere God and keep His commands, he says, for this is the duty of all mankind. Solomon's great wisdom, born now of his reverence for God, brought him to the revelation that without God at the center of his life, it was "meaningless, meaningless."

The gift that wisdom offers is better than any material riches. Material riches are often perceived by the world as more valuable. However, when we realize that the ultimate "possession" is the gift God freely gives of salvation, we will have true wisdom. This wisdom will allow us to put the things we acquire, the positions we achieve and the so-called status we attain into their proper perspective. This wisdom allows us to see, as Solomon did, that the things riches can offer are fleeting. Anything that money can buy is perishable. But the wisdom and understanding that God's Word gives is beyond measure and can never be taken away or destroyed. And true wisdom allows us to finally grasp that the grant of salvation guaranteed to each of us is a treasure that lasts forever. This everlasting peace and understanding of God's intent for our lives bring us true joy and happiness.

K. Heaven

C.S. Lewis said, "...all loneliness, angers, hatreds, envies and itchings that it contains, if rolled into one single experience and put into the scale against the least moment of the joy that is felt by the least in Heaven, would have no weight that could be registered at all."[240] This, in my opinion, is one of the best images of what heaven must be like. Can you fathom such a place? The guarantee provides *paid-in-advance admission* to this place of wonder where communion with God is finally and eternally possible.

---

[240]C.S. Lewis. The Great Divorce. P. 12. iBooks

The Bible contains many references to a place being reserved for those who have the guarantee. Jesus made reference to this on many occasions when speaking to His disciples and the people he preached to during his short time on earth. In John, chapters 13 and 14, Jesus is faced with His followers' dismay over His upcoming death. In response, Jesus told them that he was only going to be with them "a little longer" and that where He was going, they could not come. Of course, the disciples did not understand that Jesus was headed for the cross and resurrection. When Simon Peter asked him, "where are you going?" Jesus answered, "where I am going, you cannot follow now, but you will follow later" (John 13:33-36). Here again, look at the words Jesus spoke. As a lawyer, these words have special meaning. He said, "You *will* follow later." Not you "may." Not "If you do something you will gain admittance into heaven with me." He said, "You will." Jesus knew he was headed to the cross. He knew the disciples would initially deny (and one would betray) him. He knew they would scatter and lock themselves away for fear of being associated with Him. He knew they would not believe that He would rise from the dead. He knew that Thomas would demand proof before he would believe. Despite all of this foreknowledge, Jesus told them they *will* be with Him later in heaven. We who have the guarantee know that we too **will** be with Him when we die.

Jesus could tell they were perplexed with this statement, so He tried to give them the comfort they needed – the comfort only the guarantee could provide. Jesus began by telling them that their hearts should not be troubled. He said that if they had faith and trusted Him they *will* have a place in heaven waiting for them. He likened this place to a room in God's house (using an analogy that the disciples could understand). "In my Fathers' house are many rooms; if it were not so, I would have told you." Then Jesus assured them of a place in heaven. "I am going there to prepare a place for you." And then He told them the unimaginable – that He would die and come back after his death. And that He had to do this in order to lead them to heaven. (John 14:1-3).

Home is where the heart is. Home is the starting place of hopes and dreams. Home is where love resides, memories are created, friends always belong and laughter never ends. There is an old saying that goes like this, "A house is made of bricks and beams. A home is made of hopes and dreams." Jesus used this picture to illustrate for us the wonderful place where we will be happy and at peace. Ravi Zacharias[241] was able to understand and convey this vision of heaven as "home," a place where we will commune with God. In his book, *The Grand Weaver*, he said:

> Do you remember when Jesus's disciples asked him where he lived (see John 2:38)? It was a loaded question. They really wanted to know Jesus's point of origin and what He called home. The first element in reflecting Jesus's image is to understand that His home was with the Father (see John 8:14-29; 12:44-50). Jesus talked a great deal about his mission on earth, but as he drew closer to the completion of that mission, He spoke often of returning to the Father, from whom He had come (see John 13:3). Jesus told the disciples that He had prepared a place so that where He was they – and we – could

---

[241] As I have indicated before, the references to Mr. Zacharias and his books were placed in this book before his death and the revelations about the double life he led. We are all sinners who have fallen short of the standard God has set for us and by quoting Mr. Zacharias I by no means condone his conduct. Nevertheless, I have decided to keep the quotes from his books as I believe they are accurate statements about the subjects quoted.

also be (see John 14:2-4). This simple description of being at home with God is the ultimate destiny of the follower of Jesus Christ.

Home is where I am loved just for who I am, not for my name or how I preach or what books I have written — but just for being me...This is why I believe our Lord describes our presence with him in heaven as knowing him, even as we are known (see 1 Corinthians 13:12).

...when all is said and done, he calls us home to be with him. We will be at home with God! That's my destiny (see Revelation 21:3).

The respect shown in a cemetery comes not because it is home, but because it is where we bid believing loved ones a temporary goodbye. Jesus came from the Father and returned to the Father to prepare a place for you and for me. That's home. That is our eternal dwelling. We cherish the tender metaphor of home because there we will unpack our suitcases for the last time. [242]

The apostle Paul repeated this assurance in Ephesians, explaining to that church that believers actually have a "seat with [Christ] in the heavens" (Eph. 2:6, NCV). You don't have a seat at the Supreme

---

[242]Ravi Zacharias . The Grand Weaver. P. 221-26. iBooks.

Court or in the House of Representatives. You have one far more strategic; you have a seat in the government of God."[243]

Another metaphor used by Jesus to explain to His believers that they were granted admittance into heaven was the use of a gateway or door. Jesus continually referred to himself as a shepherd and His followers as sheep. People of that day understood that reference because sheep were a valuable commodity – one that shepherds must take care of and lead. Jesus used this analogy to explain the guarantee of eternal life in heaven, through belief in him. In John 10:7, Jesus referred to Himself as the gate the sheep must use to enter into the safety of the shepherd's care. "He is the entrance to the pen (v. 9) that leads to proper pasture." This section echoes Jesus's words in John 14:6 that He is the only way to the Father. His point is that He serves as the sole means to approach the Father and partake of God's promised salvation."[244]

Later in chapter ten, Jesus was reinforcing that He had the authority from God to make this guarantee. He did so by reminding his followers of His divinity, by using tangible evidence of the miracles He performed and they saw.[245] Then, as the divine Son of God, He assured them of their place in heaven. "My sheep listen to my voice; I know them and they follow me. I give them eternal life and

---

[243]Max Lucado, Before Amen. P. 74. iBooks

[244]John F. MacArthur. One Perfect Life. Part VI notes. iBooks

[245]Just some of these miracles performed by Jesus and witnessed by his disciples included: healing leprosy (Matt. 8:3), healing the centurion's servant without going to the servant's bedside (Matt. 8:13), healing Peter's mother-in-law (Matt. 8:15), calming a violent storm at sea (Matt. 8:26), healing a paralytic (Matt. 9:6–7), curing a woman who had been sick for twelve years (Matt. 9:22), raising a girl from the dead (Matt. 9:25), driving out an evil spirit (Mark 1:25), healing a demon-possessed man in a cemetery (Mark 5:15), turning water into wine (John 2:9), and healing a man who had been unable to walk for thirty-eight years (John 5:9).

they **shall never** perish; no one can snatch them out of my hand" (John 10: 25-28, NIV). Again, these words have legal significance and are important and powerful. "Shall never" is not capable of being misconstrued. Jesus guaranteed that believers will have a place in eternity and will have everlasting life. The use of the words "shall never" is the assurance of eternal fellowship with God in heaven.

C.S. Lewis explained the guarantee of admittance into heaven of God's people (the church) as a metaphor, using the analogy that each Christian is a part of the body of Christ. "[A]s organs in the Body of Christ, as stones and pillars in the temple, we are *assured* of our *eternal* self-identity and shall live to remember the galaxies as an old tale." Lewis is using his wonderfully visual language to show us that we will be one with God forever. We will exist perpetually with our Creator[246]. Emphasis added.

L. Communion with God

How would it feel to be admitted to the most exclusive club in town? Would you want to be a member of a club that had great service, delicious food, beautiful amenities, and an atmosphere where you could feel totally relaxed? A place where you were at peace and everyone you encountered in this place was happy and welcoming? A club where you were warmly accepted and fully embraced? A place where you could take a permanent "break from all your worries." Wouldn't you like to belong to a place "where everybody knows your name, and they're always glad you came"?[247] Such a fellowship would have no cliques, no prejudices, and no alienation. This ideal

---

[246]C. S. Lewis. "A Year with C. S. Lewis." HarperCollins. iBooks. P. 217. From "Membership" (The Weight of Glory)

[247]Excerpted from the theme song for the TV show Cheers.

place would make sure each person is valued, no matter their race, ethnicity, or social status. Here, one would enjoy fellowship with a group of people who had no cares, worries, or pain. In this place, you would be totally loved and accepted while envy, hatred and feelings of inferiority would never be experienced.

Well, I have good news, such a place exists. Another thing that the guarantee provides is fellowship with God. Where every tear is wiped from your face and all worry is erased from your mind. This place is heaven. As I previously explained, God is holy and cannot have anyone in his presence if they are defiled by any sin. Therefore, in order to commune with God in eternity, we can only gain entrance into heaven if we have been washed clean of sin. "Just as Abraham was called the 'friend of God' (2 Chron. 20:7; James 2:23), so also those who follow Christ are privileged with extraordinary revelation through the Messiah and Son of God and, believing, become 'friends' of God also. It was for His 'friends' that the Lord laid down His life (John 10:11, 15, 17).[248] In this place called heaven, we too are called *a friend of God*. This process of Jesus taking on our sins and therefore purging sin from our soul, allows us to be in fellowship with God the Father. When we are given the guarantee, we are able to move from a place exiled and forever separated from God into the place were God "resides." We will move into heaven: into the presence of God.

> Reading David's psalms, with all their emotional peaks and valleys, it may even seem that he writes them as a form of spiritual therapy, a way of talking himself into faith when his spirit and emotions are wavering. Now, centuries later, we can use these

---

[248]John F. MacArthur. One Perfect Life. Part IX Notes. iBooks

very same prayers as steps of faith, a path to lead us
from an obsession with ourselves to the actual presence of God.[249]

We are finally able to approach God because our sins have been
wiped clean. Once we enter into God's presence, we are able to commune with God in a way we were barred from doing before. Like
friends, we are welcomed into God's presence. "God may be the
Sovereign Lord of the universe, but through His Son, God became as
approachable as any doting human father. In Romans 8, Paul brought
the image of intimacy even closer. God's Spirit lives inside us, he says,
and when we do not know what we ought to pray "the Spirit himself
intercedes for us with groans that words cannot express."[250]

Barbara Brown Taylor is an American Episcopal priest, professor, author, and theologian and also one of the United States'
best-known preachers. She once said that, based on her lifelong
study of the Bible, "I have looked for an overarching theme, a summary statement of what the whole sprawling book is about. I have
settled on this: 'God gets his family back.' From the first book
to the last the Bible tells of wayward children and the tortuous
lengths to which God will go to bring them home. Indeed, the
entire biblical drama ends with a huge family reunion in the book
of Revelation."

You will be welcomed by God into the heavenly realms as a
good friend or family member. It is a place where we are loved,
where we can be ourselves and feel relaxed. Our family home is a
place of refuge. God brings us home to commune with Him. The

---

[249]Philip Yancey & Brenda Quinn. "Meet the Bible." P. 724-25. Zondervan.
iBooks.

[250]Philip Yancey, What's so Amazing About Grace? P. 156-57. iBooks

guarantee of salvation assures us that we will be part of that great family reunion. The invitation has been issued and the way home to this reunion is well-documented and clearly laid out. Jesus, our Shepherd, calls us home. And, when we get there, He is waiting for us with arms spread wide.

C.S. Lewis tells it this way – speaking from the point of view of an inhabitant of heaven: "We know nothing of religion here: we think only of Christ. We know nothing of speculation. Come and see. I will bring you to Eternal Fact, the Father of all other fact-hood."[251]

M. Peace

One of the first things Jesus said to his gathered disciples after his resurrection was "Peace be with you" (Luke 24:36; John 20:19, NIV). This shalom greeting, I believe, emphasizes a very important gift that Christ's resurrection provides to all believers. "A peace that surpasses all understanding" is promised to every recipient of the guarantee. Philippians 4:7. God gives this peace to us when we need it the most. I received this peace when I went through my cancer ordeal. However, I did not connect this verse in the Bible to the emotional shock to my system when I first received my diagnosis.

As I was researching this book I was searching my Bible for references to the peace of God being gifted to those who put their faith in Him. This research led me to Philippians 4:7 and the stories of Christians experiencing the peace that surpasses all understanding. First, I read the context within which this statement, made by the apostle Paul in his letter to the church at Philippi, was placed. The preceding verse was just the contextual background I needed. Verse 6 says

---

[251]C.S. Lewis. The Great Divorce. P. 4. iBooks

that we should not be anxiety-ridden when the expected storms of life blow through our lives. In such situations, Paul advises, we should turn to the lifeline used by Christ in his periods of angst and turmoil.

In Jesus's most painful period of time on earth, the night he was betrayed and turned over to the Jewish and Roman authorities, He retreated to the Garden of Gethsemane. There, sweating drops of blood, He asked that the mission He was sent to earth to fulfill be taken away. Knowing that He must be sacrificed, He was in terrible pain and anguish. His loving Father, thankfully, chose the fate of all mankind over His son's anguish. However, angels were sent by God to comfort Jesus and strengthen Him for the task that lay ahead. Luke 22:41-44, NIV. Jesus's prayers were heard and answered by God, who knew that allowing His Son to suffer and die was the most important thing that could happen for His creation. Jesus, strengthened for the burden He had to bear, then submitted himself to human authorities and gave us the gift that could never be repaid.

That is why Paul urges all who are filled with anxiety and pain to seek God, just as Jesus did. "...[B]y prayer and petition, with thanksgiving, present your requests to God." Philippians 4:6. Peace is therefore received through the vehicle of prayer. That is why communicating with God on a regular basis is so very important. "The path to peace is paved with prayer. Less consternation, more supplication. Fewer anxious thoughts, more prayer-filled thoughts. As you pray, the peace of God will guard your heart and mind."[252]

When I searched the stories of God's peace having been given to people in their darkest hour, I was overwhelmed. One of the stories that struck me was this:

---

[252]Max Lucado. Anxious for Nothing. P. 87. iBooks

Just a few days before Thanksgiving 2014, my husband left our home, our marriage, for a woman he had met at work. I was devastated, as you can imagine. Betrayed by the one who I trusted to love me forever, until death do us part.

I was saved as a teenager, and had been in and out of church throughout my life. I knew God and His Word, yet the world always pulled me back in. A month or so before my husband left, I felt this calling by God to come back to Him. I started seeking Him more and more, yet not totally surrendering. It wasn't until a few days after my husband was gone that I finally did so.

I hadn't eaten or slept in days. My family stayed with me in our home, trying to comfort me and be there by my side as I drowned in my grief. But nothing they said penetrated the pain. Their hugs fell on a numb body. Then one evening I went into the bathroom and fell apart. I laid on the floor and sobbed from the deepest part of me, unable to breathe for the physical weight of pain that bore down on my chest. In a moment, I found myself crying out to God. I begged Him to remove the pain. I told Him I couldn't take it anymore, it hurt too bad and I didn't want to go on. I pleaded for comfort. Suddenly, my son came into the bathroom and laid down beside me. He placed his hand on my back and said, "It'll be okay, Mom." That was it! Something happened like nothing I had ever felt before all of a sudden came across my body. From head to toe, I was filled with peace! The tears halted completely and the pain in my chest was gone. I felt God's presence in that bathroom as I was covered with warmth. It was that peace which surpasses all understanding. God heard my plea and sent me comfort. He came to me and touched me through my son. Every word my family spoke to comfort me before that had failed, every touch was unpalpable. It wasn't until I called upon the Lord that I got what I needed. And He delivered in an instant![253]

This guarantee of peace is a part of the blessings bestowed on believers. But it comes with a cautionary explanation. While I believe every prayer is answered by God, the responses are not always answered in the way we want or when we want. I am reminded of the scene in *Bruce Almighty* when, endowed temporarily with God's powers, he was given the power to grant "requests" of people who pray. While his powers were restricted to a certain section of Buffalo, NY, he was nevertheless inundated with a flood of prayer requests. At first, he sought to answer each one separately. However, the avalanche of prayers was too much. He therefore, chose to hit "control all" on his prayer spread sheet (which he was using to organize all the prayers on the website "Yahweh") and in doing so answered all prayers "Yes." What followed was chaos. There were thousands of people who won the lottery jackpot, which, because so many people chose the right number, paid out $12 to each! Everyone got a yes to their prayers and no one was happy. In fact, there was rioting in

the streets and everyone was furious with their meager lotto win-
nings. Bruce was perplexed. After all, he gave them the answer they
wanted. What went wrong? Later he asked God why answering
everyone's prayers with a "Yes," didn't work. "God" (portrayed by
actor Morgan Freeman) tells Bruce in response, "Since when does
anyone have a clue about what they want?"

Bruce begins to understand this because he answered many of
his own prayers. He gave himself a fancy sports car, a head anchor
position on the evening news, and plenty of new clothes. He was
able to find the street gang that beat him up and he made fools out
of them. Everything he wished for came true. But he was not happy.
Bruce didn't have a clue as to what he really wanted. However, as
the movie comes to its climatic scene Bruce finally realized what he
reallt wanted. He eventually asked God to give his girlfriend (the
love of his life) true happiness. Instead of his desires, he wanted
what made her happy, even if that meant she did not choose Bruce.

Peace does not mean that God answers all our prayers in the way
that we want them answered. Peace is knowing that your sins are
forgiven. Peace is freedom from guilt. Peace is knowing that you will
die sin-free. Peace is our eventual freedom from pain, tears, anxiety,
and hurt – not on our schedule and when we want – but ultimately
with a lasting peace that "surpasses all understanding." That is the
type of peace that only God can give! A peace that is guaranteed to
those who put their faith in Jesus. God does His part. He bestows
upon us His peace. "Our Father gives us the very peace of God.
He downloads the tranquility of the throne room into our world,
resulting in an inexplicable calm. This kind of peace is not a human
achievement. It is a gift from above. "Peace I leave with you; my

peace I give you. I do not give to you as the world gives. Do not let your hearts be troubled and do not be afraid" (John 14:27 NIV)."[254]

Most people think they can get peace by controlling their world. They believe peace will be attained by accumulating enough money so their worries disappear... until the stock market crashes and a pandemic hits the world with such power that it erases half of their business overnight. Every time you think you have things "under control" God reminds us, yet again, that control is an illusion. Control cannot bring peace - even if you are the richest, most powerful person on earth (e.g. Solomon).

> [T]he most stressed-out people are control freaks. They fail at the quest they most pursue. The more they try to control the world, the more they realize they cannot. Life becomes a cycle of anxiety, failure; anxiety, failure; anxiety, failure. We can't take control, because control is not ours to take. The Bible has a better idea. Rather than seeking total control, relinquish it. You can't run the world, but you can entrust it to God. This is the message behind Paul's admonition to "rejoice in the Lord." Peace is within reach, not for lack of problems, but because of the presence of a sovereign Lord. Rather than rehearse the chaos of the world, rejoice in the Lord's sovereignty, as Paul did. "The things which happened to me have actually turned out for the furtherance of the gospel, so that it has become evident to the

---

[254]Max Lucado. Anxious for Nothing. P. 103-04. iBooks

whole palace guard, and to all the rest, that my chains are in Christ" (Phil. 1:12–13).[255]

N. Humble and Contrite Heart

One of my favorite jokes involves the importance of humility. The local Kiwanis club gave an annual award to the member that most embodied the virtue of humility in his everyday life. Jim, a member of Kiwanis for over thirty years, was to receive the award that year. The president of the club began his introduction of Jim by describing what he had done to earn the award. Jim had worked behind the scenes with Meals on Wheels for ten hours every week, cooking and packaging meals for shut-ins. He was a mentor to two young men, helping them advance in their jobs and supporting them in difficulties they experienced in their marriages. He had given generously to his church – insisting that the donations were referenced as anonymous. Jim made a very large grant to the local food bank, which allowed it to purchase three commercial-grade refrigerators. This gave the food bank the ability to provide, for the first time, fresh refrigerated food to the needy in his town. Upon receiving this grant, the food bank wanted to name its dining room in his honor, but he declined, wanting to remain anonymous.

Jim had also chaired the Kiwanis club's good government committee for the past five years and in that time had been instrumental in establishing open county government meetings and registering many thousands of new voters of all ages and political affiliations. When Jim was asked by local governmental leaders to run for an open county commission seat he politely declined, saying he wanted

---

[255]Max Lucado. Anxious for Nothing. P. 24, iBooks.

to work behind the scenes and remain unbiased in the work of the Kiwanis committee he chaired.

After this glowing introduction, Jim rose and slowly walked to the podium to accept his award (a beautiful gold medal, tethered by a blue Kiwanis silk ribbon). His head was humbly bowed as he made his way to the dais. As he approached, the crowd erupted with a standing ovation, showing their gratitude and pride in all that Jim had done to make his community a better place to live for everyone. As Jim reached the podium the Kiwanis club president fittingly motioned for him to bow his head so that the award could be placed around his neck. With a flourish, the beautiful medallion was slowly placed over Jim's head. He looked up to beam at the audience, acknowledging their continued applause and cheering with a wave of his hand. In that instant, the room grew quiet ... and Jim's award was promptly taken away.

This is a satirical way of showing that true and pure humility can never be achieved because simply accepting and proudly donning the award for humility shows a lack of the characteristic it was meant to acknowledge. Jesus embodied these qualities of humility. In order to save us from our sins, Jesus gave up his seat on the throne of heaven to take on human form. He came to earth as a helpless baby who had to depend on sinful humans for His very existence. Can you imagine the supreme humility it took to trade your crown for a diaper? As he grew, He began to preach the good news and attracted a following. Instead of claiming an earthly position of authority, He demonstrated the heart of a humble servant so that He could teach us the value of a meek and contrite heart. By becoming "one of us" he was able to relate to the human condition. During the celebration of Passover, during His last supper, the King above all kings knelt before each of His pupils and washed their dirty feet. Everything Jesus did on earth was out of a humble and contrite heart. In "payment" for his sacrifices for us, he was arrested, falsely accused, wrongfully convicted, humiliated, beaten, mocked, scourged, and executed in one of the most brutal methods ever devised. He literally died to save us from the death sentence of sin. Before his death, Jesus tried to explain the importance of a contrite and humble heart to His followers through the use of a parable.

He told it like this: two men went up to the temple to pray, one a Pharisee and the other a tax collector. The Pharisee stood up and prayed about himself, "God, I thank You that I am not like other men – robbers, evildoers, adulterers – or even like this tax collector. I fast twice a week and give a tenth of all I get." But the tax collector stood at a distance. He was ashamed of his sins and could not even look up to heaven. Instead, he beat his breast and said, "God, have mercy on me, a sinner!" Jesus then told his disciples that the sinful and despised tax collector, rather than the self-proclaimed holy Pharisee, "went home justified before God." Jesus told them, "[f]or everyone who exalts himself will be humbled, and he who humbles himself will be exalted" (Luke 18:10-14, NIV). Jesus emphasized the primacy of this concept many other times during his ministry on earth (see e.g., Matthew 23:5-12; Luke 14:8-11, NIV).

The guarantee, once accepted, provides all the tools necessary to work toward a state of humility and contrition. Even though such perfection cannot be achieved (see the awardee Jim's example above) we can still strive for such through the process of sanctification. Sanctification comes from acceptance of Jesus as our gate to salvation. From our belief in Him and our plea for forgiveness of our sins, we receive the guarantee of eternal life. Sanctification is the process we go through as we mature as Christians. This is a result that we strive to achieve by putting God's commands at the center of our lives, working to remake ourselves in the image of Jesus. We are sanctified by reading the bible and expanding our understanding of God's Word.

Therefore, a humble and contrite heart is a benefit conferred by the guarantee. "We must work alongside God in the process of our sanctification." Paul said, "God works in us to will and do of his good pleasure." He gives us the very desire of our hearts to grow in Christ and He works in us to do it. This is why, when we get to heaven, *there will be no room for boasting*. Why? Because God did it all. However, both realities are true. We must work to do God's will in our lives while God is working in us to remake us in his image. Listen to what Paul said about this reality in his own life. "For I am the least of the apostles and do not even deserve to be called an apostle, because I persecuted the church of God. But by the grace of God I am what I am, and his grace to me was not without effect. No, I worked harder than all of them—yet not I, but the grace of God that was with me" (1 Cor. 15:9-10). Emphasis added[256]

During my time in college, I was not a model of humility or a contrite heart. In fact, my college experience at Florida State University in the early 1970s was typical of most frat boys. Drinking, partying, boasting, and bragging were staples of my behavior throughout four years of college. This was hardly the environment conducive to a humble and contrite heart. As a member of Sigma Alpha Epsilon, I was required to memorize many things associated with the rituals of fraternity life. There were drinking songs to learn, fraternity history lessons to put to memory, and rites to remember. One such thing I had to memorize was the words to a motto, written in 1856 by a founder of my fraternity. This creed, written by John Walter Wayland, is all about the virtues of humility and contriteness.

---

[256]https://bible.org/seriespage/8-work-out-your-salvation-process-sanctification

The True Gentleman is the man whose conduct proceeds from good will and an acute sense of propriety, and whose self-control is equal to all emergencies; who does not make the poor man conscious of his poverty, the obscure man of his obscurity, or any man of his inferiority or deformity; who is himself humbled if necessity compels him to humble another; who does not flatter wealth, cringe before power, or boast of his own possessions or achievements; who speaks with frankness but always with sincerity and sympathy; whose deed follows his word; who thinks of the rights and feelings of others, rather than his own; and who appears well in any company, a man with whom honor is sacred and virtue safe.

Of course, this was not me. Surely not while I was in college! However, there I stood, reciting this creed with my hand held high, pledging to the fraternity that I would be this person. Saying words that seemed so empty to a young man, fresh out of high school. Little did I know that they would come back to haunt me as I wrote this book. They never left my mind but faded into my subconscious. They are the virtues that are powered by the guarantee – they are the virtues professed much more eloquently by Jesus during His time of teaching on earth. Billy Graham, in his book *The Secret of Happiness*, cites two quotes that are appropriate here. St. Francis of Sales said, "Nothing is so strong as gentlemen; nothing so gentle as real strength." Graham also cited Charles Dickens who wrote, "A man can never be a true gentleman in manner until he is a true gentleman at heart."[257]

John Wayland based his creed on the need for people to have a humble heart like Jesus. Jesus spoke of the example of the proverbial Good Samaritan (See Luke 23:25-37) and of his encounter with the Samaritan woman at the well (John 4:4-26). Jesus, through the parable of the Good Samaritan and his discussion with the Samaritan women, showed the importance of humility and a contrite heart. "For a Jewish man [Jesus] to speak to a woman in public, let alone to ask from her, a Samaritan, for a drink was a definite breach of rigid social custom of that day as well as a marked departure from the social animosity that existed between the two groups. Further, a rabbi and religious leader did not hold conversations with women of ill-repute."[258] Jesus spoke in glowing terms about the Good Samaritan, even though a Jew was never to speak favorably of "such people." He held up this man as an example of a humble servant who saw a person in need and responded with humility and love. *"Who thinks of the rights and feelings of others, rather than his own."*

Jesus did not see a serial adulteress standing at the well but a human sinner in need of mercy. In full public view, He approached a woman of low morals and a hated person of the Samaritan sect. Jesus spoke to the woman and offered her not scorn, derision, and condemnation, but everlasting life. He encountered a despised enemy of the Jews and saw her as a sinner in need of salvation. This woman at the well and the Samaritan were people just like us!

---

[257]Chapter Four: Happiness Through Meekness
[258]John F MacArthur. One Perfect Life. Part IV Notes. iBooks

O. A Meaningful Life

In the end, the guarantee provides an assurance that nothing else can. No insurance policy, no product warranty – no government-backed promise can provide the things that God's pledge of fellowship can afford – now and forever. The assurance from God is that if we believe in His Son and ask for forgiveness, all of our sins will be forgiven. The promise is that we will dwell with God in eternity. But the guarantee does not begin with our deaths. It defines who we are now – how we should act during our lives on earth. It provides the answer to the questions that are important. *Why am I here? What is the purpose and meaning of my life?*

To understand how we can arrive at the answer to these fundamental questions, let's examine how two extremely different people went about this inquiry. The first was a great and powerful ruler and the second, a concentration camp survivor. Two very different people in two diametrically opposed environments.

King Solomon, as we have discussed, was the richest, most powerful ruler of his time. He had more possessions, was worth more money, and had the greatest influence of any living person on earth.

Viktor Frankl was a renowned physician and psychologist. In the late 1920s, Frankl was named head of the suicide prevention department of the General Hospital in Vienna. After treating thousands of people over the four years he held this prestigious position, Frankl took the job as the head of the neurological department at the Rothschild Hospital, one of the few facilities that allowed Jews to practice medicine at that time. Then, in 1942, Frankl and his parents, wife, and brother were arrested and sent to the Theresienstadt concentration camp. Frankl's father died there within six months. Over the course of three years, Frankl was moved between four concentration camps, including Auschwitz where his brother died and his mother was killed. Frankl's wife died at his third camp, Bergen-Belsen. When Frankl's camp was liberated in 1945, he learned of the death of all his immediate family members, with the exception of his sister who had emigrated to Australia. In the camps, Frankl and fellow prisoners made an effort to address the despondency they observed in other inmates.[259] Despite these extremely different positions in life, both Frankl and King Solomon were tortured with the same nagging question – what is the meaning of life?

The book of Ecclesiastes opens as Solomon looks back at his life and all that he has accomplished. As indicated earlier, he concludes that everything in life was meaningless. Pleasures, work, knowledge, wisdom, and everything he built was meaningless. Solomon searched for meaning and purpose in life and, alas, he could find none. Everything was without meaning.

Viktor and his wife Tilly, and shortly thereafter his sixty-five-year-old mother, were transported to the Auschwitz-Birkenau concentration camp. His mother was immediately murdered in the gas chamber, and Tilly forever separated from him when she was moved to the Bergen-Belsen camp. After a few days, Frankl was selected for transfer to a labor camp. He was brought to Kaufering and later Tuerkheim, subsidiary camps of Dachau in Bavaria. In these death camps, he experienced a crisis of faith. He doubted the existence of God and, like Solomon, could find no meaning to his life.

Here were two men at the opposite ends of the spectrum in their lives. Solomon, the richest and most powerful man in the world with everything he could dream of or want at his disposal. And Frankl, confined to a concentration camp, on the verge of starvation, surrounded by disease, inhumane living conditions, separated from everyone and everything he loved and haunted by the knowledge

---

[259]https://www.goodtherapy.org/famous-psychologists/viktor-frankl.html

that any minute could be his last. Yet, each had the same exact nagging question playing over in their minds and souls: how can I find the meaning of life? After much turmoil and soul-searching, each came to the same conclusion.

At the end of the book of Ecclesiastes, we find that, after much contemplation and hand-wringing, Solomon finally arrived at the truth – that in order to find the meaning of life he must put God at the center of everything. Respect God, Solomon realized, and guide your life by his commands "for this is the whole duty of man" (Eccles. 12:13).

"As Viktor Frankl explains in *Man's Search for Meaning*, he and the other victims of the concentration camps, did not dare succumb to meaninglessness, for only an enduring faith in meaning kept them alive."[260] Frankl found meaning in life through his experiences in some of the most inhuman conditions ever perpetrated on human beings. Through these events he developed the firm belief that "human nature is motivated by the search for a life purpose." As a result, he formulated a therapeutical method of treatment based on focusing a patient on the pursuit of meaning in their life. "Frankl's theories were heavily influenced by his personal experiences of suffering and loss in Nazi concentration camps."[261] Frankl found that his faith in God gave true meaning to his life. Without God squarely at the core of his soul, he concluded, life was meaningless.

Faith in our Creator and a belief that He will give us everlasting life, free of doubt, envy, pain, or worry gives life meaning. Following Jesus's commands to love one another and treat others as we would like to be treated gives us a focus that can only be achieved with God

---

[260] Philip Yancey. "The Bible Jesus Read." P. 228. Zondervan, 2017-03-01. iBooks.

[261] https://www.goodtherapy.org/learn-about-therapy/types/logotherapy

at the center of our life. Faith gives us the assurance that God will balance the books in the end.

Knowing this, we lose our need for control and come to the realization that God is in control. No longer do our plans for retirement, all the wealth and power of Solomon or the Gestapo rulers of the concentration camps have control of our hearts and minds. Only our faith in God will bring true meaning to life. As soon as we accept Jesus as our Savior, we will get the answer that Solomon searched for at the end of his life and Frankl discovered in a concentration camp.

P. Claiming the Guarantee

By now I hope I have made the case for the wonderful, everlasting, and unlimited benefits that God's guarantee provides. I trust that you can understand the things that the guarantee affords us, both immediately and for eternity. Using the auto analogy, all you have to do to claim its protections is to determine which car best suits your needs, (including the terms and conditions of the warranty), go to a dealership, sign the sales contract and pay for the car. When you get an insurance policy you seek the help of an agent and together you determine what risks need protecting and how much insurance you need to guarantee the peace of mind that these risks can destroy. But, how do you claim the guarantee of salvation? How do you determine if the guarantee that God affords you fits your particular needs? Is there a document to sign? A price you must pay? Where do you go to get assistance to claim this guarantee?

First and foremost, the decision of whether to acquire the guarantee of salvation is a voluntary choice that you – and you alone – must make. My hope is that this book may help you make an informed decision or confirm the right choice if you have already committed your life to Christ. But it is a choice that you must make – it is not something that God will force on you. You have already been endowed with the gift of free will – you received it as your birthright. This free will allows you to accept or reject this gift of grace[262].

I have mentioned the groundbreaking book, authored by C.S. Lewis, *The Screwtape Letters*. In studying this work, we learn of the trials and tribulations of Screwtape who was leading and instructing the agent on earth – a character called Wormwood. His assignment: make a Christian turn away from God. In Letter #8 Screwtape tells Wormwood why God (the Enemy) does not force His creation (us) to love Him and accept his gift of grace. "You must have often wondered why the Enemy does not make more use of His power to be sensibly present to human souls in any degree He chooses and at any moment. But you now see that the Irresistible and the Indisputable are the two weapons which the very nature of His scheme forbids Him to use." In the annotated version of Lewis' book, his son then adds a footnote to further explain that "…humans always have a choice in their salvation or damnation. Notably, in chapter 9 of Lewis's novel, *The Great Divorce*[263] the character of George MacDonald says, "There are only two kinds of people in the end: those who say to God 'Thy will be done,' and those to whom God says, in the end 'Thy will be done.' All that are in Hell, chose it."[264]

Of course, I couldn't have said it better! In your life, you always have the choice when it comes to believing in God. It is a choice that God will not force on you. It's a choice you must freely make. I love how Lewis put it: you can accept the guarantee and tell God

---

[262] I will explain how free will works and how it relates to your relationship with God in the next chapter

[263] New York: Macmillan, 1946

[264] Excerpt From: C. S. Lewis. "The Screwtape Letters: Annotated Edition." HarperCollins Publisher, 2013-08-29. iBooks.

"Your will shall be done in my life" or you can reject the gift of grace and forgiveness and decide "My will shall be done." In the end you can reject the guarantee and decide, as Frank Sinatra sang, "I did it my way." Or you can surrender your will and claim the guarantee.

From my years of observation of people through the lens of court cases and my observations of the world at large, the people who most often reject the guarantee are successful people who acquire great wealth and power. They are convinced that they achieved this enviable position in life because they did things their way. They thump their chests and proudly claim that success is all due to their hard work and creative initiative.

Some think that they can "earn" the guarantee by being good and following the "laws and rules" laid out by the church. Instead of claiming that they did it their way, they claim they *earned* the right to be in fellowship with God because they followed the rules. They went to church each week, they tithed a tenth of their pre-tax earnings, they volunteered at the local food bank, and never cheated on their spouses.

But these people don't understand the story of the prodigal son. They forgot the sermon on the mount and they failed to take into account those *white lies* they told because, after all, they were only tiny lies. They, like the Pharisees, love to extol their superiority and boast that they are not sinners, like the tax collectors. But we can never be "good enough" to earn the guarantee. We can never stand before a Holy God and claim to be without sin.

Using Jesus's parable that we previously discussed of the righteous man and the tax collector, Yancey describes the dichotomy between the two this way:

> One man thanked God for his blessings, that he was not a robber, evildoer, adulterer, or tax collector.

He fasted twice a week and tithed his income. The other had a questionable morality, not much in the way of a resume and a thoroughly inadequate theology. One prayed eloquently; the other said seven simple words, "God, have mercy on me, a sinner". Yet which one went home justified?

Curiously, the righteous Pharisees had little historical impact, save for a brief time in your remote corner of the Roman Empire. But Jesus's disciples – an ornery, undependable, and hopelessly flawed group – became drunk with the power of a gospel that offered free forgiveness to the worst sinners and traitors. Those disciples managed to change the world. [265]

I believe the way to claim the guarantee is like a take-home self-test. Only God and you will know the results. However, the world should see the changes in you. Billy Graham was probably the best known (and probably the most successful) preacher of my lifetime. And by success, I do not mean in financial or power terms. I mean that he changed hearts for God and brought the good news of salvation to billions of people. In fact, it is estimated that He preached to approximately 2.2 billion people. He preached in 185 countries and territories. And, most importantly, it is believed that 2.2 million people at his crusades responded to the invitation to accept Christ and turn their lives over to Him[266]. Graham ended each of those

---

[265]Philip Yancey: *I was just wondering* (P. 98–1 01)

[266]factsandtrends.net. Billy Graham's Life & Ministry by the Numbers. Aaron Earls. February 21, 2018

crusades with an "altar call" which extended to attendees a path to fellowship with God. I could not create a better map to claim the guarantee than the Reverend Graham. Simply and directly He said we must:

1. Admit our need (we are sinners).
2. Be willing to turn from our sins by acknowledging them (repent).
3. Believe that Jesus Christ died for us on the cross and rose from the grave. (ask God for forgiveness)
4. Through prayer, invite Jesus Christ to come into and take control of our life. (Receive Him as Lord and Savior.)

"If we take these steps," he said, "we have the <u>assurance</u> that '... whosoever shall call upon the name of the Lord shall be saved'" (Rom. 10:13). Emphasis added.[267]

Graham based this simple four-step process on the words of Jesus. This is no magical formula. This was not something Graham made up.

Jesus gave us this key to unlock the guarantee. He said:

> I have come as a light into the world, that whoever believes in Me should not abide in darkness. And if anyone hears My words and does not believe, I do not judge him; for I did not come to judge the world but to save the world. He who rejects Me, and does not receive My words, has that which judges him – the word that I have spoken will judge him in the last day. For I have not spoken

---

[267]Billy Graham. The Secret of Happiness, Chapter 8. iBooks

on My own authority; but the Father who sent Me
gave Me a command, what I should say and what
I should speak. And I know that His command is
everlasting life. Therefore, whatever I speak, just as
the Father has told Me, so I speak. John 12:47–50

Therefore, the guarantee comes through belief and acceptance.
It is accepted only by a contrite and broken heart; by acceptance
of the fact that we can never be good enough to be acceptable to
God and by repentance through asking Christ to enter that broken
heart and heal it by the forgiveness of our sins. And by letting God
change us from the inside out, remaking us in His image so that His
will shall be done in our lives. We will claim the guarantee by surrendering control to God, by placing God at the center of our lives.
And, by doing so we will be changed persons and lights to the world.

Does this process make us perfect? No, just forgiven. Acceptance
of God's will in our lives, however, is a process called sanctification. It requires us to continually examine our hearts and repeatedly return to God to ask for forgiveness and guidance. But we do
so with the absolute confidence that we will be forgiven and that
we have been saved!

I want to conclude this chapter with a quote from Václav Havel,
the first democratically elected president of Czechoslovakia. Havel
grew up under a communist regime that is based on atheistic principals. Havel came to faith following the overthrow of this authori-
tarian form of government. After his conversion to Christianity and
his election as president, he traveled to Washington DC to address
a joint session of Congress. He told the assembled congressmen and
senators that "[t]he salvation of this human world lies nowhere else
than in the human heart... The only backbone to our actions, if they
are to be moral, is responsibility. Responsibility to something higher

than my family, my firm, my country, my success – responsibility to the order of being where all our actions are indelibly recorded and where, and only where, they will be properly judged." He went on to say that his heart was changed when he accepted Christ and that this faith lead to his own rebirth. That rebirth also carried him forward in transforming a nation and its presidency. In examining this transformation of Havel and Czechoslovakia, Philip Yancey answered the question: "Does faith matter to an individual or a society?" His answer: "Apparently, yes."[268]

---

[268]Philip Yancey. Vanishing Grace, P. 172. iBooks

CHAPTER 10

WHAT THE GUARANTEE
DOES NOT PROVIDE

In the interest of fairness, I should point out what the guarantee of salvation fails to provide to believers. I do not want to leave you with the notion that once you give yourself to Christ everything during your life on earth will be roses. Just the contrary; there will be difficulties, trials, disease, broken marriages, deaths of loved ones, despair, hurt, depression, and sadness. In other words, Christians will have the same problems that the rest of the population experiences. God never promised that life on earth would be carefree. Look at what happened to his Son. While God loves us and cares for us, we can get an idea of why suffering occurs by examining the history of Jesus's life on earth. God so loved us that He allowed His only Son to suffer and die so that our sins could be forgiven. John 3:16, NIV.

There was a purpose to the suffering endured by Christ for us. However, we also know that after Jesus went through His ordeal he was united in heaven with God, His father, and was glorified because of the suffering and death He endured for us. This death resulted in the reuniting of all believers with God. As we have already seen, we are guaranteed this fellowship forever.

To try to fully answer the question of why a loving God allows suffering would take a book of its own. I struggled with this question when I was just a child. My young life was carefree, until one bright, cold New Year's Day.

On January first, I was playing with my younger brother, John, after a snowfall. As we played in the woods across the street from our house in Bethpage, NY, we saw a police car approaching. We continued to watch as it pulled up to our house. "What are they doing here?" we asked each other. We watched the police officer get out of his patrol car and head for our front door. John and I were transfixed as we continued to watch from the woods as my mom came to the door. She appeared to greet to the policeman and stood facing the officer for a minute. Then she clasped her hands to her face and became wobbly. We were scared and stunned and didn't know what to do. Within a few minutes neighbors appeared at our house and the world seemed to spin out of control. Without much warning, we were called home and without even seeing our mom, were whisked away to a neighbor's house. Two young boys, ages eight and six, couldn't comprehend what was happening. We were shoved in front of a TV with one of my best friends as the adults in the next room were talking in hushed tones. Although we tried, we couldn't make out what they were saying. John and I just sat in front of the TV, scared and silent.

What was going on? Where was our mom? Was she sick? Why were we here? Where was our sixteen-month-old sister, Lisa? What were the police doing at our house? Why wasn't anyone telling us what was happening?

It seemed like we sat there in front of the television for a long time with no answers to our questions. After an interminably long wait, the door to the den opened and my friend's dad walked in. His eyes looked down and didn't meet ours until he knelt down and softly delivered the words that hit us like a ton of bricks. Our dad was not coming home tonight. He was dead. Those words came like a bolt from the blue. The man we'd said goodbye to that morning as he left for work would never be coming home again.

The next several days were a blur. We were not allowed to attend the funeral or burial. My mother did not want to expose my brother and me to that and my sixteen-month-old sister was too fidgety to sit still. Nevertheless, a parade of mourners came through our house, culminating in a post burial "reception." There in our small house, jam-packed with family and neighbors, one adult after another came up to me saying what a great dad I had and how sorry they were. Each one tried to hold their emotions in check, but they were unable to do so. I couldn't comprehend what had happened. Why wasn't he coming home? What happened to him? No one gave me answers. Mom just told us that our dad went to heaven.

The people who showed up at the reception included aunts, uncles, cousins, and neighbors, yet no one had answers for me. The priests from our church came and offered blessings and hugs. But my questions went unanswered. But one rather strange thing did happen. As mourners took their leave, a number of the men took me aside, patted me on the back and told me that I was now "the man of the house." I was stunned. I was eight years old but somehow I was magically changed into the man of the house. *How would that work? Did I need to get a job? What exactly did I need to do? What about playing ball with the guys from the neighborhood? Would I still play right field?* I could not, for the life of me, understand or comprehend what my new duties would be. I couldn't ask my mom, she was devastated. She cried all the time. I couldn't ask my buddies, they were just kids like me. If I had to be the man of the house, I would have to figure it out for myself. I would do my best. After all, I had watched my dad be the actual man of the house and I could do some of what he did. I finally decided that the answers did not matter.

It didn't matter because I didn't believe my dad was really dead. For the next four years, my life was like a nightmare. I was absolutely convinced that I was dreaming. I knew that I would wake up "in the morning" and everything would be, once again, as it was on that first day of January.

Very shortly after the funeral, my mom sold our house and moved us from Long Island to Sarasota, Florida. We moved right next door to my very Italian grandpa and grandma. Grandpa was going to be our surrogate dad. I loved my grandparents, they always treated us like we were special. Grandpa would take my brother and me fishing and we would help him tend his vegetable garden in the back yard. He wasn't much into playing sports but he did let us cook with him.

Life was getting back to some semblance of normal and I tried not to think of how and when my dad would return. Nevertheless, the lingering pain of my father's sudden death continued to haunt me. But I kept most of the pain inside. After all, I was now the man of the house. In my prayers, however, I would share my torment with God and ask many questions, without a seeming answer. These were questions that my mother, grandma, and grandpa never answered for me. Did he die or was he just away for a time? When would he return? If he did die, why did God make my dad die? If God made him die, how did he die? Why, if he died of a heart attack as my mom said, why did he die so young?[269]

---

[269]My mother never told my brother, my sister and me that my dad committed suicide. It wasn't until some 36 years later (after my mother passed away) that my brother John found the news article in the NY Times describing how my dad, on his lunch break from CBS in New York, went to the top of a building and jumped to his death.

The pain, however, never left for long. These questions and the long-simmering hurt of my dad's sudden death, came to the forefront again just four years later when my beloved grandfather died of cancer. This second loss really sent me into a tailspin of despair. The pain of loss was compounded and the rug was again pulled out from under me. I was terribly distraught and ran away from home, making it just about a quarter-mile away to one of the vacant pieces of wooded land that dotted my neighborhood. After searching all afternoon and into the night my mom and grandma found me curled up under a tree, my face streaked with sweat, and my eyes reddened from hours of crying. The grim reality of death suddenly became very real. The dream of my dad being there when I woke up was shattered by harsh reality.

Why would God let this pain invade my life again? Why was my grandpa, my surrogate dad, also taken away from me? Was I now the man of two houses? How could I take care of my mom, grandma, brother, and sister? Questions asked...but no answers given.

About two years later, my mother's brother settled in Sarasota with his family and opened an Italian restaurant. He gave me my first job at age fourteen as a dishwasher and bus boy. It was great to have another man in my life. After school and on weekends we would work, side-by-side, in his restaurant – him cooking and me cleaning. It was hard work but it was actually fun. My grandmother loved having her son and his family close and everything seemed like life was, once again, returning to another type of "normalcy."

However, after a year or so something strange happened. My mom drove me to my uncle's restaurant to work one Saturday morning and all the lights were out. The door was locked and my uncle's car was not in the parking lot. We immediately went home and my mom and grandma tried calling him. In the days before answering machines and voicemail, that was all they could do.

Hours passed without any answer so we decided to go to the house my uncle Tony and his family were renting. No one was home. His car was not in the carport. My brother boosted me up to peer into the living room window and there was no furniture there. Three days later we found out that he and his family suddenly left one night without any notice or warning. They cleaned out their bank accounts and just up and left. No note from my uncle, no forwarding address, no warning... nothing!

What I didn't know then was that my mother had co-signed as a guarantor on the equipment loan and the lease for his restaurant. When my uncle took off he did leave us something – he left my mother all of the liability for his debt. The bank foreclosed on the note and we lost everything. We had no nest egg and couldn't pay either the lease payments on his restaurant or the mortgage on our house. We spent the next six years moving in and out of small apartments and tiny two-bedroom villas, barely getting by. And, as a bonus, I also found out two months before I was to start my freshman year in college that my college fund was gone. I had to work and borrow my way through college and law school. It was, without exaggeration, a very difficult childhood experience. How could a loving God let all of these tragedies happen to my mom, grandma, brother, sister and me? I had no answers.

A horrific, life-changing event occurred to most of us twenty years ago on September 11, 2001. We watched in real-time as terrorists attacked our country and killed almost 3,000 of our fellow citizens. A shaken country asked, "Why?" How could God allow this to happen? Two weeks later, Billy Graham stood in the pulpit at the National Cathedral during a service to remember the dead.

I still remember everything about the planes hitting the towers in New York and the Pentagon. I remember the crater left by United Flight 93 after the brave passengers rushed the cockpit to save a further attack on Washington. Seared into my brain forever are the life-shattering images of the aftermath. I will never forget, however, the healing words of the Reverend Graham. "We come together today to affirm our conviction that God cares for us, whatever our ethnic, religious, or political background may be. The Bible says that He is 'the God of all comfort, who comforts us in all our troubles.'" He went on to say that "[n]o matter how hard we try, words simply cannot express the horror, the shock and the revulsion we all feel over what took place in this nation on Tuesday morning. September 11 will go down in our history as a Day to Remember."

Graham however did not waiver as he addressed the nation with the question on all our minds and hearts.

But how do we understand something like this? Why does God allow evil like this to take place? Perhaps that is what you are asking. You may even be angry at God. I want to assure you that God understands these feelings that you may have.

We've seen so much that brings tears to our eyes and makes us all feel a sense of anger. But God can be trusted, even when life seems at its darkest.

What are some of the lessons we can learn?

First, we are reminded of the mystery and reality of evil. I have been asked hundreds of times why God allows tragedy and suffering. I have to confess that I do not know the answer. I have to accept, by faith, that God is sovereign, and that He is a God of love and mercy and compassion in the midst of suffering.

The Bible says God is not the Author of evil. In 1 Thessalonians 2:7 the Bible talks about the mystery of iniquity. The Old Testament Prophet Jeremiah said, "The heart is deceitful above all things and beyond cure."

The lesson of this event is not only about the mystery of iniquity and evil, but, second, it's a lesson about our need for each other. What an example New York and Washington have been to the world these past few days! None of us will forget the pictures of our courageous firefighters and police, or the hundreds of people standing patiently in line to donate blood.

...

Finally, difficult as it may be for us to see right now, this event can give a message of hope—hope for the present and hope for the future. Yes, there is hope. There is hope for the present because the stage, I believe, has already been set for a new spirit in our nation. We desperately need a spiritual renewal in this country, and God has told us in His Word time after time that we need to repent of our sins and return to Him, and He will bless us in a new way.

...

Here in this majestic National Cathedral we see all around us the symbol of the cross. For the Christian, the cross tells us that God understands our sin and our suffering, for He took them upon Himself in the Person of Jesus Christ. From the cross, God declares, "I love you. I know the heartaches and the sorrows and the pain that you feel. But I love you." The story does not end with the cross, for Easter points us beyond the tragedy of the cross to the empty tomb. It tells us that there is hope for eternal life, for Christ has conquered evil and death and hell. Yes, there is hope.[270]

This hope has, as its bedrock, the guarantee of salvation that is marked by the cross and the empty grave. We know that no matter what happens, God has promised us that all who claim the guarantee will be with Him in eternity. Eternally feeling nothing but pure joy. No tears, no death, no fears, no evil, no anxiety, no betrayal.

In my years of research on this book, I have heard God's answers to all my "why" questions and they all point to the cross upon which He allowed His Son to suffer. His answers point to the type of love that requires no tit-for-tat, no quid pro quo. The type of love that is unending and unconditional. That love is revealed on Easter morning by the empty tomb.

A. A Long Journey

Once we have decided to put our faith in Christ we have committed ourselves to a life of service. Christ asks us a question, "Do you love me?" When we answer, "Yes, Lord," He then tells us to feed

---

[270]https://billygraham.org/?s=remarks+at+the+National+Cathedral+on+September+14%2C+2001

and take care of his sheep and lambs. John 21:15-17, NIV. There are no "strings attached" to the guarantee but a response to the agape[271] love shown by God through Christ.

What would you do for someone who lays down his life to save yours? This situation was addressed by the great author Alexandre Dumas in his book *The Count of Monte Cristo*. In the movie, based on the book, the main character, Edmond Dantes[272] is framed and sent to prison for a crime he did not commit. Languishing in prison, he befriends a man (who he refers to as "the priest") who teaches him about God's love and forgiveness. Dantes later escapes this island prison and is washed up on a seemingly deserted island. There he encounters pirates and is forced to provide entertainment for his captors by agreeing to a knife fight – a fight to the death – with a pirate named Jacopo.

Jacopo was brought to the island to be buried alive for stealing from the pirate captain. Jacopo, it seems, is an expert knife fighter. Edmond Dantes is given a choice; fight to the death (and possibly save his own life) or refuse to fight and be killed by the pirates. The fight to the death ends when Edmond gets the better of Jacopo and, with the knife at his throat, Edmond shows mercy and spares Jacopo's life. The penalty for this result was supposed to be the life of Edmond, however he convinces the captain of the pirate ship to spare the life of Jacopo by Dantes agreeing to become indentured to the pirates. The captain agrees and Jacopo is set free. Dantes shows grace by wagering his life to spare the life of Jacopo, a man he never met or knew. Jacopo, who moments before tried to kill

---

[271]This is one of several Greek words for love. When the word "agape" is used in the Bible, it refers to a pure, willful, sacrificial love that intentionally desires another's highest good.

[272]In the movie, Edmond was played by the actor Jim Caviezel, who fittingly also played Christ in The Passion of the Christ.

Dantes in the fight, is overcome with humility and gratefulness. In return, Jacopo looks into the eyes of Edmond and vows, "I swear I am your man forever."

Christ rescued us from death by agreeing to be a substitute for our sins. In return we should pledge to be "His men and women forever." The guarantee therefore promises a long journey of faith. However, it does not provide an easy shortcut to heaven. "There is a great market for religious experience in our world; there is little enthusiasm for the patient acquisition of virtue, little inclination to sign up for a long apprenticeship in what earlier generations of Christians called holiness."[273] Christ asks us if we love Him. Do we love Jesus for dying on the cross to guarantee the forgiveness of all our sins? Do we love Jesus for being the willing substitute for the punishment we deserve for our sinful nature? If you believe Jesus died for your sins, your easy answer is "I am your man (or woman) forever." If you love Him you will do all in your power to obey His commands. If you love him, you will feed His lambs, take care of the widows and orphans, shelter the homeless, treat your enemy as you would your cherished neighbors. In short, we will love God with all our hearts and minds, and bodies.

B. Delayed Gratification

One of the virtues I have tried to teach my children is the value of delayed gratification. In today's world, this is a rare commodity. The world teaches us that immediate gratification is the best way to live our lives. Easy access to credit based on a thin piece of plastic in our wallets or purses gives us the ability to "buy now and pay later."

---

[273]Eugene H. Peterson. "A Long Obedience in the Same Direction." P. 22. InterVarsity Press, 2012-04-25. iBooks.

Growing up as a kid in Bethpage, I was taught that delayed gratification was the only way to acquire something I wanted. Following my mother's example, if I wanted to buy my mom a Christmas gift I would put it on lay-away. I would pick out her present at the Five-and-Dime in early October and make weekly payments until the pink bedroom slippers were paid off in full by mid-December. This system caused me to pay for something before it be could be acquired. It was clearly a matter of doing errands, picking up bottles to return to the store for money, and saving my pennies so I would be able to retrieve my mom's Christmas gift by Christmas Eve. It seems this is a novel concept in today's world.

"Delay of gratification [is] the act of resisting an impulse to take an immediately available reward in the hope of obtaining a more-valued reward in the future. ... The ability to delay gratification is essential to self-regulation, or self-control."[274] This was an important concept to my mom and one that she instilled in me. It became a way of life as I grew into an adult, married, and raised children. Ilene Strauss Cohen Ph.D., wrote in an article published in *Psychology Today* that "[c]hoosing to have something now might feel good, but making the effort to have discipline and manage your impulses can result in bigger or better rewards in the future. Over time, delaying gratification will improve your self-control and ultimately help you achieve your long-term goals faster." The author goes on to explain how delaying gratification, even when it causes pain, helps us achieve greater goals.

But what happens when you want to be instantly satisfied in all areas of your life? What happens when you only avoid pain? What results from

---

[274]https://www.britannica.com/science/delay-of-gratification

needing to have the newest and most expensive car, even though you're in horrible credit card debt? Living for a purpose becomes impossible at that point because *a life spent avoiding pain doesn't result in goals getting accomplished*. It might be an easier life in the short term, but it won't necessarily be a better life in the long run. When we live in pursuit of immediate pleasure – needing to have the newest gadget or accessories the moment they're available or wanting the perfect job without getting an education or working our way up from the bottom – we become just like toddlers again, completely incapable of delaying gratification. (emphasis added)[275]

Paul, in prison again in Rome, wrote to Timothy, reassuring him of the hope and conviction that yet filled him, "I know whom I have believed, and am convinced that he is able to guard what I have entrusted to him for that day" (2 Tim. 1:12). Paul is able to look ahead with such confidence because of his bedrock belief in the God who has walked with him and shown himself real in so many ways. Despite the beatings, stonings, imprisonments, shipwrecks, and times without food, water, or clothing, Paul knew he could trust God. *Something wonderful awaits him*, and his present suffering will be redeemed and will one day seem as nothing. Paul knows God and the love of Jesus, through the Holy Spirit. This relationship gives him strength no matter what he experiences."[276] He knows this delayed gratification is worth it because he has the

---

[275] Ilene Strauss Cohen Ph.D., The Benefits of Delaying Gratification. Psychology Today, December 26, 2017

[276] Philip Yancey & Brenda Quinn. "Meet the Bible." P. 2111-12 Zondervan. iBooks, emphasis added

guarantee of eternal fellowship and bliss with God. Paul is "all in" on the notion of delayed gratification, despite the urgency of his present condition.

We are God's creation. He has created us to have pain, even though our bodies and minds want us to avoid pain. Pain has its purpose. It warns us that something is wrong. As we grow up we learn to understand the important place that pain has in our lives. More on this later.

God, in a sense, is asking us to delay gratification. He tells us that we will experience pain and disappointment in the short run (our life on earth) but in the end, we will have eternity waiting for us. Jesus, in his Sermon on the Mount, referred to this when He tried to explain the concept of treasures in heaven. "As Jesus explains it, we are accumulating a kind of savings account, 'storing up treasures' in heaven rather than on earth – treasures so great that they will pay back any amount of suffering in this life. The Old Testament has dropped a few scant hints about an afterlife, but Jesus speaks plainly about a place where "the righteous will shine like the sun in the kingdom of their Father" (Matt. 13:43).[277] Matt. 6:1-34.

In the eleventh chapter of the book of Hebrews, we get a view of faith through the tool of delayed gratification. "The picture of faith that emerges from this chapter does not fit into an easy formula. Sometimes faith leads to victory and triumph. Sometimes it requires a gritty determination to 'hang on at any cost.' Hebrews 11 does not hold up one kind of faith as superior to the other. Both rest on the belief that God is in ultimate control and will indeed keep his promises – whether that happens in this life or in the next."[278]

---

[277]Philip Yancey & Brenda Quinn. "Meet the Bible." P. 1443. Zondervan. iBooks.
[278]Philip Yancey & Brenda Quinn. "Meet the Bible." P. 2145 Zondervan. iBooks.

As I explained in the story about my three good friends discussing the subject of death on the deck of our Canadian fishing lodge, I confidently spoke of my lack of fear of death because I *know* what awaits me on the other side. Like Paul, I *try* not to ruminate about my present troubles because God's covenant promise to me, fulfilled in Jesus, is guaranteed. "Apart from Christ, we live in constant fear of death and in constant bondage to our failures, or sins. Only Jesus can set us free, that's why he is worth the risk." [279]

C. Answered Prayers?

Prayer is one of the most difficult issues in my mind when it comes to being a Christian. As a boy, I cried out to God about the death of my dad and grandfather and he seemingly was quiet in response. At times I have struggled with my prayer life. Other times I pray fervently but lose track of my thoughts. I have had, over my life, many questions about prayer. *Does God listen to our prayers? If God does listen, why doesn't He answer? Once I have the guarantee will my prayers be answered? Why should I even pray if God already knows what my prayers will be? How do I know if my prayers are answered?*

If this sub-section about unanswered prayers is in the chapter about what the guarantee does not provide, does that mean these questions are already answered? To give you a lawyerly answer... it depends!

In an attempt to answer these questions, I think we need to start with the bedrock question – what is prayer? "The real value of persistent prayer is not so much that we get what we want as that we become the person we should be. A person prays, said Augustine,

---

[279] Philip Yancey & Brenda Quinn. "Meet the Bible." P. 2130-31. Zondervan. iBooks.

'that he himself may be constructed, not that God may be instructed'. Prayer offers an opportunity for God to remodel us, to chisel marble like a sculptor, touch up colors like an artist, edit words like a writer. The work continues until death, never perfected in this life."[280]

Therefore, prayer is a mode of communication between God and his children. It is a form of Christian therapy, where we tell God our deepest desires and problems and He reworks our hearts and souls from the inside out. If we think of prayer this way, most of the answers become clear(er).

Does God listen to our prayers? Yes, according to Jesus, He does. Jesus is quoted as saying that God listens to our prayers and "whatever you ask in prayer, believe that you have received it and it will be yours" (Mark 11:24, NIV). Jesus didn't mean that God will grant you whatever you ask in the exact manner you envision. Just like every part of the Bible, we need to read this statement in the context of everything Jesus said. He also said that God will listen to your payers and will give "... good gifts to those who ask" (Matt. 7:11, NIV). Jesus did not promise that God will give us anything we want, just that He will listen to our prayers and give us what is good for us.

When my dad committed suicide I prayed that God would turn back time so that life would be like it was before he died[281]. I desperately, continually, and fervently prayed for God to bring my father back. But of course, my father did not come back. How can that prayer not be a "good thing" that God should give me?

---

[280]Philip Yancey. "Prayer." Zondervan. iBooks.

[281]My recurring dreams actually followed this prayer. I would be walking down a street and would see my dad on the other side. I would rush to him only to find that he had disappeared from my sight. These dreams had different settings but always had the same result. They lasted well into my thirties.

Well, what if God had granted that prayer? What would my life be like? What would my dad's life be like? When I think of these things I understand that perhaps answering that prayer may not have been what was good for me or my dad. You see, about a year before he committed suicide, my dad was in a serious train accident. We lived on Long Island and dad would commute every day into New York City to work at CBS Television. He took the Long Island Railroad from Bethpage to NYC. One day, on the trip back home, the train derailed and he sustained a very bad back injury. He was treated for weeks in the hospital. When he came home he was not the same. He couldn't play with me. He couldn't work on finishing the attic – where my brother's and my bedrooms were going to be. He was *different*. He was in constant pain. He had to go to therapy sessions and get pain shots. Eventually, he went back to work but his life – and the lives of my mom, brother, and baby sister – were never the same. He worked through the pain, came home, sat in a chair, and tried to engage with his family. He tried… until he apparently gave up and ended his pain.

If God granted my prayer, would my dad's life have been a joyous one? Would his pain have ever gone away? Or would he have endured a life in constant unremitting pain? Would that have been good? What would our family life be with a dad in this condition? And if he lived and we stayed in Bethpage, I would never have moved to Florida, never attended Florida State University, and never would have met the love of my life. If Mary Alice didn't marry me I would never experience the sheer joy brought to me by my children and grandchildren.

George Bailey, in the movie *It's a Wonderful Life* (a staple of my Christmas), found out what would happen if his urgent prayer was answered in the way George wanted it to be answered by God. He was at the end of his rope, his family's savings and loan was being taken over and he was wanted for embezzlement (a crime he did not commit) by the authorities. He tried a plea for help from the bitter old man who ran the rival bank – but was told that he would be "better off dead." In his desperation, he ran to a bridge and tried to end his life in the same way my dad did. Everything that George had accomplished in his life suddenly seemed to be meaningless. He felt that he was nothing – his entire life seemed as if it were crashing down around his feet[282]. He prayed to God and wished that he had never been born. As he stood at the highest point on the bridge, ready to jump into the icy waters below, his guardian angel, Clarence, hovered nearby. And Clarence was devising a plan.

Clarence wondered, what if God granted George's prayer? What if George Bailey could be shown what life would be like if he had never been born? Suddenly everything changed. Clarence was able to show George what life would be like if he never graced the earth. The result was a gut punch. Clarence showed George the housing development that he had funded for the working-class people of Bedford Falls. But it was not how George remembered this beautiful community. It was not filled with children playing and neighbors talking and laughing on their front porches. It was totally changed. This idyllic middle-class housing development was gone and replaced by a slum.

This slum was filled with broken-down shanties owned by the hard-hearted bank president, Mr. Potter. The beautiful houses Gorge had financed for the working-class people of Bedford Falls were now a series of tenement houses rented by a Scrooge-like landlord. The town of quaint shops, movie theaters, and churches was gone; replaced by rough speakeasies, bars, and dance halls. The pharmacist that George worked for as a young boy, who George prevented from

---

[282]Does that sound a little like Solomon?

making a catastrophic mistake with a wrongly filled prescription, was now a ruined, broken-down drunk. Angel Clarence explained that since God granted George's prayer that he was never born, he was not there to save the pharmacist from giving the wrong prescription to a child who was poisoned. Clarence also revealed that 300 Americans died because George's brother Harry, who George saved from falling through the ice as a child, didn't live to join the Air Force. Clarence tells George that Harry Bailey died as a child and did not grow up to be a flying ace in WWII. As a result, he was not there to save a transport ship of soldiers heading to Europe. All 300 men lost their lives to a German submarine.

George was grief-stricken and horrified. He never dreamed that he had affected so many lives. The harsh reality of his answered prayer came home to roost. Clarence made him see that no matter how hard his life was, no matter how much pain and anguish he was currently experiencing, he did not want God to answer his prayer in the way George wanted. George Bailey realized that if God answered his prayer, terrible things would happen to the lives of the people he touched and loved. George realized that the ordeals and traumas he endured in life all served a purpose. And that, in reality, his was truly *A Wonderful Life*.

Back in 1990, Garth Brooks had a number one hit with his song, *Unanswered Prayers*. In this haunting song, he delivers the news that sometimes it's better *not* to get what you ask for because you often don't really know what's best for your life. In one of the great lines from the chorus, Garth tells us that God does listen to all of our prayers. He then reminds us that God just doesn't give us the answer that we want. He tells us that "[j]ust because He doesn't answer, doesn't mean He don't care." But, do we really believe that? I mean, do we believe there are prayers that God just answers with a "No"? Or do we get troubled that God doesn't answer prayers in the way that we want them answered?

I wonder if this was what Jesus meant when He said that God will answer prayer in a way that provides good gifts to those who ask. I believe God answers every prayer, but that doesn't mean the answer has to be yes. Sometimes, just like any parent on earth, our heavenly Father has to say, "No, that's not good for you," or "No, I have something better in mind."

This calls to mind a scene from the sequel to *Bruce Almighty*. In the sequel, Bruce's old rival in the newsroom, Evan, has left the TV anchor position in Buffalo and gone into politics. He heads to Washington and is promptly thrust into a position where a powerful senator is trying to force him to vote in favor of a bill that will open up a nature preserve to development. If this land gets developed, there will be an adverse impact on water rights. During all of this political maneuvering, Evan gets a visit from God. Seems that God has other plans for Evan. In the movie, God turns Evan into a modern-day Noah, complete with the burlap toga and beard. God asks Evan to build an ark to save the animals from a flood that the development is going to bring forth.

Evan resists God and questions God's power. He uses prayer as an example and says that God doesn't even care enough to grant prayer requests. In response, God takes Evan to a diner and tries to show and explain how prayer works. "God" puts it this way:

> Let me ask you something. If someone prays for patience, you think God gives them patience? Or does he give them the opportunity to be patient? If he prays for courage, does God give him courage, or does He give him opportunities to be courageous? If someone prays for the family to be closer,

do you think God zaps them with warm fuzzy feelings, or does He give them opportunities to love
each other?

Evan finally understands prayer and how God intends prayer
for our good.

D. Freedom from Discipline?

I was born in 1953 and really grew up in late fifties, the six-
ties and early seventies. My parents believed in discipline and they
showed love by providing a firm understanding of right and wrong
through the discipline they provided to my brother, sister, and me.
After my father died, my mother had the burden of raising three kids,
ranging in age from one to eight, all by herself. She did not fail to
show her love for us by shirking her responsibility of providing the
discipline we needed. Yes, love for us through discipline. Without
discipline, we would not know right from wrong. Without discipline, we would not have been able to grasp how to navigate a life
based on the proper way to conduct ourselves. Without discipline,
we would not be able to live in a country governed by the rule of
law. The discipline that we received from our wonderful mother was
borne of love for us and it gave my sister, brother, and me a great
perspective on how to succeed in life. This discipline, I believe, had
its foundation in God's love for us, His children.

I was raised with some kids who didn't have this same form of
love shown to them. Their parents believed in giving their children
the freedom to make their own choices. These parents, in a well-in-
tentioned effort to raise independent children, *spared* their kids
from the *burdens and rigors* of discipline. These children turned out
to be like sailboats without keels, drifting through life and "winging

it" – making decisions without any sense of the right or wrong way of doing things. In my observation, children who fly by the seat of their pants lack the necessary tools required to make correct and informed decisions. I have a sense that they were not loved like I was. Their parents seem removed and remote, disassociated with their lives.

The guarantee does not free us from being disciplined by our Father in heaven, it allows us to experience the love God has for His children. As we see in Hebrews 12:1-28, "God disciplines us for our good, that we may share in his holiness. No discipline seems pleasant at the time. In fact, at times it may seem painful or punitive. Later, however, it produces a harvest of righteousness and peace for those who have been trained by it."[283]

E. Freedom from Pain and Suffering?

As mentioned above, God has not promised to free us from pain and anguish... on earth. If he refused to prevent His Son from experiencing these things, we should not expect that, as believers, we will be spared. Jesus said as much to His disciples. He likened the pain that we are all to expect on earth as something that will lead to joy. What? Pain leading to joy? In the Book of John, chapter 16, Jesus analogizes this transformative experience to the pain a woman experiences giving birth. He reminds the disciples (and us) that a woman giving birth experiences a great deal of pain and anguish. However, when her child is born she forgets the pain because she is overcome with extreme joy. v. 22.

I was present at the birth of all three of my children. While I will never truly know how much pain my wife experienced, I could

---

[283]Philip Yancey & Brenda Quinn. "Meet the Bible." Zondervan. iBooks.

see the strain on her face and in her body while holding her hand, rubbing her back, and trying to coach her to breathe through the contractions. When Carol Burnett was asked by a male reporter to describe the pain of childbirth, she told him to try and imagine what it would feel like if he took his lower lip and stretched it over his head. My wife bravely and willingly experienced this ordeal to get to the utter joy she felt as a beautiful infant was laid in her arms. Pain was necessary to experience the unrivaled joy of bringing forth a new life.

After Jesus alludes to the pain and joy of childbirth, He turns the focus on Himself. Jesus told His disciples that He was going away very soon. He predicted that His death would bring them grief and fear. He told them that they would watch Him die a horrible death and as a result, they would weep and mourn. But Jesus also told them that their grief and pain would transform into joy when they saw the empty tomb and experienced His resurrected body.

He also promised that their futures would include further turmoil and pain. They would be rejected and they would experience hatred. They would be scorned for their beliefs. Upon hearing this they must have been wondering just how a lifetime of pain could lead to joy. Just how and when will these travails lead to happiness? Jesus assured them that "I have told you these things so that in me you may have peace. In this world you will have trouble. But take heart! I have overcome the world." (v. 33)

He was telling them this so they could "rest assured" that this life on earth will end with a grand reunion with Him in heaven. Because Christ overcame the world, we will experience the joy of knowing that our transgressions are forgiven. It is guaranteed! We too will overcome the world and will be at peace with God in heaven one day. In heaven, all our aches, pains, anxieties, heartaches, and anguish of every sort will be wiped away. We will experience sorrow no more. We will have everlasting peace and joy. Just as Jesus gave this assurance to His disciples, He gave the guarantee to us as well.

C.S. Lewis experienced a great deal of pain in his life. This pain was punctuated by the death of his mother when he was a child. Lewis was no stranger to pain and overcame a series of crushing ordeals that caused him to doubt his faith. He spoke openly about these travails and wondered aloud about the question of whether God was, indeed, good. The death of his mother when he was a small boy was only the first blow.

As mentioned earlier, Lewis was long a bachelor. He, however, eventually met a woman and fell headlong in love. The time they spent together was, according to Lewis, the very best years of his life. He transformed from a stalwart bachelor to a happy and devoted husband overnight. But then the love of his life succumbed to cancer. Lewis dealt with the pain of her death by shaking his fist at God and looking inward in an effort to try to make sense of it all. His struggles are reflected in his book, *A Grief Observed*. He writes that God was either who He said He was or a cruel being who took delight in the pain that he inflicted.

> The terrible thing is that a perfectly good God is in this matter hardly less formidable than a Cosmic Sadist. The more we believe that God hurts only to heal, the less we can believe that there is any use in begging for tenderness. A cruel man might be bribed—might grow tired of his vile sport—might have a temporary fit of mercy, as alcoholics have fits of sobriety. But suppose that what you are up against is a surgeon whose intentions are wholly good. The kinder and more conscientious he is, the more inexorably he will go on cutting. If he yielded

to your entreaties, if he stopped before the operation was complete, all the pain up to that point
would have been useless. But is it credible that such
extremities of torture should be necessary for us?
Well, take your choice. The tortures occur. If they
are unnecessary, then there is no God or a bad one.
If there is a good God, then these tortures are necessary. For not even [a] moderately good Being could
possibly inflict or permit them if they weren't.

You can't see anything properly while your eyes are
blurred with tears.

These struggles with the realization that this pain was allowed
by a Holy God troubled Lewis to the point of questioning his faith.
God, however, had other plans for him. This painful struggle would
lead Lewis to deeply search his faith and, as a result, he wrote some
of the best books on the subject of pain. In the forward to Lewis'
ground-breaking book, *A Grief Observed*, his stepson wrote: "C. S.
Lewis, had written before on the topic of pain (*The Problem of Pain*,
1940), and pain was not an experience with which he was unfa-
miliar." However, he goes on to explain, "all human relationships
end in pain - it is the price that our imperfection has allowed Satan
to exact from us for the privilege of love." To paraphrase a famous
quote, Lewis determined that it was better to have loved and experienced pain then to have never loved at all! Pain was the price paid
for the privilege of loving another deeply.

The disciple Peter is another "case study" in the power of pain
and anguish. As you know, he denied Jesus three times on the night
Jesus was betrayed. When the rooster crowed at the conclusion of
the third denial the pain and utter torture Peter experienced was

manifest when he realized what he had done. Earlier that very night Peter had promised Jesus that he would be a steadfast disciple, even if it meant Peter's death. And here he was, just a few hours later, denying his Christ and Lord to save his own skin. What a hypocrite. And what a coward. As the realization of what he had just done swept over him, he felt the pain of betrayal that he had inflicted on the Son of God and the hatred and anguish he felt toward himself. He was inconsolable.

However, that pain led to joy when he was forgiven by Jesus after the resurrection. This experience of the joy of forgiveness affected Peter deeply. This is evident in his writings. He relates this experience of pain leading to joy in his letter to the first-century churches (1 Peter). The historical events surrounding this letter involve the persecution of Christians by the Roman authorities. The churches were under assault and Christians were being jailed and killed. The new Christians were wondering why Jesus did not return to earth and vindicate His church.

> Most likely, Peter is writing this letter during an out-break of persecution under Nero. Urgent questions stir up within the embattled Christian community. Should they flee or resist? Should they tone down their outward signs of faith? Peter's readers, their lives in danger, need clear advice. Beyond that, they also want some explanation of the meaning of suffering. Why does God allow it? Does God care?

> Peter attempts to answer these questions in the first chapter of his book. He, like Christ before him, deals not with the question of the cause of the anguish and pain the church is experiencing (the

why question) but instead deals with the results achieved by the suffering they were going through. He answers that suffering can 'refine' faith, much as a furnace refines impure metals. Suffering shifts attention from the rewards of this world – wealth, status, power – to more permanent, "imperishable" rewards in the life to come.[284]

I was interrupted with my writing just now by an email from the daughter of a good friend and colleague of mine. I was informed that his pancreatic cancer had spread to the lining of his brain. This was a very rare progression of his cancer and the doctors had just informed the family that there is no treatment that can be given. This man is an excellent lawyer and well respected by everyone who knows him. We were both members of an international association of trial lawyers focused on the defense of civil litigation. This group would meet twice a year to educate, socialize, and keep our bonds of camaraderie strong. The email from his daughter caused me to reminisce about the times we spent together. One of my favorite traditions within this group of hard-working and driven lawyers took place each meeting during an after-dinner dessert social.

On the night of the social, each of the members of our federation would go to dinner at area restaurants in groups of eight to ten people and later reconvene at the meeting location for drinks and dessert. In the corner of each post-dinner dessert social room sat a piano. As the night progressed many of our members (my wife and I included) would gather around that piano. The pianist would play

---

[284]Philip Yancey & Brenda Quinn. "Meet the Bible." P. 2190-91. Zondervan. iBooks.

familiar songs and we would sing as we followed the lyric books with pages worn by many years of use.

At once, these hard-charging and focused lawyers would transform into a choir of esquires as piano notes filled the room. My friend, an excellent baritone, would join in the singing and enthrall all those who gathered. His rich melodic tones surrounded everyone's voices as we sang songs from Broadway to the Beatles. His strong voice would rise above the rest as we all tried to match the chords emanating from the piano. Our friend, Rich, the "Boise Baritone" was loved by all.

As we sang with him, our spirits were lifted as Rich carried the tunes (and us) in joyous melodies. My friend always had a twinkle in his eye and loved telling jokes and stories to amuse all those gathered 'round the piano. His talent made our lives happy and light and generated broad smiles. The joyous moments often spilled into the early hours of the next day as we swapped stories of our children and battles won in the courtroom, between singing songs of triumph and love.

I find it strange that I heard of Rich's diagnosis as I was writing this section on pain and suffering. But, I am reminded by Jesus that the anxiety being experienced by my friend, his family, and colleagues is temporary. If I know Rich, he is telling jokes to the nurses and doctors through the pain and spinning stories of victories won and battles joined. I trust that my friend, though he was experiencing angst in the last days of his life on earth, will have his faith refined and strengthened as he awaits his final reward[285].

Many other Christian authors have tackled the question of why a loving God either inflicts pain upon his children or allows pain

---

[285]Rich Hall died in Hospice care within weeks of my writing these words. I know Rich was a man of faith and I believe he is in eternal peace and his soul rejoices as he is now in the presence of God

to be heaped on those who believe. Philip Yancey penned a book that took a sideways look at the question of pain and suffering. Instead of asking the question of "why" God allows us to suffer, he asked (then answers) the question "Where is God When It Hurts?" Yancey discussed the question of why the sensation of bodily pain is needed by God's creatures. Pain, he reminded us, indicates that something is wrong. If we sprain our ankle the pain makes each step a conductor of further agony. Our natural response to this pain is to avoid inflicting more pain. We use crutches and make accommodations to take the weight off our foot. Pain, in this way, prevents further damage and hastens the healing process by getting us off our feet. Pain causes us to act in a way that lets the damaged joint heal – instead of further deteriorating that area of our body. In the same way, God uses our suffering to heal and protect us from further emotional, physical, and spiritual damage. "Pain is a part of the seamless fabric of sensations and often a necessary prelude to pleasure and fulfillment. The key to happiness lies not so much in avoiding pain at all costs as in understanding its role as a protective warning system and harnessing it to work on your behalf, not against you."[286]

Just as in the case of the sprained ankle, God uses our pain to protect us from further damage and "... from the larger view, from the view of all history, yes, God speaks to us through suffering – perhaps in spite of suffering." Taking this point and developing a cohesive answer, Yancey concludes, "God is in *us* – not in the things that hurt – helping to transform bad into good. We can safely say that God can bring good out of evil; we cannot say that God brings about the evil in hopes of producing good[287]." Yancey (and I) there-

---

[286]Philip Yancey. "Where is God When It Hurts?". P. 54-55. iBooks

[287]Philip Yancey. "Where Is God When It Hurts?" P. 95; 109. iBooks

fore believe that God does not inflict the pain but uses pain for His (and our) good purposes.

As can be seen from the words of the Apostle Peter, C.S. Lewis, and Yancey, God does not create the pain and anguish that each of us experiences but He is with us as we deal with these turbulent times in our lives. Further, God does not turn His back on us as we go through terrible trials but He takes the bad times and creates good from them.

The deaths of my father and grandfather were something that I would never wish on anyone, even my fiercest enemy. Their deaths devastated me. Coming in close succession, these losses left me wondering why God hated me. Why God would take away my father when I was so young and my grandfather so soon thereafter? However, through the lens of time and the perspective that it brings, I have come to realize that these traumatic events helped shape me into the man I have become. I believe these heartbreaking experiences gave me a mental and emotional toughness that I would need in my later life. They also brought me closer to God. I came to realize that the comfort I needed at this pivotal time was provided by my family who surrounded me with love. I came to feel a sense of peace that surpassed my eight-year-old ability to understand.

In my later teenage years, I grew to recognize that peace was actually the presence of God – who was with me the whole time. God was with me, even when I had my emotional breakdown after the death of my grandfather. God did not cause these deaths, but He used them to mold me into a person who could withstand the storms that would blow through my later years and create in me the ability to love deeply and believe fervently. The deaths of my father and grandfather and the healing that resulted therefrom strengthened the keel that kept me on a straight and narrow path and led to a deeper understanding of God and His plans for me.

These bouts of pain also taught me that I was equipped to assist others in their moments of crisis. I realized that the plans God had for me were present in the storms that blew through my young life. Weathering these storms of pain and anguish gave me the ability, as an adult, to empathize with others going through such experiences.

As Christians, we are to be the presence of God in a hurting world. God taught me this through the ordeals I suffered as a child. Through my experiences I have gained an understanding of pain and loss. As a result, I believe I am able to help people who may go through the same experiences. How we should care for people in pain is part of God's plan. Christians are to be His eyes, feet, hands, and heart in a hurting world. "A university conducting research on pain recruited volunteers to test how long they could keep their feet in buckets of freezing water. They observed that when a companion was allowed in the room, the volunteer could endure the cold twice as long as those who suffered alone. 'The presence of another caring person doubles the amount of pain a person can endure,' the researchers concluded.[288]"

If we were to look only at the trial, torture, humiliation, beating, and brutal death of Jesus, we could conclude that God does not care for us and lets the world inflict pain on us at will. If God did not stop such treatment of His Son, how much less does He care for us? If we looked at pain this way we would have properly come to this conclusion. However, if we only look at the surface level of pain and the problem of pain under this perspective, we will miss the point. The only way God could show humanity the ultimate example of total and unconditional love was through the death of His Son on the cross. The only remedy for the terminal illness of our sin is that atoning death.

---

[288]Yancey, Philip. "The Question That Never Goes Away". P. 57. iBooks

God took the evil acts of this world and made them the ultimate gift of love for us. He was with His son through His ordeal and resurrected Him to usher us into heaven. If we look at the ordeal of Jesus from the perspective of time, we can gain an understanding of how much God loves us. Looking back on the death and resurrection of Jesus allows us to get the proper picture of how God views pain and its purpose.

"We may not get the answer to the problem of pain that we want from Jesus. We get instead the mysterious confirmation that God suffers with us. We are not alone. Jesus reconstructs trust in God. Because of Jesus, I can trust that God truly understands my condition. I can trust that I *matter* to God and that God cares, regardless of how things look at the time. When I begin to doubt, I turn again to the face of Jesus and there I see the compassionate love of a God well-acquainted with grief."[289]

Funerals are society's way of saying goodbye to those we love. Funerals are also communal gatherings where people share their pain and grief over the loss of loved ones. It is therefore appropriate that one of the most quoted portions of the Bible at funerals is Psalm 23. This Psalm, written by King David, has different phrases for different needs that we have. During times of peace and calm David credits God with allowing these waves of serenity to comfort us – using words such as *green pastures* and *quiet waters*. But David reminds us that we will also go through pain, anguish, and trials as well. Our lives will experience cancer, financial ruin, unrequited love, betrayal, and death. We are told that we will walk through the valley of the shadow of death and will come face-to-face with evil – the cause of this pain. God will not bring these things upon

[289]Yancey, Philip. "The Bible Jesus Read." P. 320-22. Zondervan, 2017-03-01. iBooks.

us, David said. God's gift of free and unfettered will allows pain and evil to enter our lives.

Satan and the forces of evil on this earth inflict these calamities. However, David reminds us that when these tragedies befall us, God is right there at our side. "I will fear no evil, for you are with me; your rod and your staff, they comfort me." v. 4.

God's rod and staff comforted my soul by helping me to overcome the grief that broke my heart when my father and then my grandfather died. God was with my family and me when my uncle bankrupted my mother and her three young children. "Enemies are still present, as is evil, but 'I will fear no evil, for you are with me...' In times of pain, God comes close. Those few words, 'you are with me,' reveal the one thing we can count on in calamitous times. Always, no matter the circumstances, we have the ***assurance*** of 'Emmanuel,' which simply means 'God with us.'"[290]

As C.S. Lewis came to realize, the cancer that took the life of his new bride came about as a result of the evil of cancer that exists in this world. However, the peace that surpasses all understanding comes about as a result of God being with us as we go through our battle with cancer. Lewis came through the darkness of the pain and grief he experienced and saw the light that was God's presence. "In a modern world that presumes God's absence or lack of concern, Christ is God crying 'I am here.' Because of Jesus, we have the ***assurance*** that whatever disturbs us, disturbs God more. Whatever grief we feel, God feels more. And whatever we long for, God longs for more."[291]

---

[290] Yancey, Philip. "The Question That Never Goes Away". P. 84. iBooks. Emphasis added.

[291] Supra, P. 91

God never intervenes in our lives. This is so because He is already present there. We may not feel His presence all the time but when we feel He is absent, it is because we do not look or search for Him. Every time I have fervently searched for God I have felt His presence. The problem is that we do not search for Him. We become distracted by our own suffering and fail to look for Him. Only when we "come to the end" of ourselves, do we find God. We are driven to our knees by pain because that is exactly where we need to be to find God.

There is a great story by an unknown author that explains why we fail to find God in our time of pain. It goes like this:

> One night a man had a dream. He dreamed he was walking along the beach with the Lord. Across the sky flashed scenes from his life. For each scene, he noticed two sets of footprints in the sand: one belonging to him, and the other to the Lord.
>
> When the last scene of his life flashed before him, he looked back at the footprints in the sand. He noticed that many times along the path of his life there was only one set of footprints. He also noticed that it happened at the very lowest and saddest times in his life. This really bothered him and he questioned the Lord about it.
>
> "Lord, You said that once I decided to follow You, You'd walk with me all the way. But I have noticed that during the most troublesome times in my life,

there is only one set of footprints. I don't understand why when I needed You most You would
leave me."

The Lord replied, "My son, My precious child, I
love you and would never leave you. During your
times of trial and suffering, when you see only one
set of footprints, it was then that I carried you."[292]

You see, God is with us when the world inflicts pain on us. He
is always there, even when we fail to see Him.

If we can agree that God is only good and cannot create or allow
anything evil to come from Him, that still doesn't answer the question of why, when evil, pain, or suffering comes our way, God doesn't
do something about such things. Once a baby is diagnosed with
cancer, why doesn't God simply do something good and cure the
child? I do not think there is any definite answer to this question
as it is not directly addressed in the Bible. Here, however, is how
Yancey attempts to answer this difficult question:

Often when people pose a question like "What
good is God?" they are asking why God doesn't
intervene more directly and with more force. Why
did God let Hitler do so much damage, or Stalin
and Mao? Why doesn't God take a more active role
in human history? I can think of several possible
reasons. According to the Old Testament, God did
take an active and forceful role in the past, yet it
failed to produce lasting faith among the Israelites.

---

[292]http://www.knowjesus.com/Encourage.shtml

And, as earthly powers have learned, force and freedom make uneasy partners and an emphasis on one always diminishes the other; God consistently tilts toward human freedom. In the end, though, we have no sure answer and only fleeting glimpses of God's ultimate plan.[293]

This brings me full circle to where I started this chapter. One of the things that the guarantee of salvation does not provide is freedom from pain, suffering, anguish, and anxiety. We will continue to suffer and have to abide these things during the time we spend on earth. That is because, for whatever reason, God has allowed disease, evil, betrayal, anguish, and anxiety to enter this world through the sin of Adam and Eve – and by our continued sin to this very day. God has, however, taken our suffering and assured us that He will use it for our good and will never leave us in the process. "[T]he major New Testament passages on suffering all focus on the productive value of suffering, the good that it can produce in us (perseverance, character, patience, hope, and so on)."[294]

While life in the United States is far from perfect, there are many other places on earth that are worse. One of the worst places in the modern-day world for suffering is Somalia. According to World Health Organization (WHO), the leading causes of death in Somalia are illnesses that have either been eradicated or are under control in this country. Lower respiratory infections are the leading cause of death in Somalia. Others, in order of prevalence, are diarrhea, measles, malnutrition, tuberculosis, meningitis, and maternal-fetal conditions. As a result, the population growth rate

---

[293]Yancey, Philip. "What Good is God". iBooks
[294]Yancey, Philip. "Prayer". iBooks

in Somalia is <u>negative</u> 2.3%[295]. This poor African country has seen famine, disease, and civil war for the past twenty years. Billions of relief dollars have flooded this country with very little effect.

With this background information, I found an interview with a Christian nurse relief worker who spent a long time caring for God's children in Somalia. Her words proved very instructive on the proper perspective that pain and suffering should have in our lives. She said this, "Perhaps one day I'll be back in America working the night shift at a comfortable suburban hospital. Then I'll probably struggle with new issues, such as how to be selfless and grateful in a land of plenty." This humbling and frank statement reveals how God can put our pain in perspective. This nurse's statement is a vivid reminder of how, with all our stress and anguish, we may need a reminder of God's goodness.

We need to be able to see how our trials may be used for good by God. I believe that the trials and sorrow we experience can only be a source of good when we are able to view them from the perspective of time. When these storms hit we can only view them through a microscope or with blinders on. Blinders cover the rear vision of the horse, forcing it to look only in a forward direction and keeping it on track. Blinders are also useful to reduce the chances of the horse being spooked and making a run for it while still attached to the wagon[296]. Blinders have a way of preventing us from putting these trials in their proper perspective. All we can see are the waters rising around us as the winds are whipping our sheltered lives. They blind us from seeing God, who is right there with us at these lowest points in our lives.

---

[295]StatistiC.S. are from the WHO's analysis in 2018

[296]http://www.dallasequestriancenter.com/why-do-horses-wear-blinders/

Just like George Bailey, we can't understand how the storms in our lives are used by God for good. When George was forced to forgo college and world travel by the storm that occurred in his life following the death of his father, he could only see loss and tragedy. It was only when he was forced to look at his life through the perspective of time that God was able to show him how important those storms were in changing, for good, not only his life but the lives of hundreds of people. Only time will allow us to see that God was right there with us through the trials and pain we had to endure.

Philip Yancey wrote about the value of pain when he encountered and formed a great bond of friendship with Dr. Paul Brand. Dr. Brand had made the care and treatment of the poor who are afflicted with leprosy his life's work. Working primarily in India with the lowest members of their caste system he took care of people who suffered from the *lack* of pain. The primary symptom of this dreaded disease is a total lack of feeling from areas of the skin that would eventually turn into ulcerated and necrotic flesh. This lack of pain prevented the body from reacting to these diseased skin areas and resulted in patients simply continuing to put pressure and tension on the affected skin. The result of the patients' actions caused the skin to further deteriorate, leading to further decay. This, in turn, required the amputation of limbs and the loss of organs. The inability to feel pain by leprosy patients directly leads to these losses. In chapter 20 of their co-written book, *In His Image*, they describe the benefit of pain to our body – and the Body of Christ (His Church):

> As rehabilitation director of the hospital, I strive
> to remind the patients of parts of their bodies they
> might "forget about" in the absence of pain. I have
> spent much of my life repairing the damage that

results when patients lower their guard. I would give anything to awaken in such people a sense of their body's unity, but overcoming this peculiar sense of detachment seems impossible without the sensation of pain. Just as pain unifies the body, its loss irreversibly destroys that unity.

..."If one part suffers, every part suffers with it," says Paul (1 Cor. 12:26). [297]

F. The Guarantee of Evil?

The guarantee provides the assurance of everlasting life. It does not provide assurance that evil will not be encountered during our time on earth. In fact, we are told by God that we will have to face and contend with evil. Since God is purely good and nothing bad or evil can come from Him, where does the evil come from? The evil in this world comes from you and me – from men, women, and even children. You ask, then, if God created us and God can only bring about good things, why did God allow us to commit evil acts? How can a purely good God allow His creation to be bad? Weren't human beings created in the image of God? I have struggled with these questions.

The answer to all these questions is found in two words: free will. God did not create us to be robots whose only choice is to follow a pre-programmed existence. No, God so loved us that He gave us the gift of free will. Free will gives all of us the license to do as we please. Free will permits us to turn away from our Creator. Free will allows us not to love the loving God that gave us everything good. It

---

[297]Yancey, Philip & Brand, Dr. Paul. "In His Image." Zondervan. iBooks.

provides us the ability to reject the grace of God. Grace that cleanses us from our sins.

Eugene H. Peterson described this dilemma thusly, "We have been told the lie ever since we can remember: human beings are basically nice and good. Everyone is born equal and innocent and self-sufficient. The world is a pleasant, harmless place. We are born free. If we are in chains now, it is someone's fault, and we can correct it with just a little more intelligence or effort or time. How we can keep on believing this after so many centuries of evidence to the contrary is difficult to comprehend, but nothing we do and nothing anyone else does to us seems to disenchant us from the spell of the lie." [298]

What would make my loving father take his own life, leaving a wife and three children to fend for themselves? Free will allowed my father to make his own decisions. Free will gave my father the power to end his life and forever scar the lives of his family and friends. Did God allow this to happen? No, God is not the author of bad things. God gave my father free will and he chose to end his life.

C.S. Lewis has a way of putting the "gift" of free will into perspective.

> God created things which had free will. That means
> creatures which can go either wrong or right. Some
> people think they can imagine a creature which was
> free but had no possibility of going wrong; I cannot.
> If a thing is free to be good it is also free to be bad.
> And free will is what has made evil possible. Why,
> then, did God give them free will? Because free

---

[298]"A Long Obedience in the Same Direction." P. 36-37. InterVarsity Press, 2012-04-25. iBooks.

will, though it makes evil possible, is also the only thing that makes possible any love or goodness or joy worth having. A world of automata—of creatures that worked like machines—would hardly be worth creating. The happiness which God designs for His higher creatures is the happiness of being freely, voluntarily united to Him and to each other in an ecstasy of love and delight compared with which the most rapturous love between a man and a woman on this earth is mere milk and water. And for that they must be free.[299]

I often brought a smile to the faces of those in my Bible study group when I referenced the "gospel of Bruce Almighty". But this movie, I believe, illustrates many biblical principles with satire and evocative warmth. I have mentioned this movie many times in this book but it bears repeating when tackling the subject of free will.

When "God" endowed Bruce with His "powers" he warned him that there were only two things that Bruce could not do with those powers. The first was that he could not tell anyone that he was God and the other was that Bruce could not make someone love him. This latter admonition escaped me at first but it came very clear in one pivotal scene. Bruce and his longtime girlfriend had a fight and she left the apartment they shared. Bruce realized what he had done to her and was despondent as a result. He, therefore set about trying to get her back. He tried everything. He carved love notes to her in the trees that lined her street. When she went to her favorite coffee shop and looked up at the TV playing in the corner,

---

[299]excerpt from Mere Christianity. C. S. Lewis. "A Year with C. S. Lewis." P. 99. HarperCollins. iBooks.

a commercial for a new record collection was being advertised. The album included songs such as "All You Need is Bruce" and "If You Can't Be With the One You Love, Then Love Bruce." Bruce tried using all his powers to get his girlfriend to love him. He even "listened in" on her prayers to God in an effort to understand how he could win her back. Nothing worked.

Finally, in a fit of desperation, he showed up at the elementary school where she taught and tried to *will* her to love him. In that scene on the playground of the elementary school Bruce tries to pull his girlfriend back into a relationship with him. He stretches out his arms toward her and pleads "Love me, love me, love me."[300]. She thinks Bruce is insane and simply walks away. He concentrated all of his "godly" powers on her in a last-ditch effort to get her to change her mind. Bruce screwed up his face and held his breath as he tried to make her love him. But nothing could cajole or force her to love him.

It was at this point that Bruce remembered what God had said about the only real limits on the powers he was given. He could not "force" anyone to love him. Bruce, in frustration, looks up to heaven and says, "I know... free will!" Bruce eventually asks God "How can you make someone love you without affecting free will?" *There is no answer*, God explains. There is no answer because free will is the opposite of making anyone do anything. God so loved us that he gave us free will. Free will, however, allows us to forsake that love.

Free will is the author of evil. This is so because God allows us to think, feel and do as we please – without any divine constraints. C.S. Lewis in Letter #2 of *The Screwtape Letters*, describes a dialogue between Screwtape, the devil's lieutenant, and Wormwood,

---

[300]Remember the meeting with Peter and Jesus after his resurrection where Jesus asked Peter this same question, three times! John 21:15-16

his operative on earth. In it, Screwtape advises his operative to "[w] ork hard, then, on the disappointment or anticlimax which is certainly coming to the patient (the new Christian) during his first few weeks as a churchman. The Enemy (God) allows this disappointment to occur on the threshold of every human endeavor. It occurs when the boy who has been enchanted in the nursery by Stories from the Odyssey buckles down to really learning Greek. It occurs when lovers have got married and begin the real task of learning to live together. In every department of life, it marks the transition from dreaming aspiration to laborious doing." God allows us to use our free will in any manner we choose. I believe this is the price of free will and the reality of the world.

Therefore, God gives us the freedom to choose. This freedom has its costs and choosing the wrong path allows evil to creep into our lives. In fact, this freedom to choose is something that God does not waiver on, even if it means that his creation turns away from Him. Even if it means that we fall out of love with God! "God conducts Himself in keeping with His righteousness. He will never violate our freedom to choose between eternal life and spiritual death, good and evil, right and wrong. His ultimate goal is not only to glorify Himself but also to make a happy relationship with His crowning creation—man. Never will He make any demands which encroach upon our freedom to choose."[301]

G. The Guarantee of Doubt

Once we realize that we have the guarantee of God's forgiveness and the resulting salvation that it provides, does that mean we will never waiver in our faith? Will this book and the references cited

---

[301]Billy Graham, The Secret of Happiness, Chapter 4. iBooks

within its pages remove any lingering uncertainty over our claim to eternal fellowship with God? I would hope that to be the case but my own experience tells me the answer is, unfortunately, *no*. When doubt and questions crept into my heart I wondered if my certainty about God's salvation was misplaced.

Then I read the story of how Martin Luther dealt with his moments of doubt and pain. I remembered how Peter denied Christ. How Thomas would not believe Christ rose from the grave, despite all of his fellow disciples giving him eyewitness testimony. How the apostle Paul had to be struck blind on the road to Damascus before he would believe. How Jonah ran away from God and had to be cast into the sea and swallowed by a whale before his doubts were erased. And the list goes on.

> Doubts and complaints are valid responses, not symptoms of weak faith – so valid, in fact, that God made sure the Bible included them all.
>
> ...
>
> And, because of Jesus, perhaps God doesn't understand. At Gethsemane and Calvary and some Inexpressible Way, God himself was forced to confront hiddenness of God. "God striving with God" is how Martin Luther summarized the cosmic struggle played down onto crossbeams of wood. On that dark night, God learned the full extent of what it means to feel God-forsaken. [302]

---

[302]Philip Yancey. Disappointment with God p. 232-33. iBooks

I believe that God expects us to have moments of doubt. He knows that we will have some questions that cannot be answered. He knows we will struggle with our faith. I don't know how you feel about learning of the struggles that some of the titans of faith had, but for me – they give me comfort. Perhaps misery loves company, but seeing persons of greater faith than I struggling with questions and doubt makes me feel less guilty when I question my faith. If one of Jesus's closest disciples can deny Christ in a moment of panic (where he thought he might be the next one arrested) then God understands that His fallible creation will falter.

By now, it is clear that one of my favorite Christian writers is Philip Yancey. He has a way of making difficult subjects understandable. His portrayals of complex biblical principles have given me comfort and enlightened my understanding of God. His biblical education and vast knowledge of God have led to a prodigious body of work and his prolific writing has provided people all over the world with a deepened and abiding faith.

Imagine my shock when I read of his own struggles with God and the guarantee of salvation. Surely, he was steeped in an understanding of God's grace and how we are forgiven. How then could he have any lingering doubts? In his book "Reaching for the Invisible God" he talks about his own moments of uncertainty. He says:

> My struggles with faith have at least this in their favor: I come from a long, distinguished line. I find kindred expressions of doubt and confusion in the Bible itself. Sigmund Freud accused the church of teaching only questions that it can answer. Some churches may do that, but God surely does not. In books like Job, Ecclesiastes, and Habakkuk the Bible poses blunt questions that have no answers.

In an odd way, the very failures of the church prove its doctrine. Grace, like water, flows to the lowest part. We in the church have humility and contrition to offer the world, not a formula for success. Almost alone in our success–oriented society, we admit that we have failed, are failing, and always will fail. That is why we turn to God so desperately. (P. 19-20)

So the very failures and doubts that we have are known and understood by a loving God and used by Him as a tool to turn us back to a right relationship with Him. This is the very nature of the guarantee.

CHAPTER 11

THE CLOSING ARGUMENT

E very case I tried ended with a closing argument. And every closing argument ended with a suggestion to the jury as to what they should do, what verdict to render in the case set before them. During my career, my closing arguments laid out all of the facts that were presented to the jury during the trial. These facts consisted of the testimony of the witnesses and the documents that were introduced into evidence. The closing argument, I would tell jurors, was my last chance to speak with them before they went into the privacy of the jury room to deliberate. I would use the little time I had left to emphasize how the evidence they heard fit the narrative that I promised I would prove when they were first selected to be jurors in the case.

The closing argument is perhaps the best part of the trial for advocates, such as me. It was the time I most looked forward to because in closing argument I was allowed to inject my passion for the case. While I had to stick with the evidence produced during the trial, I was given the latitude to stitch that evidence into a pattern of proof that I could persuasively use to create a picture that the jury could employ to find in favor of my client. The trial, as I tried to portray it, was like a jigsaw puzzle. Each word of testimony and piece of documentary proof formed pieces of the puzzle. My closing argument involved putting those pieces together so the jury could see the whole picture at the end of the case.

In a way, I looked upon my profession as a trial lawyer as similar to that of a salesperson. Instead of selling a product, I was selling a set of facts. It was my job to sell the jury on the justness of my client's case. If I did my job and they bought our theory of the case, my client would prevail. The best salespersons are those who passionately believe in the products they sell. If they don't have a thorough knowledge of their product and a firm belief in its excellence, they can't persuade a prospective buyer to purchase the product. Trial lawyers are no different. That is why closing arguments were so fun. I could let my firm belief in my case show as I presented my pitch to the jury.

I was proud to be a lawyer and felt fortunate to be a part of this noble profession. My job, as I saw it, was to provide the best arguments on behalf of my clients – just as the opposing counsel would do for his or her clients. With the judge as the arbiter of the law and the jury as the determiner of the facts, I believe that our legal system of justice is the best in the world at rendering a fair and just determination of a controversy. There are many lawyers who had a great impact on Christianity. As previously mentioned, Joseph of Arimathea was a noted lawyer in Jerusalem who was a member of the Sanhedrin. He was present when Jesus was brought before this tribunal on a charge of blasphemy. Joseph saw the trial as a sham and spoke up against the improper procedures used in that trial and the lack of proof in the prosecution's case. When 59 of the 60 members voted to sentence Jesus to death, Joseph was the lone voice in opposition. As a skilled trial lawyer, he insisted that the Sanhedrin comply with its long-established rules of procedure. Joseph passionately argued his case, yet the outcome was never in doubt.

Probably the most famous Christian lawyer of the sixteenth century was Thomas Moore. He held a high and esteemed job in the United Kingdom. His position was legal counsel to the King of England. In that post, he was charged with giving legal advice to the King. When Henry VIII decided to divorce his wife, Catherine of Aragon, the Catholic Church warned him that such an action was forbidden under the church's Canon Law. The king would have none of this. In response, he forced through a bill in Parliament that said anyone who denied him the right to divorce his wife would be beheaded. When he called on Moore for approval of this law, Thomas told the king that it was morally wrong and that he would not approve. He did so, knowing full well that the consequences of his opinion could be dire. For such conduct, Moore gave his life.

The legacy of this courageous decision has been codified in a society of lawyers, based in Chicago. This organization is "...dedicated to restoring respect in law for life, family, and religious liberty." The Thomas Moore Society "defends and fosters support for these causes by providing high-quality pro bono legal services from local trial courts all the way to the United States Supreme Court."

One of the greatest works of literature was penned by a lawyer. His novel deals with the subject of God's grace and how it is displayed by God's sons and daughters. This book tells the story of a prisoner who manages to break out of a prison work camp. Penniless and desperate, he steals food and winds up on the doorstep of a priest. The priest takes the bedraggled escapee into the parsonage and nurses him back to health. However, as soon as the man regains his strength, he steals the church's silver and takes off in the dead of night. The ex-prisoner is soon captured and brought back to the church in chains by the police. Upon seeing the man with the stolen silver the priest exclaims, "You left in such a hurry you forgot to take these silver candlesticks." Upon hearing that the priest "gave" the silver to their prisoner as a gift, the surprised gendarmes let the man go. The prisoner's hardened heart was broken by the priest's demonstration of undeserved grace in the face of his own betrayal. As a result of this act of kindness and love, the prisoner's heart is changed and thereafter he leads a different life. The man who wrote this beautiful story is the great author and lawyer Victor Hugo and his book is *Les Miserables.*

There are many other stories of how lawyers have advanced the kingdom of God through various methods of persuasion and the defiance of evil. I hope the passion I have for Christ and what He did for all of us is evident to you. I trust that the case I have laid out in the pages of this book has resonated with you in such a way as to ignite a similar flame of passion in you. I have tried to convey God's guarantee of salvation in a way that all of us can understand. In comparing and contrasting God's solemn promise of everlasting life with everyday legal documents (such as insurance policies and product warranties) I hope that I have been able to transfer to you the reassurance and comfort God's promise has given me.

When I purchase an insurance policy I do so with the hope of peace of mind in the event a calamity occurs. If I get into an accident and cause someone damage, my auto policy provides me the assurance that those damages will be paid. If I buy a new car I can drive it away from the dealership with confidence that if it breaks within the next two years or so, the dealer will repair the car at no (or little) cost to me. If the bank within which I deposit my money goes under, I can make a claim to the FDIC to seek recovery of my loss. The guarantee that God provides puts all of these assurances to shame. His guarantee is unconditional, comes without exceptions, cost or exclusions. This guarantee has no ending – it is forever.

When I rely on a policy of insurance or new car warranty I have a written contract that spells out the terms of the assurance. I can trust something other than a verbal promise or advertisement. God has provided us with such written proof of His guarantee – even though God does not need to do so. His Word is good enough. I have discussed where and why this written guarantee has been provided. The pages of the Bible are filled with the terms of this guarantee. We are also provided a complete description of what the guarantee is and how each of us can claim this wondrous, blessed assurance.

During the practice of law, I was often reminded that while the courts strive for justice through the pursuit of truth, the legal system is not perfect. While I have tried to convince you of the truth of God's promise, I concede that I cannot answer every question nor provide perfect proof. In doing so I am reminded of a case I previously discussed in chapter one and often cited to judges when I was making an argument on behalf of my clients. The great US Supreme Court Justice, Oliver Wendell Holmes, as I referenced previously, said that the law does not demand perfect knowledge or depend any less on reasonable inferences and deductions than we all do in everyday life. "[A]ll life is an experiment," he said. "Every year if not every day we have to wager our salvation upon some prophecy based upon imperfect knowledge."[303] While the law provides no such iron-clad guarantees, God does. We have a guarantee from an unimpeachable source. No guarantee by man or government can hold a candle to God's promise of eternal life.

Even though the proof I have presented is not perfect, I do believe the evidence that is set forth in this book is "clear and convincing". I believe I have shown this level of proof through eyewitness testimony (recorded not only in the Bible but in contemporaneous publications from the first century). I have shown how testimony

[303]Abrams v United States, 250 U.S. 616, 630, 40 S. Ct. 17, 22 (1919)

and writings recorded centuries before the birth and death of Jesus were consistent with the historical events of Jesus's life. C. S. Lewis summarized it this way:

> I have to believe that Jesus was (and is) God. And it seems plain as a matter of history that He taught His followers that the new life was communicated in this way. In other words, I believe it on His authority. Do not be scared by the word authority. Believing things on authority only means believing them because you have been told them by someone you think trustworthy. Ninety-nine percent of the things you believe are believed on authority.
>
> ...
>
> The ordinary man believes in the Solar System, atoms, evolution, and the circulation of the blood on authority—because the scientists say so. Every historical statement in the world is believed on authority. None of us has seen the Norman Conquest or the defeat of the Armada. None of us could prove them by pure logic as you prove a thing in mathematics. We believe them simply because people who did see them have left writings that tell us about them: in fact, on authority. A man who jibbed at authority in other things as some people

do in religion would have to be content to know nothing all his life.[304]

The testimony of these eyewitnesses has stood up to decades and centuries of cross-examination. The words of the Bible that relate to the guarantee and the fulfillment of Jesus's redemptive death and resurrection have been shown to be historically accurate and reliable. The mere fact that *none* of the hundreds of people who witnessed the resurrected Christ ever recanted their testimony is proof that their testimony is truthful. When you add the fact that these people were threatened with imprisonment or death if they did not retract what they said, it is even more astonishing. Heck, even Jesus's prosecutor, Caiaphas, attested to Jesus's divinity. It was Caiaphas who advised the Jews that it was expedient that one man should die for the people.[305] "...Caiaphas, being high priest that year, said to them, 'You know nothing at all, nor do you consider that it is expedient for us that one man should die for the people, and not that the whole nation should perish.'" Now, he did not say this on his own authority, but being high priest that year he prophesied that Jesus would die for the nation, and not for that nation only, but also that He would gather together in one the children of God who were scattered abroad. The Apostle Peter (Simon Peter) puts it this way:

> We did not follow cleverly invented stories when we told you about the power and coming of our Lord Jesus Christ, but we were eyewitnesses of his majesty. For he received honor and glory from God

---

[304]C. S. Lewis. "A Year with C. S. Lewis." P. 47-48. This excerpt from Mere Christianity. HarperCollins. iBooks.

[305]John 11:45–54

the Father when the voice came to him from the Majestic Glory, saying, "This is my Son, whom I love; with him I am well pleased." We ourselves heard this voice that came from heaven when we were with him on the sacred mountain. 2 Peter 1: 16-18 (Emphasis added)

As an eyewitness on the Mount of Transfiguration, Peter heard God positively identify Jesus as His Son – the same identification the crowds heard at Jesus's baptism by John.

As indicated, the proof offered at any trial is both testimonial and documentary. The proof set forth in the documents I have provided in this book attests to God's promise of eternal salvation. This proof is also significant in that it builds on and fortifies the testimonial evidence presented.

I have provided proof that shows the authenticity of the Bible. The timeline of the writing of the gospels, for example, proves the matters asserted therein. I have provided you instances of how John's gospel was accurate through the confirmation in analogous Roman writings of the same time period. I have shown how accounts in all of the gospels of Jesus's arrest, conviction, method of execution, burial, and resurrection are independently verified by authentic texts published contemporaneously to the biblical accounts. I have also proved the reliability of the Bible by showing that the Bible, when viewed as a whole document, is consistent throughout. Furthermore, I have also given you evidence of how portions of the Bible that were published centuries before the life of Jesus are consistent with His life, death, and resurrection. This internal historical accuracy and consistency is further proof of the reliability of the Bible – and thus the veracity of God's guarantee of salvation. The Old Testament's "history foretold" shows how the words of the prophets, written centuries before the birth of Christ, came true in the life of Jesus. This is convincing proof, I would submit, of the historical accuracy of the Bible.

I believe I have also provided expert testimony proving the existence of God, the creator of the universe. This proof was subject to rigorous cross-examination and has withstood the challenge. I also provided proof that God was the creator of you. I presented the celebrated mathematician, Pascal, and his famous wager. This rational and logic-based approach is used in modern-day game theory and was used as the basis for debate about whether or not to believe in the guarantee of salvation.

In the last chapters in this book I devoted my arguments to the things that the guarantee provides...and the things it does not. I provided my viewpoint in an effort to enable you to make up your own mind as to whether you wish to accept God's unmerited gift of grace, His forgiveness of sin, and guarantee of eternal life.

As I have attempted to outline in this book, there are three basic things that God's guarantee provides. First, it gives you an acquittal from the penalty of sin. Second, the indwelling of the Holy Spirit is provided to counsel you throughout your life. And third, the guarantee assures that you will have eternal fellowship with God in heaven. These things are guaranteed, if only you accept them. God guarantees the forgiveness of sins if we simply confess those sins sincerely and humbly to Him. We have this guarantee of forgiveness by our belief in the death and resurrection of His Son as the atoning sacrifice for our sinful character and actions.

This forgiveness wipes away the sin we have committed (and will continue to commit) and cancels the debt that our sin has accrued. God provides mercy instead of punishment. We are no longer condemned for our sins but are redeemed through the blood of Christ, shed for us. Jesus took our place and withstood the worst the world could give – dying an excruciating death to atone for our disobedience. This act simply and powerfully demonstrated the glory of grace, unmerited and undeserved, and given by God to us. The grace is epitomized by the welcome the prodigal son was given after squandering his inheritance and taking up with prostitutes. Amazing grace, how sweet the sound that saved a wretched sinner like me!

The guarantee does not alleviate pain but it does transform pain into healing. God does however guarantee that He will be there, at your side, when you are hurting even if His presence may not be perceived by you. God was at my side throughout my six-year ordeal of pain – even when I felt abandoned. His presence was there the whole time but I didn't comprehend it until the healing took place. This healing, in fact, allowed me to get through my battle with melanoma.

So, you may ask, what happens once we accept God's gift of grace and live our lives under the protection of the guarantee? In providing my answer, I am reminded that we cannot claim the guarantee by being good enough. We can never live up to the standard of being without sin. However, take a deep breath. We can never be bad enough either. No matter how many times we sin, we will never be prohibited from claiming the grace offered by God.

Remember the song *Amazing Grace*, written by John Newton, the slave ship owner, and captain? He treated God's children like cattle, tore them away from their families, and confined them in atrocious conditions before selling them into a life of slavery. He was about as evil as it gets. Despite all the pain and anguish he inflicted on hundreds of thousands of human beings, He confessed his sins, was offered and accepted God's wondrous grace, and was forgiven.

If we truly put our trust and faith in Christ we are new creatures. If the Holy Spirit dwells in us and becomes our counselor it is

God's will that shall be done in our lives and not our own. "We are not saved by serving Him, but we are saved to serve Him. From the moment we are saved, we ought to live in the service of our Lord. If we refuse to be His servants, we are not saved, for we evidently still remain the servants of Satan."[306]

When we don't serve God we are serving our own interests and are pursuing things of this world. The fruit of belief *is action*. In loving our neighbors as ourselves we do the hard work of following God's commands. We show God's love for us by giving it to others. By feeding, clothing, and sheltering the poor, we are becoming God's hands in a world where people need compassion and caring. By being a kind and gentle person, we acknowledge God's great and unending grace in our lives. By being humble and contrite we become servants – just as Jesus modeled for us. Basically, by acting in a manner diametrically opposed to what the world is telling you to do we are saying to God, Thy will shall be done!

Because it is impossible for us to do the will of God by ourselves, God provides the gift of forgiveness. This is the type of grace the priest showed to Jean Valjean, the escaped prisoner who deserved punishment for his theft of church property. He repaid the kindness of the priest with betrayal. Instead of getting what he deserved, Jean Valjean received unmerited and undeserved grace.

Someone once said that perhaps the best way to convey the values we (ought to) cherish is not to talk about them incessantly or try to legislate them, but to cherish the literature and art in which they are firmly embedded.

I have tried to imbed in this book a great many quotes and the work of scholars who understand this subject much better than I.

---

[306]Charles H. Spurgeon. "Following Christ." P. 7. Aneko Press, 2018-11-23T20:24:24Z. iBooks.

As a lawyer this is the way we are taught to make a legal argument – by citing case law, legal journals, and statutes to underpin and bolster the arguments we are making for or against a proposition. The philosopher William James advised that "in the metaphysical and religious sphere, articulate reasons are cogent for us only when our inarticulate feelings of reality have already been impressed in favor of the same conclusion." In the first chapter, I asked you to try your best to avoid making your mind up on the question of God's guarantee before hearing all the evidence and listening to my closing argument. This, I hope, you have done.

My fondest wish for you is to experience the type of love you can find nowhere else. You can't find it where Solomon looked. It was not present in his great wealth, power, influence, or possessions. You can't locate this type of love by attaining great fame or acclaim – just ask the relatives of the many celebrities who drank or drugged themselves into the grave. No person, thing, position, possession nor accomplishment can bring you the type of ultimate joy that a personal relationship with your Creator can provide. And nowhere is that love expressed so vividly and poignantly as God's Son, bearing your sins on the cross and taking on sin through death to set you free.

And that, ladies and gentlemen of the jury, is my closing argument. I believe if you have listened to all the evidence you will conclude that we are all sinners who have fallen short of God's standard of purity and goodness. But the good news is that our guilt has been expunged before this trial even began. The sentence has been commuted before it could be handed down. And all of us have been granted a full pardon. Our guilt has been washed clean and we are forgiven, now and forever. *Guaranteed!*

Acknowledgments

My journey in writing this book spans fifteen years of research followed by three years of writing, re-writing and editing. Now at the end of this trip, I can reflect on the path that brought me here. This is the perspective that I mentioned as I made my way through the points in this book. This entire process has been a labor of love. It was helped along the way by many people I love and who cared for me - friends, colleagues, and especially family.

First and foremost, I must provide my eternal thanks to my wife, Mary Alice. Mac, as I have called her since our first date in January of 1975, has been my best friend, constant companion, love of my life and editor. She is a much more talented and proficient writer than I. She graduated with a communications degree the day before I graduated from law school, as our first two years of marriage coincided with our last two years of education. In fact, Mac was the reason I stayed in law school. After that brutal first year I was ready to quit, as many first-year law students do. But Mary Alice reminded me why I went to law school. Her gentle and sweet words gave me the encouragement I needed to stay the course and complete my degree.

Over the next two years, Mac edited all of my law school papers, briefs and arguments. She was my sounding board during my Moot Court and Mock Trial competitions. Throughout my 41-year career, she also advised me on my trial strategy and continued to edit the many articles I authored. She did this while writing for the Sarasota Herald-Tribune and raising our three children. I simply would not have been the lawyer I was without her! As you can probably imagine by now, she helped edit this book. I could not have written or completed it without her love, support and encouragement.

My three children, Courtney, Sara, and Luke, served as my inspiration and the underpinning of confidence that I needed throughout the process of getting my book started and pushing it across the finish line. They constantly asked me how the writing was progressing and gave me words of encouragement as I wrote chapter after chapter. They were the first people to read the completed book – after their mom completed her revisions. Their love and support can never be repaid.

Jay Crouse, the man who first introduced me to the Bible study Raising a Modern-Day Knight, should also be thanked. Jay, who asked me to be a spiritual mentor for his son, has been a source of invaluable assistance. Jay, a published Christian author and men's ministry leader, graciously offered to read and provide input on this work. I appreciate his wisdom and opinions, without which I could never have put the finishing touches on the completed manuscript.

Throughout my life, I have been influenced by too many people to mention in this acknowledgment - priests, pastors, teachers, and fellow Christians traveling a path with me that leads to salvation. Father Dougherty at Incarnation Church in Sarasota was a great teacher and comforter to me as I struggled with the storms that blew through my early childhood. Pastor Larry Edison of Covenant Life church in Sarasota was a wonderful teacher I encounteredI encountered when I left the Catholic Church and took the next step in my faith journey. He guided me with his leadership and sermons and eventually encouraged me to become an Elder in the church. I appreciate the insight provided by Randy Ashcraft of Bayshore

Baptist Church in Tampa. He taught me that we should not fail to perceive the beauty that God provides in our lives and that we not miss "The Dance." Pastors Jim Harnish and Magrey deVega's sermons at Hyde Park UMC in Tampa caused me to rethink many of the ways I viewed Christian tenets and doctrines. My thanks to them for broadening my horizons.

I was also blessed when Paul Butler came into my professional life. Paul, who received a divinity degree before completing law school, was a perfect example of what a Christian lawyer was supposed to be. By his counsel and example, I became a better lawyer who lived by the standards that Jesus laid out for each of us. With Paul, there is no separating the lawyer from the Christian: they are two in the same. He was and continues to be a great role model.

The Bible studies that I have participated in and led have been a constant source of joy and learning - especially the Tuesday morning men's group, Fathers of Knights. I have been privileged to be associated with these men for over ten years as we have shared our faith, struggles, joys, and sorrows. We have laughed and cried together as we continually join arms and move toward sanctification – each week growing closer to God. The mission we agreed to accept when we first came together was raising godly children. I believe I am a better father because of the men that I have been honored to be yoked with while on my spiritual journey. I also have been encouraged by the bible studies I participated in during our summer and fall days in Highlands, NC. These wonderful and encouraging men have walked with me on this journey of faith.

The collection of authors that I have cited throughout this book have educated me on topics that have been difficult to understand. These authors have written on this subject far better than I had the capacity to do. I hope that my references to their works will lead you to read these thoughtful and insightful books.

Last, but not least, I so much appreciate the many people who have encouraged me along the way including my sister Lisa and her husband Dave, my sister Lori and my son's godfather Jim, who first introduced me to the works of Philip Yancey.

God provides many people to light the way along the narrow path! Amen!

About the Author

Lewis F. Collins, Jr. was born in Jamaica, NY on September 13, 1953. He attended Florida State University where he received a B.A. in Business in 1975. He then attended Loyola University School of Law, graduating in 1978 with a Juris Doctor degree. He practiced law from 1975-1997 in Sarasota, FL and from 1997-2018 in Tampa, FL. He  was Board Certified in Civil Trial Law by the Florida Bar and represented defendants in civil litigation throughout the state of Florida. He was a founder of the Sarasota Chapter of the American Inns of Court and a Founding Fellow of the American College of Coverage Counsel. He served as the Dean of the Litigation Management College at the Kellogg School of Business at Northwestern University. During his legal career, he authored over thirty published legal articles and presented seventy-eight lectures to legal groups on a variety of substantive legal and trial tactics topics.

Mr. Collins served in many leadership capacities during his legal career, including President of the Florida Defense Lawyers Association (1995-96); President of the Federation of Defense and Corporate Counsel (2005-06), and President of Lawyers for Civil Justice (2009-10). He also served his community as an Elder in the

Presbyterian PCA Church; as Board Chair of the Sarasota Family Counseling Center (1990-91) and as a mentor with the Taking Stock In Children program in Tampa, FL.

This is Mr. Collins's first book.

CPSIA information can be obtained
at www.ICGtesting.com
Printed in the USA
LVHW020226020622
720196LV00012B/850

9 781662 843099